CW01334196

UP IN SMOKE

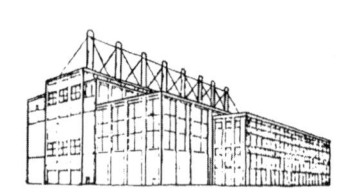

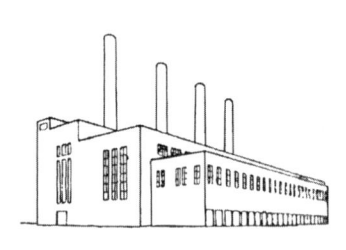

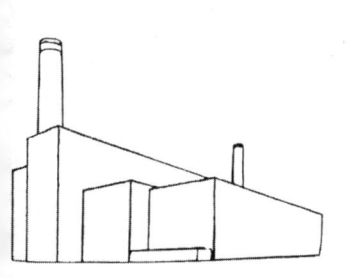

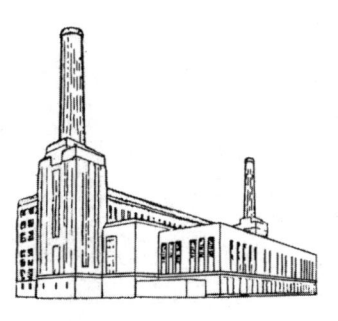

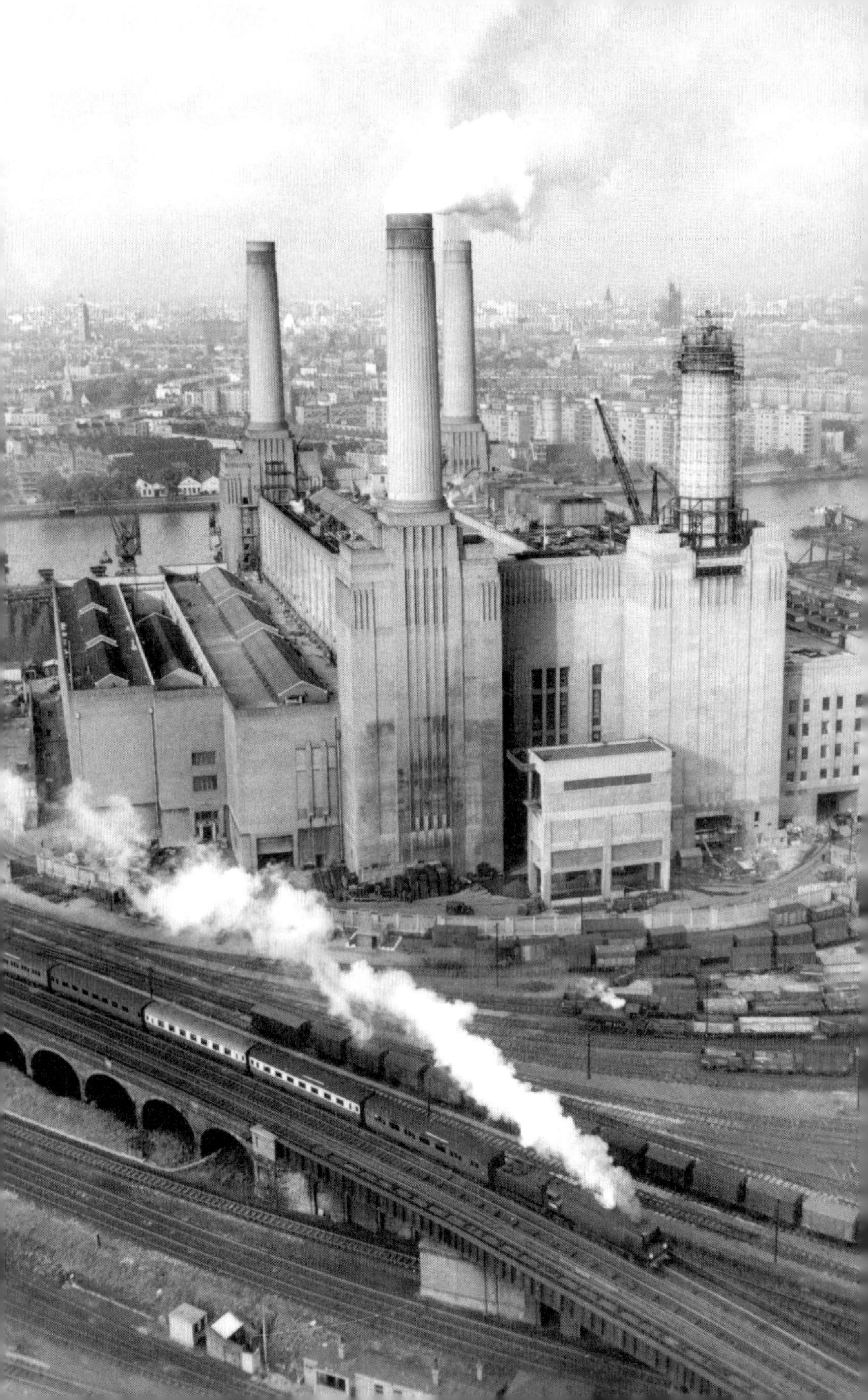

UP IN SMOKE
The Failed Dreams of Battersea Power Station

PETER WATTS

First published in Great Britain by Paradise Road 2016

Copyright © Peter Watts 2015

Peter Watts has asserted his moral right under the Copyright, Designs and Patents Act 1988 to be identified as the author of this work.

All rights reserved. No reproduction, copy or transmission of this publication may be made without written permission.

A CIP catalogue record for this book is available from the British Library.

ISBN 978-0-9935702-0-9

www.paradiseroad.co.uk

Commissioned and edited by Andrew Humphreys
Designed and typeset by Gadi Farfour
Proofread by Omer Ali

Printed by TJ International, Padstow, Cornwall

PREVIOUS SPREAD
A coal-fired locomotive steams by the coal-fired power station in 1953 as the fourth chimney is in the process of being erected. © TopFoto

> "Nothing is more beautiful than a great humming power-station"
>
> Filippo Tommaso Marinetti,
> *The Manifesto of Mechanical and Geometrical Splendour*, 1914

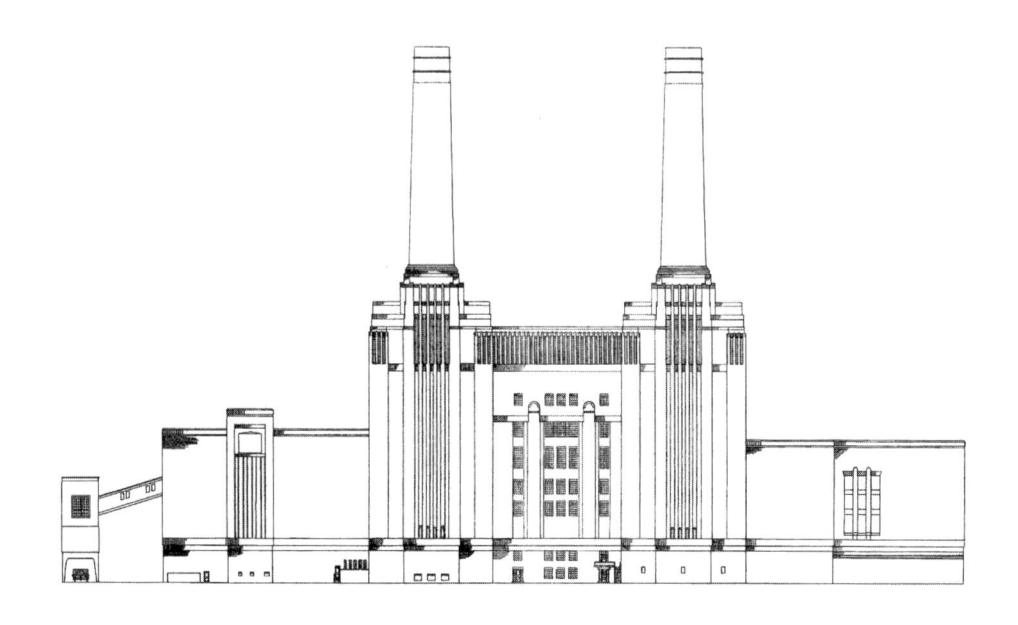

CONTENTS

	Preface	10
	Introduction	14
1	Together in Electric Dreams	22
2	An Evil Scheme	36
3	A Flaming Altar	48
4	New Power Generation	62
5	Pigs Might Fly	80
6	Powering Down	94
7	A Cunning Plan	110
8	The Broome Years	130
9	The Parkview Years	154
10	The Treasury Years	182
11	A Good Thing for Londoners	206
12	Power to the People	220
	Afterword	238
	Battersea Power Station Timeline	242
	Bibliography	246
	Filmography	248
	Notes	249
	Acknowledgements	261
	Index	262

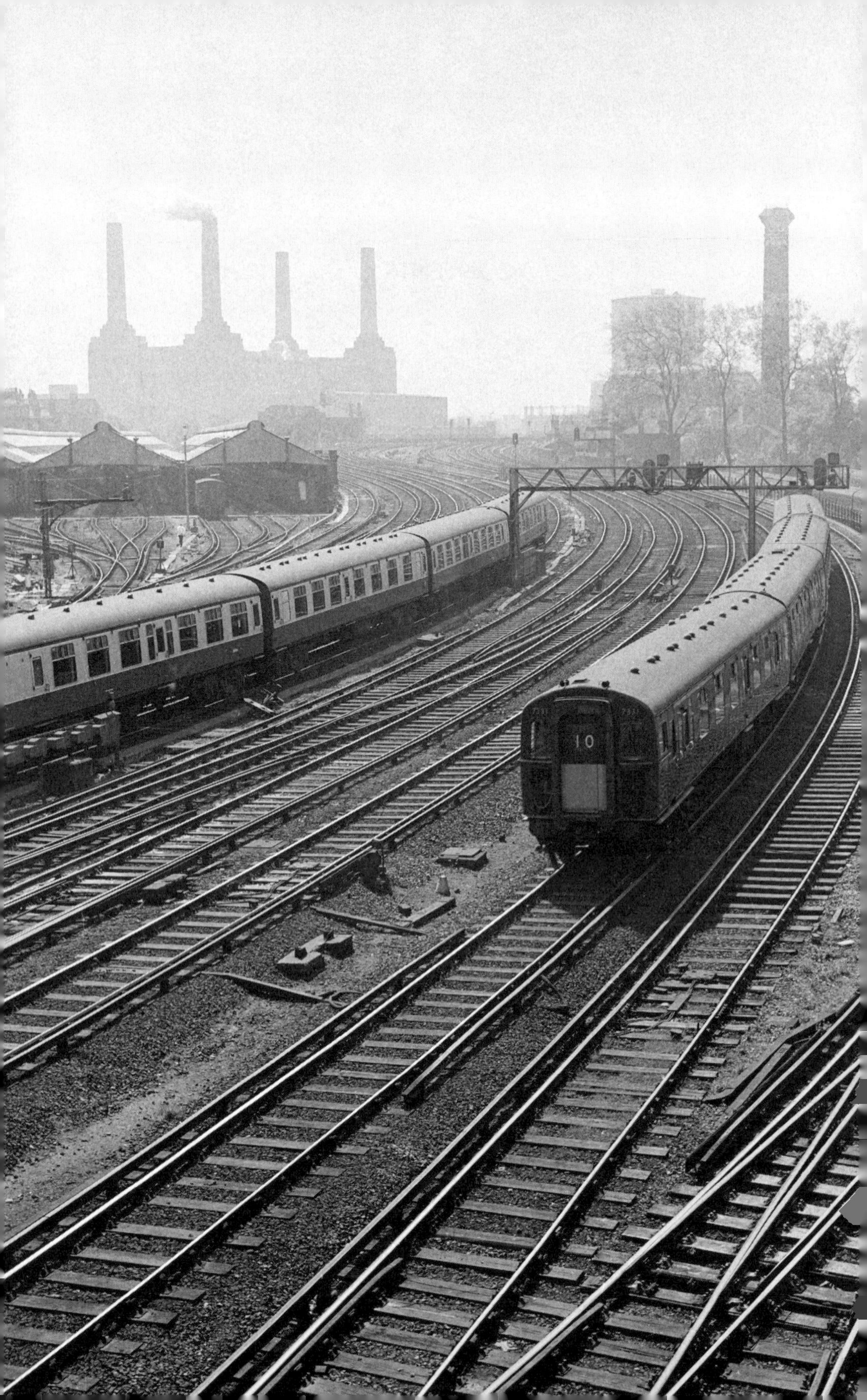
10

PREFACE

WHEN I WAS A CHILD travelling from the suburbs into the centre of London, the looming presence of Battersea Power Station beside the railway track as we approached Victoria train station was the signal that we had arrived in the city. It was like the ruin of a medieval river citadel, a towering gatehouse that warned we had left behind the security of home, where everything was familiar and of comprehensible scale, and were about to enter the big smoke. It was a thrilling moment, every time.

I am now an adult with two young children and the sight of the building still triggers in me a surge of excitement. So when the publisher suggested I write a book about Battersea Power Station, I was surprised to realise that it hadn't been done before. This is one of London's most loved buildings, a landmark not just in its own city but around the world thanks to its appearance on the cover of an album by one of the world's biggest bands.

It also happens to be one of the city's most contentious buildings. For more than thirty years, in plain sight of thousands of commuters who pass it every day on trains in and out of Victoria, the power station has stood derelict and decaying. In that time barely a week has gone by that a newspaper, magazine or website has not carried a story on the building, fascinated by its teetering but not yet terminal decrepitude, like a booze-wasted rock band that still might get it

PREFACE

together for one almighty comeback. There have been gossipy articles about the parties and events Battersea has hosted, and the surreal assortment of celebrities and organisations whose names have been linked with it. There have been recurrent tales about the damage being done by the weather to its vast brickwork frame. But the best stories have been those that reported on grand future plans for the power station's use. Over the years, these have been many and varied. For three decades now, periodically the media has been summoned to the Battersea riverside to be dazzled with a sparkling new vision for the empty building, typically delivered with all the hyperbole of a party leader on the campaign trail. Then things would go quiet before the next round of stories, which would inevitably be carried in the financial pages and deal with bankruptcy and buyouts as yet another Battersea dream crashed and burned. These failed projects and missed opportunities have been a constant background to London life for so long that most of us lost track of what was going on a long time ago. This book is an attempt to piece it all together, to find out what has kept going wrong. Was the building itself to blame, as so many developers insisted, or was there more to it than that?

I quickly came to realise that the recent history of Battersea very much mirrors what has been going on across London at large. The power station has been subject to buffeting by popular trends and fashions, and has alternately suffered and benefitted from every fluctuation in the political and economic climate that has affected the wider city.

Rather than a straightforward history, this is a journalist's book. Over the past two years I have interviewed as many people as possible who have been involved with Battersea, most of whom have never previously spoken on the

PREVIOUS SPREAD
Battersea Power Station as border post, in the 1970s (with just one chimney smoking), when the author was a youth travelling into central London on the train.
© Historic England

subject. There were several who declined to talk – as I said, the power station is contentious – and one or two others who would only do so off the record.

The story that results will, hopefully, shed some light on the question asked by so many Londoners over the past few decades: namely, what is going on with Battersea Power Station?

What I discovered is that there is no simple, concise answer but any considered explanation might include elements of greed, pride, lust, envy, betrayal – all the ingredients, I hope, of an excellent story.

London, January 2016

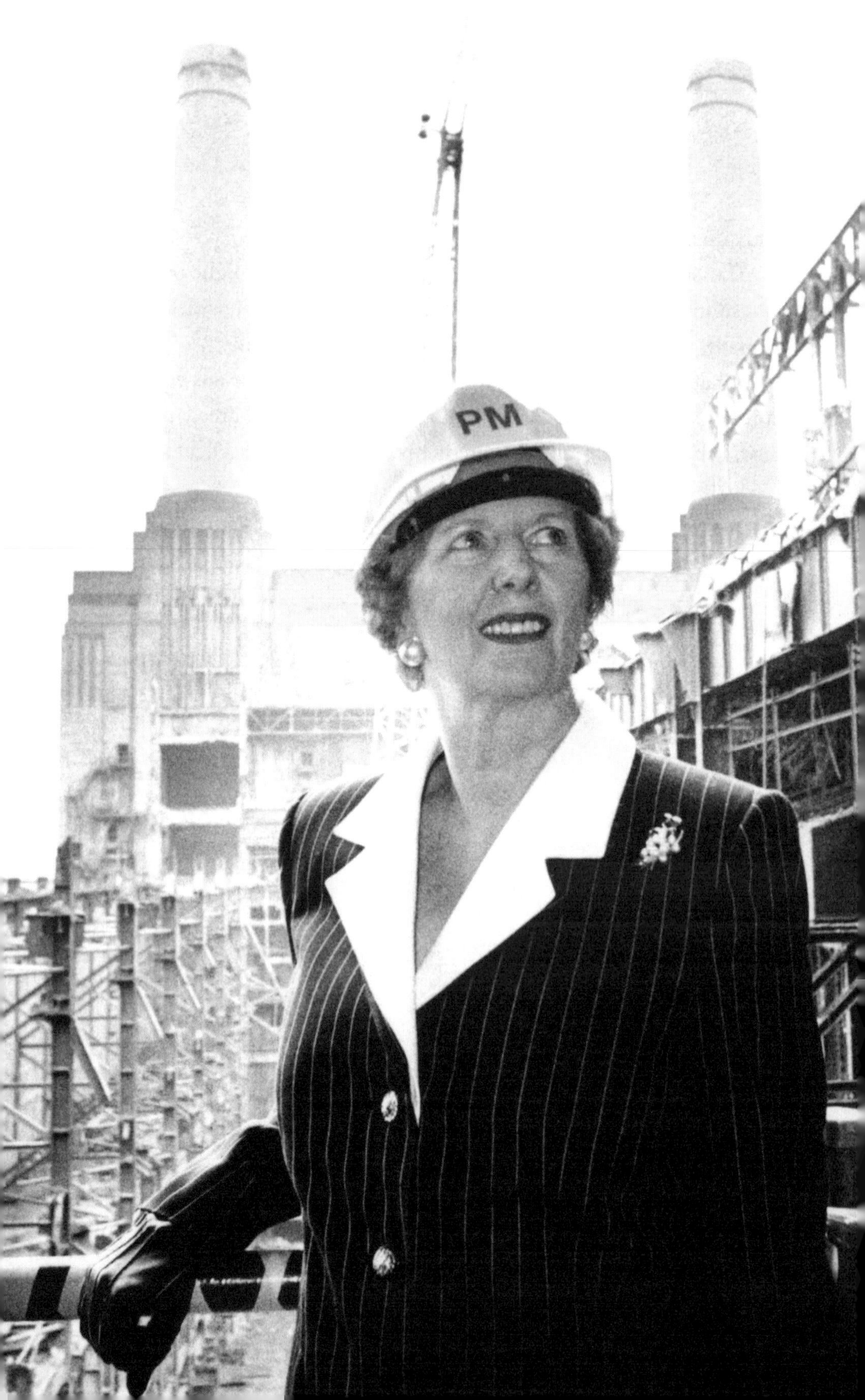
PM

INTRODUCTION

WEARING A WHITE HARD HAT and brandishing the biggest laser gun in Britain, Margaret Thatcher took aim at the wall of Battersea Power Station and fired. It was June 1988 and the occasion was the naming ceremony for The Battersea, an elaborate and heavily publicised plan to turn the defunct 1930s coal-fired power station on the Thames into Europe's answer to Disneyland. The Prime Minister was developer John Broome's guest of honour. She told reporters that The Battersea was a "wonderful example of private enterprise and local government working hand in hand for the benefit of Britain", and that Broome should be praised for "seizing the opportunity not only to save this magnificent building but to put it back to work for the nation". She was effusive in her praise for Broome and his project: it was possessed she said, of "that touch of pure genius, tinged with English eccentricity, that has always made Britain great".[1]

Thatcher was almost certainly fonder of Broome than she was of Battersea Power Station, of which she is said to have once insisted, "I never want to see smoke coming out of those chimneys again."[2]

At the launch, she gamely did her bit for the cameras, for Britain, for Broome. Surrounded by journalists and local politicians, she posed with her gun. The laser beam she fired detonated fireworks and triggered the dropping of a white curtain dramatically revealing

INTRODUCTION

the building's new name picked out in flame. Purple smoke poured from the great white chimneys – presumably the PM did not object to the smoke in this instance. The explosions were so loud that local residents called 999. Four fire engines and a fireboat were sent to the scene, ensuring even more coverage in the following day's newspapers for the grandstanding Broome, who boldly told the press that The Battersea would open in two years at precisely 2.30pm on 21st May 1990. "And if you think this is good," a beaming Broome told his project manager John Gidman, "wait till the opening ceremony. I've got twenty-five members of the royal family coming down river by barge."[3]

The royals never came. John Broome's scheme, already deemed something of a fantasy by local politicians on the day of that launch,[4] came to nothing. "It was once a testament to British industrial power and confidence. It is now a shrieking monument of twelve years of shyster government," sniped MP Tony Banks in the House of Commons in 1991,[5] as Broome's plans unravelled. In the coming years Banks and a great many other parties would have plenty more to provoke their ire as Broome's was only the first of several grand plans for Battersea to fail spectacularly.

Today, the power station remains a heroic ruin, albeit one surrounded by the beginnings of a long-term building project as the land around this monumental pile is readied for the construction of a series of landmark luxury developments by a starry array of international architects. Like so many London buildings, Battersea Power Station is now entirely owned and operated by a foreign state, a sad fate for a British institution but not an unusual one.

Battersea has always had an uncanny knack for reflecting the changing preoccupations of the UK capital. In the late 1920s, when the

PREVIOUS SPREAD
Prime Minister Margaret Thatcher, resplendent in pinstriped suit and personalised hard hat, is the guest of honour at the launch of The Battersea in June 1988. © Rex Features

plans for a gigantic power station close to the centre of London first went public, the rich citizens of Chelsea and Westminster were terrified at the prospect of the damage the smoke might cause. So began a furious campaign to halt construction that wound up involving everybody from the Archbishop of Canterbury to the king of England. Industry prevailed and the scheme went ahead. To plans finalised by celebrated architect Giles Gilbert Scott the power station was built in two phases – it is, in fact, two power stations built back-to-back, each the mirror image of the other. The first phase was the A Station, which, viewed from the Thames, is the right half of the current building. It took the form of a large, rectangular boiler house topped by two chimneys, with a lower, adjacent wing containing the turbine hall and switch house. In the latter was a control room designed by James Theodore Halliday of Manchester-based architects Halliday & Agate, with marble walls, coffered and glazed ceiling bays with decorative lights, and semi-circular desks from which foremen would monitor operations.

It represented the best of British industry and design, providing electricity to the masses through state-of-the-art technology from within elegantly composed surrounds. It demonstrated the ingenuity of British builders and adhered to the still prevalent old Victorian notion that utilitarian public buildings could and should be decorative and appealing.

Recognition of the building's strategic value was almost immediate. When politicians discussed the dangers presented by Oswald Mosley's Fascist Blackshirts in 1936, the government was told, "There is always the danger in the modern state that these men may be used in time of revolutionary ferment to occupy key positions – the Bank of England, the Battersea Power Station, Broadcasting House – and from there they might well be in a position, although a minority of the country, to capture the machinery of government."[6]

INTRODUCTION

Already, Battersea Power Station was considered to be one of the three most important buildings for the function of the nation.

The power station's importance grew from 1939, when it produced electricity in support of the war effort. However, the war slowed construction of the B Station – essentially a symmetrical copy of the A Station, albeit in cheaper materials due to the cost of the conflict. It began operation when the third chimney was raised in 1941; a fourth arrived almost as an afterthought in 1955. It was only now, more than twenty years after Battersea first began operating, that the power station took the dramatic, four-pronged form familiar to all today. With its distinctive profile, it has been described as an upside-down billiards table, "a great upturned plug straining to suck voltage out of the clouds" [7] and an overturned elephant. Less charitably, the art critic of *The Sunday Times* Waldemar Januszczak compared it to "a dead dog lying by the side of the road with its legs in the air". But really it looks more like a modern castle, a 20th-century counterpart to the medieval Tower of London six miles downriver.

Yet paradoxically, within a year of its completion, the power station would be seen as an outdated relic as a new age of atomic energy dawned; the UK's first atomic power station, at Windscale in Cumbria, became operational in 1956. Wandsworth's vast brick building, belching fumes over the river, now became a symbol of a country whose economic and imperial ambitions were on the wane. The A Station was closed down in March 1975 and the building began a slow journey into the realm of living history. As its industrial role diminished, its cultural and symbolic status grew, exemplified in 1977 when the power station was immortalised by Pink Floyd for the cover of their album *Animals*. In the autumn of 1980 it was hastily listed by English Heritage as people began to confront its inevitable closure, which happened three years later.

The power station had been built with private money but after the war it passed into public ownership following the nationalisation of the electricity industry by the Attlee government. This was in keeping with the post-war political consensus, which determined that public utilities like electricity should be provided by the state for all, the same ideological commitment that led to creation of the National Health Service around the same time. But by 1983, public ownership was increasingly regarded as an unwanted burden on government, especially in Wandsworth, a flagship borough for privatisation. In this climate, it was essential that the issue of what to do with a giant abandoned power station was made somebody else's problem.

A flawed competition was organised by the Central Electricity Generating Board after which the power station was more or less given away for £1.5m, entering private hands and immediately becoming the subject of the first of many property battles. It has remained in private hands ever since. In that time, its potential future has been subject to the whims of whatever the current owners have deemed profitable or fashionable. It was going to be an English Disneyland; a casino; a football stadium; a giant cinema complex; a permanent home for an international circus troupe; a horse-racing track; a religious theme park. The plans were often fascinating, accompanied by bold words and beguiling architectural visuals in national newspapers but, as in the case of John Broome's scheme, nothing came of any of it. The power station passed between owners (or their banks), all of whom threw sacks of cash at architects, designers and planners in a bid to solve this gigantic problem while London and the press watched from the sidelines, horrified that one of the most famous buildings in the world could be so hideously neglected, its roof ripped off, walls collapsing, chimneys decaying. Some wondered whether it could survive. Others wished it wouldn't.

INTRODUCTION

Detractors included Prince Philip, who once asked one of the power station's owners, Victor Hwang, "Why don't you just knock the bloody thing down?"[8] Luckily for London, it never quite reached the point where demolition was possible, however tempting it may have been for the owners.

Despite everything, the building has only grown in the affections of Londoners and, indeed, the wider world. This is partly down to a post power-production career as a bit-part player in countless films and TV shows, and its enduring popularity with photographers, artists and image-makers. It has appeared in computer games, complete with pixelated flying pig in the fiendish ZX Spectrum 1980s classic *Jet Set Willy*. Its likeness adorns cufflinks and T-shirts, American Apparel romper suits and Converse trainers. When the power station featured in September 2013's Open House, the annual festival in which some of London's private buildings open their doors to visitors, 40,000 people queued for five hours for the chance to look around inside.

London's current obsession is luxury housing. When – or if – Battersea Power Station finally reopens it will be as the central feature of what is essentially a gigantic gated community for London's rich, investors who are happy to spend more than £1m on a studio flat purchased sight-unseen, off-plan. It is easy to feel that at this point, the power station's long, close relationship with Londoners will have effectively come to an end. As with so many recent developments along the river, the overriding impression is that this building is no longer meant for the likes of me and you.

How did we get to this point? The story of Battersea Power Station that unfolds in this book is a tale of flamboyant developers, arguably well-intentioned but frequently ill-advised, of greed, bad luck and broken dreams, and of London's rampant property speculation. It is about the value we place on heritage and history, and who we ask to bear that cost. It is about local campaigners, unelected and high-minded, but often more imaginative than the wealthy and powerful cabal they confront. It is about an ideology that backed the free market despite repeated failures, and never thought to question whether it got things wrong. It is about the future of London, the legacy we are leaving as we sell our skyline to foreign investors. And it is about a flying pig, a symbol that has become increasingly appropriate as time has gone on and successive promises about Battersea Power Station's future have dissolved in the London air like the smoke that once billowed from those four gargantuan chimneys.

PARK ENTRANCE

CHAPTER ONE

TOGETHER IN ELECTRIC DREAMS

Why London needed a giant power station and how Battersea was chosen as the site

IN DECEMBER 1907, an American engineer named John Walter Frink Bennett, together with architect Francis Swales, presented the British public with proposals for a fantastical scheme called "Dream City". Modelled on Coney Island's Dreamland, it was a theme park that would feature lakes and promenades, a water chute, an illuminated tower, a pageant based on a very American idea of Elizabethan England, the tasteful-sounding "midget village" and "Esquimaux settlement", as well as gardens laid out to represent those found in different European countries. The *Daily Mail* described the scheme as "a veritable fairy land".

The site chosen for the scheme was beside the Thames at Battersea; the very spot, in fact, to which John Broome would later invite Margaret Thatcher to help publicise his own Disneyland-inspired theme park set in an obsolete power station. Dream City, Bennett promised, would open by May the following year.

Bennett proposed to develop Dream City on a fifteen-acre plot recently vacated by the Southwark and Vauxhall Waterworks Company, once famed for producing the most polluted water in London. Arthur Hill Hassall, a chemist who diligently examined all London's water supplies in 1850, reported on the Southwark and Vauxhall for medical journal *The Lancet*. He wrote that, "This water was in the worst condition in which it is possible to conceive any water to be… in a worse state even than Thames water itself, as taken from the bed of the river."[1]

It was also lethal. Physician John Snow was horrified by the quality of the water from Battersea when conducting his groundbreaking studies into cholera; he discerned that Southwark and Vauxhall water had killed hundreds during the 1854 epidemic. Partly as a result of the findings of these two public-health pioneers, it became illegal to draw water from below Teddington Lock after 1855. Southwark and Vauxhall built new waterworks in Hampton, upriver of Teddington, but did not abandon Battersea completely. Instead, they pumped water from Hampton to Battersea, where it passed through a new system of filtration beds before going out to the public. However, by 1903, the waterworks in Battersea were obsolete, clearing the stage for Bennett and Swales.

John Bennett was born in Chicago and educated at the University of Michigan, where, in addition to excelling as an American footballer, he graduated as a civil engineer in 1899. He moved to London finding work with the Waring-White Building Company,

PREVIOUS SPREAD
A bird's-eye view of Dream City, the World's Fair-inspired attraction proposed by John Bennett for the site of the former Battersea waterworks.

a leading contractor with involvement in projects including the Ritz and Waldorf hotels, and a number of Underground stations. It was at this company he met Swales, a Canadian who was educated in New York and Paris, and who would later consult on the great Beaux-Arts frontage of Selfridges department store on London's Oxford Street.

Original drawings of the Dream City scheme suggest that what the pair had in mind was something very like a scaled-back version of the 1900 World's Fair, or Exposition Universelle, in Paris. Bennett and Swales had acquired a lease on the land for twenty-one years and promised to provide "an up-to-date, healthy and popular-priced place of amusement".[2] Visitors would enter from Battersea Park Road via a monumental iron arch modelled on the Paris Exposition's Porte

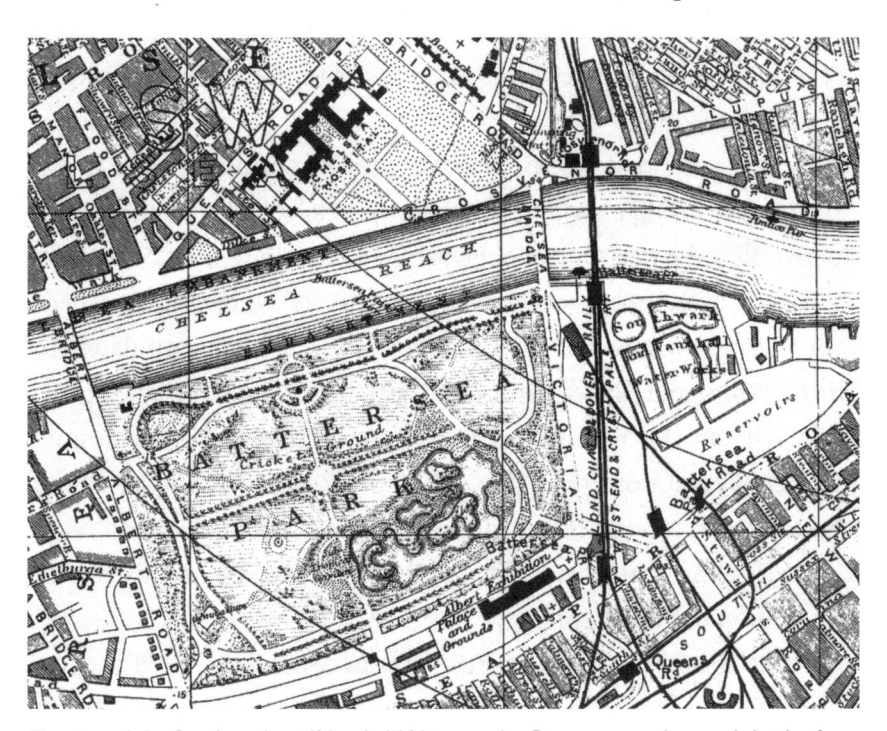

The site of the Southwark and Vauxhall Waterworks Company on the south bank of the Thames, with Battersea Park to the west, separated by the line into Victoria railway station. From an 1888 map of London.

Monumentale, except at Battersea a water chute plunged from the top of the gate's dome into the vast monumental lake that filled the centre of the southern half of the site. The lake ran up to the foot of a giant, square tower, like St Mark's Campanile at Venice, which was to be illuminated at night; the architect's drawing shows rays of light being beamed from the top, like an urban lighthouse. At the base of the north side of tower is a massive bandstand and auditorium that, oddly, slopes away from the stage and down to an enormous parade ground. This is flanked by all manner of pavilions including one fashioned like a mosque, another like a Chinese temple and pagoda. There is a large rollercoaster beside a park containing a circus tent, both abutting the railway line. The site presents a grand colonnaded facade to the river, where there is a wharf for the paddle steamers that would deliver visitors from central London (a covered walkway at the south-west corner connected the site to Battersea Park station for those arriving by rail).

Press reports describe further attractions not discernable in the drawing including a switchback railway, helter-skelter, a submarine that would take passengers beneath the lake where they could gaze on "weird ocean monsters, wrecks and divers", and a subterranean rollercoaster that would carry riders along a track populated by ghosts, animated skeletons and a cave featuring "strange reptiles [that] will crawl across the track in front of the car". In what sounds like a challenge from the 1970s TV show *It's a Knockout*, there was also to be a revolving beam that visitors had to run across to reach a platform and win a prize. The entire site would be illuminated by one million electric lights.

A music-and-dancing licence was successfully applied for and Dream City was approved by the London County Council (LCC). But it never happened; the reasons are unrecorded but it could well be that Bennett and Swales's scheme was squeezed out by competition from the hugely successfully – and similarly styled – Franco-British Exhibition, which opened at White City in west London in 1908. Bennett returned to New York where, ironically, he served as acting commissioner of water supply.

The waterworks remained derelict for a further twenty years, until the site attracted the attention of the London Power Company. This was then one of the city's biggest providers of electricity and it was looking for a suitable location for a landmark new power station that would illuminate not just a theme park but half of London.

In retrospect, it was a rather daft idea, to plonk a power station by the river so close to central London, but it was also a marvellous one. It happened thanks to Francis Fladgate, a Harrow-educated solicitor and former vice president of the Law Society who had retired from legal practice in 1920 at the age of sixty-seven to concentrate on his position as chairman of the Charing Cross Electricity Supply Company. This was one of several small private companies competing to satisfy the increased demand for electricity in the ever-expanding metropolis.

Electricity had started to replace gas as the primary means of providing light in London during the 1880s, largely thanks to the invention of the vacuum filament lamp (precursor of the light bulb), developed separately in America by Thomas Edison and in Britain by Joseph Swan at around the same time. Sporadic experiments with electrical lighting had taken place earlier – the portico of the National Gallery had been lit in 1848, arc lights were installed along the Embankment between Charing Cross and Westminster in 1878, and there had been an attempt to light Billingsgate Fish Market in 1879 – but these were all of limited success because the harsh light produced was expensive, unreliable and so painful on the eyes that it was said to induce headaches. The light bulb changed that: this was the invention that made electric light suitable for internal

Crowds gather to marvel at some of the earliest electric lighting, installed on the Embankment in central London in December 1878.

illumination. In 1881 it was used to illuminate the Savoy Theatre on the Strand, said to be the first public building lit entirely by electricity. That same year an International Exposition of Electricity was held in Paris, the purpose of which was to establish the superiority of electricity over gas. Edison and Swan were both present, two of four inventors exhibiting their lamps (another was the American Hiram Maxim, who would later gain fame as the inventor of one of the earliest machine guns), with Edison taking top honours for what was judged to be the most efficient device.

Looking to corner the UK market after his Paris triumph, Edison built the world's first public power station at 57 Holborn Viaduct. It went into operation on 11th April 1882 with steam-driven generators named "Jumbos" after the elephant of the same name, which had just been sold by London Zoo to American showman PT Barnum. It supplied the Old Bailey and main post office, and some neighbouring businesses, and also lit the length of Holborn Viaduct and Newgate Street. For the briefest period, London was at the forefront of electrification. However, just four months later the government passed the Electric Lighting Act and the advance was fatally stalled. The act encouraged private companies to supply electricity but, at the same time, forbade anybody from digging up streets in order to lay cables. The government would regulate power-generating operations by requiring them to apply for a licence but these would only be granted for a fixed, limited period of seven years. The intention was to avoid the monopolies that had occurred in the provision of gas, but the effect was to deter serious investment ensuring the supply of electricity in London, in the words of historian Gavin Weightman, remained "parochial".

Throughout London, small power stations became commonplace, some so tiny they serviced only a single business. Typical was the one that grew out of an art gallery in New Bond Street. The Grosvenor Gallery, which had been founded to exhibit the work of the Pre-Raphaelite painters, began using arc lights in 1883. The experiment was a success, to the extent that local shop-owners asked if they could be connected too. Inevitably a more powerful generator became necessary, which was designed for the gallery by a young engineer called Sebastian Pietro Innocenzo Adhemar Ziani de Ferranti, who, despite the name, was born in Liverpool, albeit the son of an Italian-Belgian photographer with a lineage he could trace back to the doges of Venice. Ferranti's generator, housed in the gallery's basement, was soon powering thousands of buildings as far away as Trafalgar Square and Lincoln's Inn Fields through cables slung from roof-to-roof.

Operating under the new name of the London Electric Supply Corporation, the gallery managed to attract large sums of capital investment for its power-generating schemes, which Ferranti now proposed to use for the construction of the world's largest power station. This was built at Deptford. In many ways, this was Battersea's predecessor – a huge building that was intended to supply many households from a riverside location chosen for the convenience of the boats that brought in the coal. It went into operation in 1891 but almost immediately suffered an accident that caused a two-week blackout followed by further problems resulting in a three-month shutdown. Ferranti left the business.

At this point, London had fallen far behind cities like New York and Paris when it came to electrification, and Berlin, which Thomas Edison considered then the best lighted city in Europe. The American also expressed astonishment that London's underground railway was steam-powered rather than electric. In America, he explained to a reporter from Britain's *Daily News*, electricity was used for far more than just lighting. "The same wire that brings the light to you will also bring power and heat. With the power you can run an elevator, a sewing machine or any other mechanical contrivance that requires a motor, and by means of the heat you may cook your food." In August 1890 the US would also carry out the first legal execution by electrocution, taking eight minutes to fry William Kemmler, who had been convicted of murdering his lover with an axe.

As the 19th century gave way to the 20th, more and larger power stations were constructed in London, which, as Edison had suggested, now served more than just the needs of lighting.

MORE AND LARGER POWER STATIONS

Sebastian Ferranti's Deptford Power Station, the first large-scale plant in London for the generation of electricity, portrayed here in an engraving from *The Illustrated London News* of 26th October 1899.

In 1903 a new station at Greenwich brought electrification to the city's tram system; in 1904 a station at Neasden began supplying the Metropolitan Railway; and in 1905 Lots Road went online to provide power for the Underground. Even so, by the start of the First World War there were still seventy different power stations operating in London, some run by local councils or the municipal LCC, many still in private hands, like the one at Notting Hill which employed dogs to lay cables through tunnels. Many areas were not connected at all.

Sir Harry Haward, former comptroller of the LCC, noted the frustrating lunacy of the competing systems in his 1932 book *The London County Council from Within*: "The current is alternating in some areas and direct in others; it is delivered at a number of different voltages and is charged for under a bewildering array of tariffs and rates with the result that consumers living in one street may be charged 3d a unit for lighting while those in the next street are charged 5d and electrical apparatus may become absolutely useless when its owner moves from one district to another."

In fact, the LCC had been trying to unpick the tangle of London's electricity supply as far back as 1906 but its suggested solution of putting the whole enterprise under public ownership had been rejected by Parliament. Ten years later, Parliament was forced to confront the issue itself and it came to the same conclusion as the LCC. Its recommendation in 1917 was that the state should take over generation and transmission of electricity, a decision of expedience rather than any ideological commitment to nationalisation.

Bringing the different providers together was a challenge. Local councils tended to operate generating plants in the poorer East End and outer suburbs, but electricity in the wealthy West End and central London boroughs was still in the hands of private companies. Parliament debated the issue in 1919, but a law that would have compelled electricity suppliers to reorganise was watered down by the House of Lords.

There was a recognition, though, that somebody needed to step in and resolve the issue. Francis Fladgate took on the task in 1920, when he pushed through a plan that would eventually unify ten of London's smaller electricity producers, including his own Charing Cross Electricity Supply Company, under the ownership of a single body, the London Power Company (LPC). As Fladgate would later write: "The express object of the establishment of the LPC was to eliminate inefficient and uneconomical stations, to improve those which were reasonably efficient and economical, to provide new stations when and where required, and generally to promote economy, efficiency and reliability in the production of electrical energy in the metropolis." By the time he was finished in 1925, the LPC controlled electricity supply across London from Paddington in the west to Greenwich in the east, north into Farringdon and south towards Camberwell. Around the same time, the government created the Central Electricity Board to work with the private companies to ensure the transmission of standardised electricity around the country.

Critical to Fladgate's plans was the construction of a grand new power station that could generate the huge amounts of power required and which would also make a statement about the ambition, reach and dynamism of the LPC. But before that could happen a suitable site needed to be found.

In 1925, Fladgate made "exhaustive inquiry negotiations"[3] with the Duke of Northumberland for thirty-five acres in Brentford. He also pursued an interest in the site of the old waterworks in Battersea. The Central Electricity Board was presented with the two options and pronounced its preference for Battersea. Consent to go ahead with the scheme was granted in October 1927.[4]

Battersea's advantage as a location for a giant power station was also its drawback: its central location. It was close to those parts of central London that it would be supplying with electricity, thus dramatically reducing transmission costs. But would the public accept an enormous industrial plant within sight of Westminster?

Battersea, cut off from fashionable Chelsea and powerful Westminster by the barrier of the Thames, had remained an agricultural area into the 1850s when it was still covered in market gardens, especially famous for their excellent asparagus, known as "Battersea bundles". Like much of London, it was transformed in the second half of the 19th century when railway lines and bridges made the suburbs suddenly accessible, and the population exploded from 10,000 in 1851 to 150,000 just forty years later.

Industry began to descend on Battersea and the area gained a gasworks, chemical and cement works and, of course, water-treatment works. Together they filled the air with noxious fumes that contributed to the area's low reputation, a taint of disrepute that stretched back to the early 18th century and centred around an establishment called the Red House. This was an inn sat in five acres of grounds across the river from Chelsea Hospital. It was famed for its louche attractions and leisure activities, where, according to a quote in the *Survey of London*, "pigeons are shot continually and sometimes men". A possibly hyperventilating gent by the name of Thomas Kirk told *London City Mission Magazine* in September 1870 that he had gone to "this sad spot" on a Sunday afternoon – in other words, on the Lord's Day – and had witnessed "from sixty to 120 horses and donkeys racing, foot-racing, walking matches, flying boats, flying horses, roundabouts, theatres, comic actors, shameless dancers, conjurers, fortune-tellers, gamblers of every description, drinking-booths, stalls, hawkers and vendors of all kinds of articles". It all sounds rather fun, but in the view of Kirk it was "a place out of hell that surpassed Sodom and Gomorrah in abomination".[5]

Battersea Park had initially been created as a way of sanitising this picaresque patch of London. It was laid out in 1858 on the marsh of Battersea Fields, and was intended to attract the well-to-do residents of Chelsea and Fulham over the river, which they would cross by Chelsea Bridge, also completed that year, as long as they were prepared to pay a small toll. Queen Victoria led by example, becoming the first person to use the bridge on 31st March 1858 on her way to open the park; it is probably safe to assume her passage was toll free. For years, the bridge – which was originally to be called Victoria Bridge – was only lit on those nights when the Queen was sleeping in London, something that, along with the toll, ensured neither bridge nor park were quite as popular with residents of the north bank as had been hoped.

Snobbery played a part too: the industry that had settled in Battersea required a labour force, which made it a distinctly working-class neighbourhood. "The area soon became as notorious as the East End for its overcrowded, insanitary conditions," writes David Rosenberg in his radical history of London, *Rebel Footprints*. Perhaps accordingly, given the spirit of the times, the borough was governed from 1889 by a coalition of radical progressives, who espoused a form of municipal socialism and built public toilets and baths, as well as an early electricity generating station on Lombard Road. They took as their emblem a gold bee, a symbol of unity and cooperation. It was amid this hotbed of industry, radicalism and low entertainment that Fladgate decided to locate his power station, on the riverside plot left empty by the abandoned waterworks. Dream City had failed to take hold but perhaps the site could now provide the foundations for a brave new electrified world.

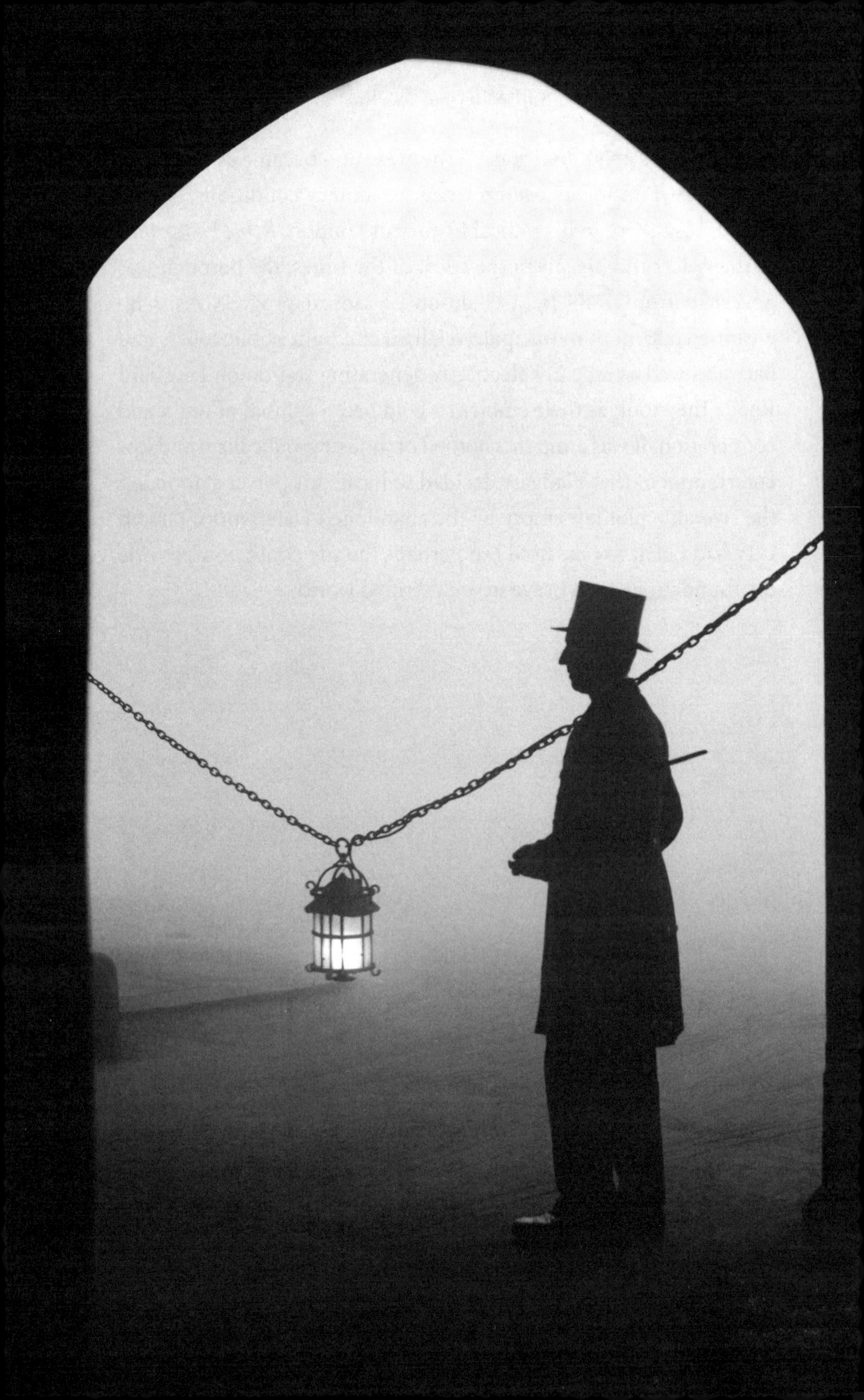

CHAPTER TWO

AN EVIL SCHEME

How the great and good of England united in opposition to the baby-bleaching threat of the proposed Battersea power station

THE MOST REVEREND COSMO LANG, Archbishop of Canterbury since 1928, would have his ill-judged moment of fame in 1936 when he took to the airwaves after the abdication of Edward VIII to label the outgoing king "misguided and disgusting". But in April 1929, he was enjoying the calm of the Mediterranean on board a yacht owned by banker John Pierpont Morgan, Jr. Although Lang was visiting peers and holy sites in Jerusalem and Greece, he was also convalescing from a recent illness, but this did not stop him firing off a pointed telegram to Chelsea Town Hall. Written for the attention of Charles Clapcott, the Mayor of Chelsea, it read:

AN EVIL SCHEME

"Please use my name in any effort against Battersea Power Station. Archbishop of Canterbury."[1] Even on holiday, God and state were uniting against the twin menaces of capitalism and industrialisation as represented by the proposed new building. The archbishop would later fulminate in more detail about "the appalling callousness which has made the infliction of the Battersea Power Station apparently inevitable, where trees and parks and historical buildings need preservation more than anywhere else, and where the health of the people should be the paramount consideration".

It was Mrs Handel Booth of Grosvenor Road, SW1, who first alerted the world at large to the horror of what was about to be raised by the side of the Thames at Battersea. For some time a heated discussion had been ongoing in the pages of the national press concerning the grimy output from the chimneys of the "Chelsea monster", the power station on Lots Road, opened in 1905 and still exciting grievance more than two decades later. Mrs Booth wrote to *The Times* on 6th September 1927 to alert readers to a new and impending threat from across the river at Battersea. She had attended a public inquiry in June held at Savoy Court on Cromwell Road for those who lived with 300 yards of what she called this "proposed nuisance" at which she had learned about a planned "super power station" with "sixteen chimneys 200-feet high" and "sixteen boilers that never go out". "It is not yet too late to prevent this abomination in our midst," she urged.

From this rallying call, an opposition grew that was to include not just the Archbishop of Canterbury but also the mayors of Chelsea and Westminster, the president of the Royal Institute of British Architects and the king's physician. Between them, these illustrious NIMBYs would cite potential damage to the

PREVIOUS SPREAD
Since industrialisation in the early 19th century, London had been wreathed in thick yellow "pea soupers". A power station on the Thames at Battersea could only worsen the problem. The photo was taken at Lincoln's Inn Fields in 1934.
© Fred Morley/Getty Images

Tate Gallery, Lambeth Palace, St James's Park, Westminster Abbey, the Houses of Parliament, Whitehall, the National Gallery and just about any other building within a five-mile radius of Chelsea Bridge. Even King George V would have his say. Much of this argument was carried out on the pages of *The Times*, unquestionably the most important and influential newspaper of the day.

In February 1927, the London Power Company (LPC) had applied for consent to build at Battersea a super-station that would have a capacity of 360,000kW, an output equivalent to its current nine power stations combined. The London County Council (LCC) approved the scheme, as did the government's Office of Works department, although with a few significant caveats relating to the management of pollution. On 27th October the government gave its final consent.

No power station had ever been built in London as large as that planned for the fifteen-acre riverside site at Battersea. The appointed designer was Somerset-born Leonard Pearce, previously electrical engineer at the Barton Power Station in Trafford Park, Manchester, and employed by the LPC as its engineer-in-chief since 1926. To assist at Battersea, Pearce brought in Henry Newmarch Allott of CS Allott & Son as his civil engineer, having worked with him in Manchester since 1915. Allott would not live to see the new power station completed, dying in 1929, after which his role was taken by his nephew Arthur Creswell Dean.

It was Pearce and Allott who established the basic concept of organising the power station in three main sections – boiler house, turbine hall and switch houses – which would be laid out in parallel, and for the station to be built in two phases, A and B, which would be the mirror image of each other, so that when complete they would make one perfectly symmetrical building. The idea behind the separation of the boiler house, turbine hall and switch houses

AN EVIL SCHEME

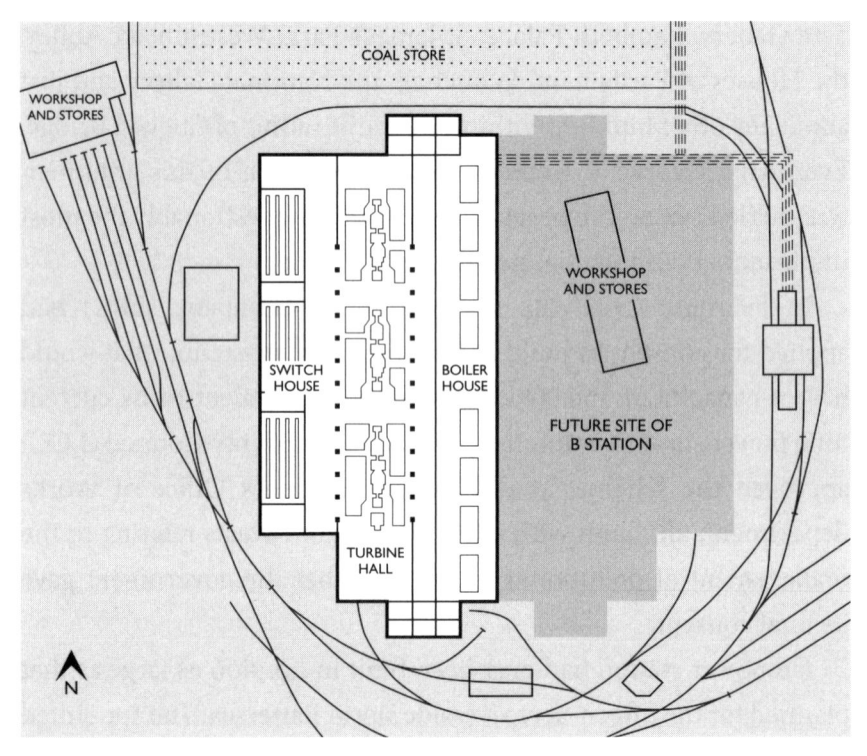

Pearce and Allott's basic concept for the new power station was for it to be built in two phases, A and B, with both stations having mirror-image arrangements of a boiler house, turbine hall and switch house.

was that it reflected the three stages of the generation of electricity in a coal-fired station.[2]

Pearce's first designs featured a steel-frame with brick exterior surmounted by sixteen relatively short steel chimneys aligned in two rows and braced by steel cables. In surviving drawings it looks much like a run-of-the-mill factory or, maybe, with its supporting cables, a little like a cantilevered football stand. The chimneys, however, were controversial. Fears continued to grow that the new power station would be hideously polluting. Higher and fewer chimneys were demanded by the government.

A revised scheme reduced the number to eight slightly taller steel chimneys, arranged in two rows of four. However, evidence from the power station in Barton now suggested that steel chimneys were prone to rapid corrosion, so in July 1928 yet another revision was produced, now with six tall chimneys of brick and concrete. The following year this was further refined and Pearce, now working with Dean, settled on what would prove to be the final arrangement of four chimneys, one at each corner. Although subsequently this turned out to be a highly aesthetically pleasing arrangement, it was born entirely of necessity.

As Pearce and Dean reworked their plans, the citizens of Chelsea worked up their indignation. The anti-Battersea campaign was now being marshalled by Reginald Blunt, a local historian and founder of the newly formed Chelsea Society. On 29th November 1927, Blunt told *The Times* of a meeting with the LPC, who "did their best to reassure our forebodings with attractive samples of gauze gritters and encouraging bottles of extracted grime… Still, I am afraid we came away without much enthusiasm." Blunt remained sceptical that it would be any more expensive to bring electricity in on overhead cables from outer London, or beyond, and believed it "impossible that this huge mass of coal can be handled and consumed without seriously affecting the atmosphere which we Londoners have to breathe".

These were legitimate concerns but as time went on the debate became increasingly incoherent. In February 1929, Sir Edward Hilton Young, a Conservative MP and future minister for health, wrote to Geoffrey Fry, the prime minister's private secretary, demanding an inquiry. The power station, he wrote in a state of shrill hysteria, would "kill every green thing within two miles of Battersea, rot all the buildings and bleach all the babies". Fry responded in similar spirit, suggesting that "you and I and our families must immediately escape to Wiltshire leaving, like Lot and his wife, the city of the plain to its inevitable destruction".[3]

AN EVIL SCHEME

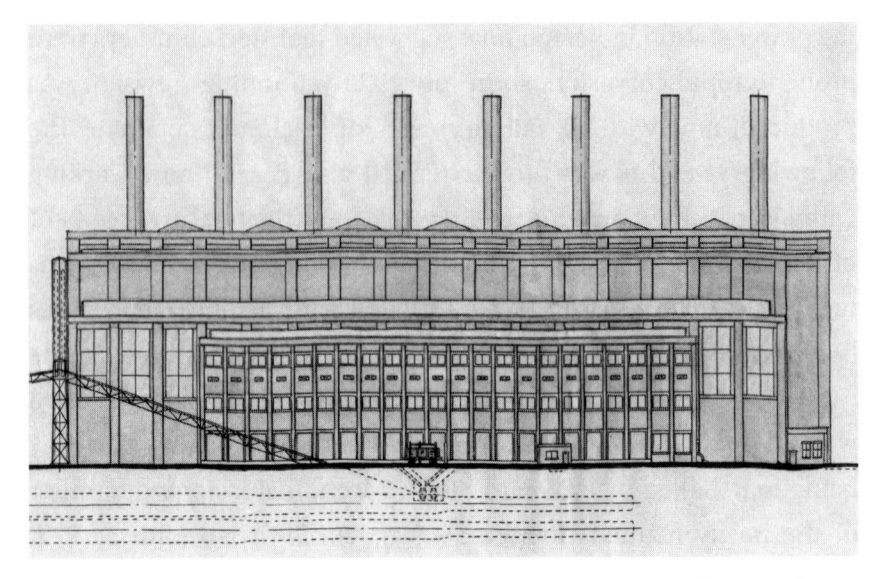

The first design for a power station at Battersea by engineers Leonard Pearce and Henry Allott, drawn up in 1927, took the form of a large brick shed with sixteen short steel chimneys. This is the west elevation. National Archives

The protests intensified on 9th April 1929, when a letter objecting to the scheme was sent to *The Times* signed by several eminent figures, including Mayor of Chelsea Charles Clapcott, Mayor of Westminster Vivian B Rogers, President of the Royal Institute of British Architects Walter Tapper and the editor of medical journal *The Lancet* Squire Sprigge. After detailing their objections, the letter concluded, "it seems manifest that the present project is ill-advised, particularly as there are alternatives which have technical and economic advantages".

The following day the newspaper ran an editorial in support of the objectors accompanied by a map of the "probable area affected by fumes", which included landmarks such as the National Gallery, Buckingham Palace, St James's Palace and the Houses of Parliament. Unsurprisingly, this triggered even more correspondence. "At least twenty square miles of artistic London will be blanketed with soot and almost impossible to live in," thundered one irate reader. "The

FROM PARADISE TO AN INFERNO

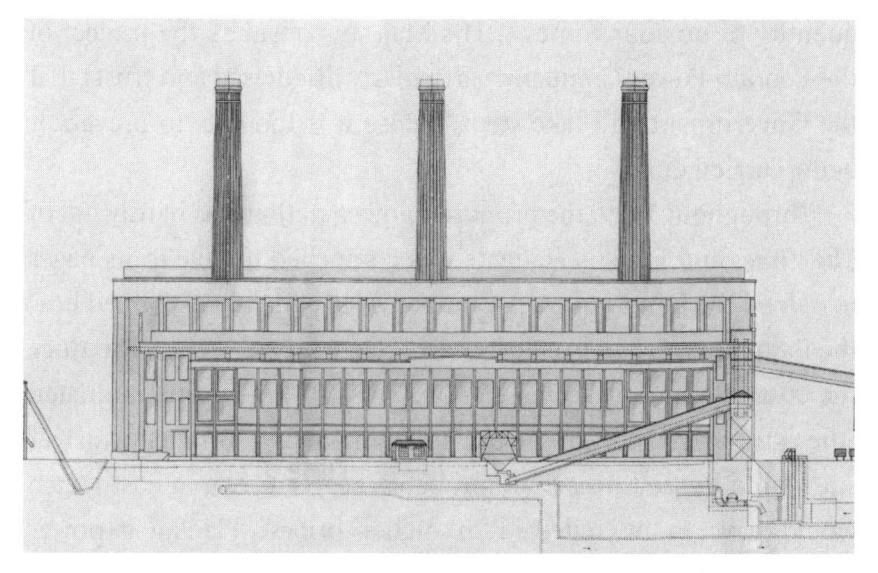

An intermediary design by Pearce and Allott, with the chimneys now reduced to six. Rather than steel, which had been discovered to be susceptible to corrosion, it is now proposed they are constructed of brick and concrete. National Archives

depreciation of surrounding property may run into millions of pounds, but the loss of sunshine and consequent ill health will be incalculable." Another feared that "Battersea Park will sink from a paradise to an inferno". A spokesperson for Chelsea Physic Garden worried that the "the emission of sulphur fumes and grit [would] exert a detrimental influence on vegetation and seriously prejudice scientific research", and the Bishop of Southwark, not wanting to miss out on the fun, condemned the Battersea power station scheme as simply "evil".

Even chain-smoking King George V, recovering from surgery on his lungs in Bognor and, perhaps, rather attuned to matters involving air quality, became involved. On 12th April, he had his assistant private secretary send a letter to Minister of Health Neville Chamberlain commenting that having followed the story in *The Times*, "His Majesty feels the greatest concern at the prospect of the atmosphere of London being still further polluted by the large quantity of noxious fumes… His Majesty considers the project of the London Power Company particularly ill-advised and trusts that the Government will take steps, before it is too late, to prevent it being carried out."[4]

Throughout 1929, the proposed power station was hardly out of *The Times* and Francis Fladgate was compelled to take to its pages to defend the London Power Company. He patiently explained how the Battersea site had been carefully selected to substantially reduce the cost of electricity transmission. The LPC, he wrote, estimated "the extra capital cost of the transmission system from a downriver site would be well over £2m, probably nearer £3m… a cost which would have to be reflected in higher prices". Placing a power station somewhere outside London – the coalfields of Kent was one popular alternative choice – would also require extensive cabling causing widespread inconvenience and disruption. The Port of London Authority refused to allow cables to be laid on the Thames, he explained, so overhead lines "would have to circle round south London and enter around the Croydon enclave where bricks and mortar are not quite so impenetrable".

But the major concern to address was pollution. Fladgate reminded readers of *The Times* of a commitment made by the LPC that stated, "The company shall in construction and use of the said generating station take the best known precautions for the due consumption of smoke and for preventing the evolution of oxides of sulphur and generally for preventing any nuisance arising from the generating station or from any operations thereat." Fladgate promised that the company would not be deterred by any considerations of cost and even as debate raged in the press throughout 1929, experiments were taking place at the LPC's Grove Road Power Station in St John's Wood to discover a method of preventing sulphur emissions from the Battersea chimneys.

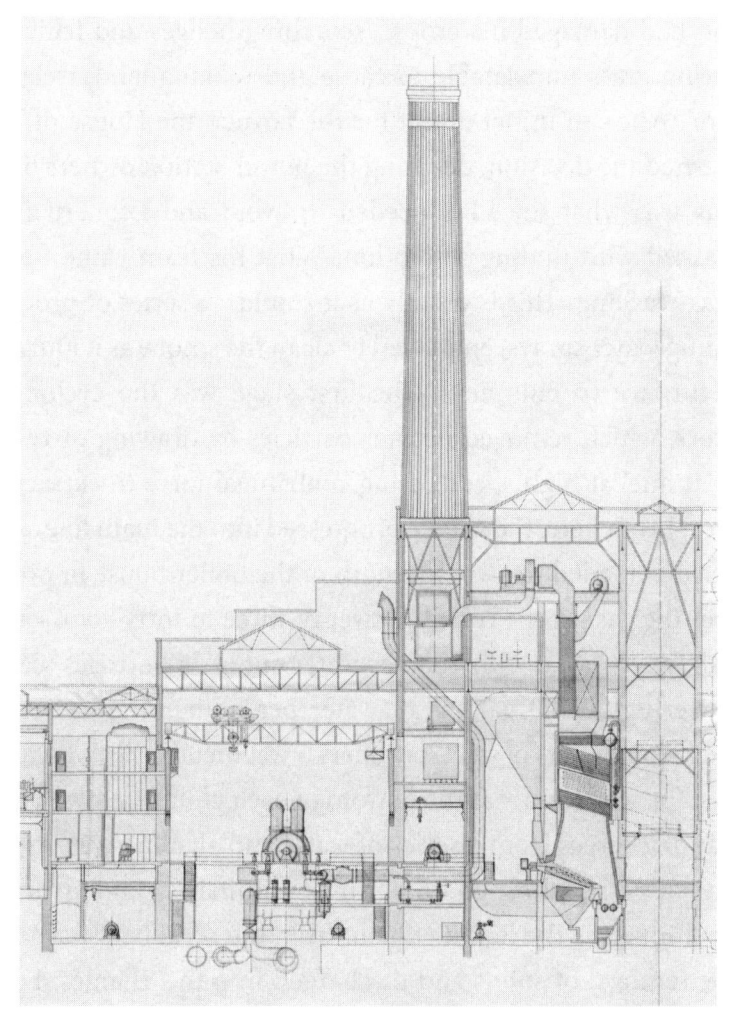

In order to eradicate polluting sulphur from the chimney emissions, Pearce and his team came up with a "gas-washing" system, running the smoke through water in order to clean it. National Archives

When the LPC agreed to eradicate sulphur from their chimneys they were whistling in the dark. Nobody had ever attempted to do this before, certainly not on such a large scale. The concerns over sulphur had arisen after a farmer in Manchester took the city corporation to court claiming that acid rain (the term may sound modern but it was, in fact, coined in 1872) from Barton Power

Station had damaged his crops, "scorching hedges and fruit trees, rendering grass unpalatable to cattle and making land useless for pasture". After an initial defeat for the farmer, the House of Lords overturned the decision, deeming the power station owners liable.

This was what the LPC needed to avoid and Leonard Pearce was tasked with finding a solution. What his team came up with was gas-washing. This is exactly as it sounds: a series of processes, including water sprays, employed to clean the smoke as it journeyed from furnace to chimneys. The first stage was the cyclone grit arrestors, which removed heavier particles by drawing dirty gases into a tunnel at high speed, using centrifugal force to extract dust and grit. From here, the smoke progressed into the main flue, a huge pipe that extended the whole length of the boiler house in order to contain the gas for the required twenty-three to forty-four seconds while it was sprayed with Thames water out of 368 nozzles (capable of delivering 60,000 gallons of water per hour). The gasses then passed through tiers of steel scrubbers – wet metal grills, providing a catalyst for oxidation – at the bottom of each chimney tower, facing regular discharges from a series of water and alkaline-water sprays. They then passed through timber mist-eliminators and up and out of the chimneys. The liquid effluent from the scrubbers was treated for the removal of solids and discharged into the Thames. For the process to function, chimneys needed to be sited at either end of the flues, which ran the entire length of the building: this would eventually give Battersea Power Station its distinctive appearance.

The gas-washing process was observed at Grove Road by representatives from the Department of Scientific and Industrial Research, the Ministry of Health and the Office of Works, all of whom were tentatively satisfied. They reported "neither acid taste nor objectionable odour could be detected by breathing the undiluted test gasses coming from the exit flue… and the absorption of about ninety-five percent of the sulphur acids in the flue gases was confirmed". Further refinements were still desired on both sides: the government wanted proof that gas-washing could work on the scale required at Battersea, while the LPC wanted to tinker with the process to reduce costs as much as possible. Essentially, though, Pearce had triumphed. In the words of the *Daily Telegraph*, the "ogre was taught to swallow its own smoke". But it came at a price. The LPC estimated gas-washing had a capital cost of £2m, or about what it was going to cost to build the station itself (this was also what it would have cost to carry the electricity had the station been sited away from central London).

Although the press continued to snipe, the LPC was given the green light to proceed with construction. It was now that Fladgate engineered his masterstroke. The scientific and economic arguments had been settled but he anticipated another possible objection to a power station being raised in such a prominent position: its appearance. He needed architecture of sufficient grandeur and majesty to silence any critics. Overtures were made to Sir Herbert Baker, former assistant to Edwin Lutyens and the architect of India House on the Aldwych and South Africa House on Trafalgar Square, but his initial concepts were rejected by the LPC.[5] Fladgate resumed his search and at the company's annual general meeting in March 1930 he had an announcement to make. Battersea Power Station was to be "projected on the most modern lines", he said: for efficiency of design, it had Dr Pearce, for clean emissions it had "the most eminent chemists that could be found" and for "distinction in its elevation" it now had one of the greatest architects of the era, Sir Giles Gilbert Scott.

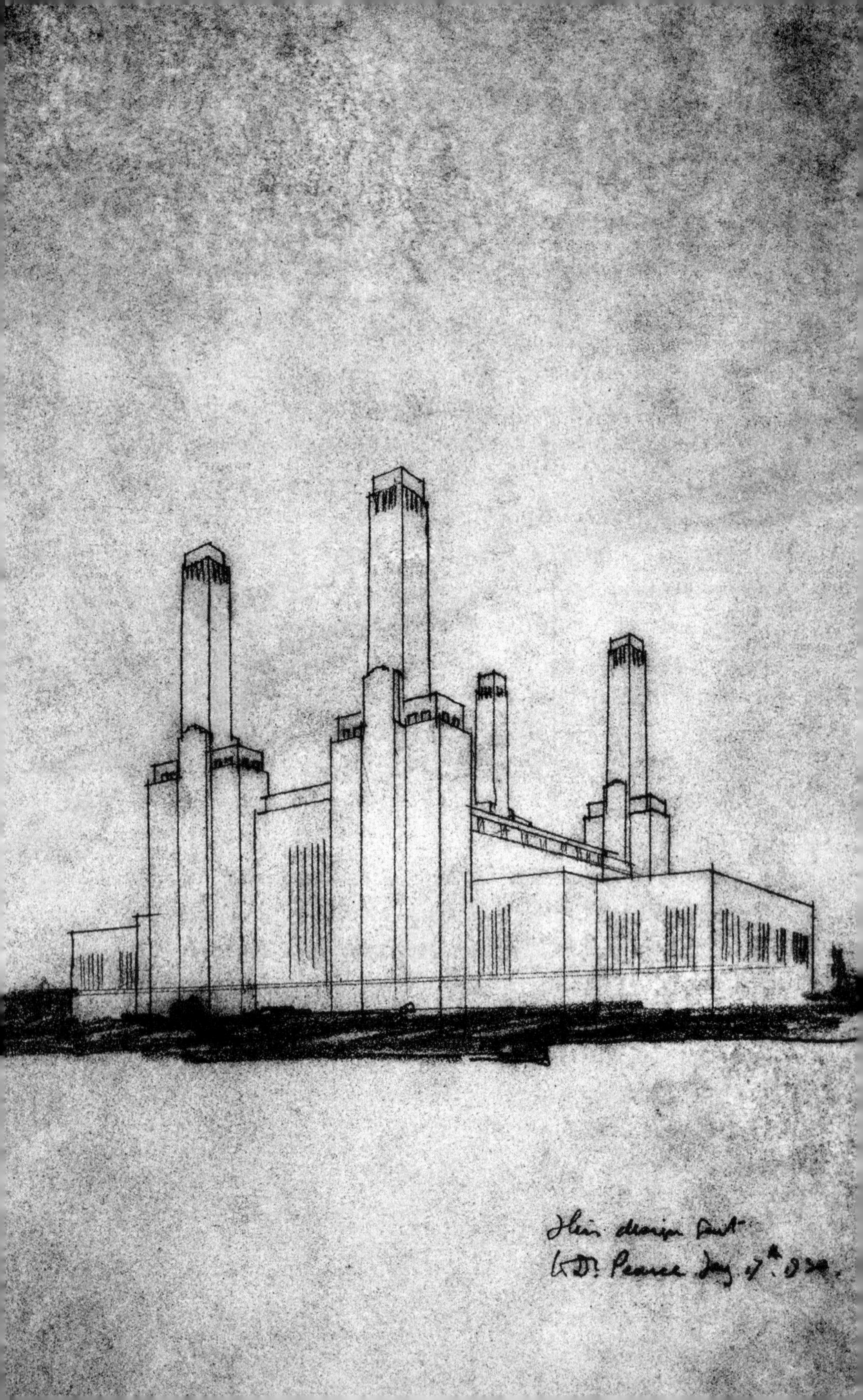

CHAPTER THREE

A FLAMING ALTAR

The architect of Liverpool's monumental Anglican cathedral – and the humble telephone box – fashions a soaring temple of power

THE LONDON CORRESPONDENT of the *Yorkshire Post* may have been the first person to record in print the unforgettable impact of seeing the soaring walls of Battersea Power Station from a passing train – a view that has since become familiar to millions. Writing in May 1932, when the steel frame of the power station was complete along with much of the covering brickwork, he wrote that "from near at hand the building is remarkably impressive… and the best view is had on approaching Victoria on the Southern Railway," continuing to say that "at present, the station looks like the beginnings of a vast cathedral".

A FLAMING ALTAR

This would certainly not be the last time Battersea Power Station would be compared to a cathedral, a common response to its grand scale and ambition, but also a nod to the man who helped shape its final form, even if he disliked the ecclesiastical comparisons. Giles Gilbert Scott was the third generation of Britain's greatest architectural dynasty, which began with George Gilbert Scott (1811–1878), the Victorian architect of great Gothic landmarks. Scott senior towered above his profession; he designed around 800 buildings including London's Albert Memorial, Foreign Office and the Midland Grand Hotel at St Pancras (another building that remained a ruin for far too much of its life). His eldest son, George Gilbert Scott, Jr (1839–1897), was also an architect, principally of churches, but sadly his career was derailed by mental instability and alcoholism. He fathered six children of whom four survived childhood, including Giles and his younger brother Adrian, both of whom became architects.

Giles claimed that he only met his father twice as he was declared insane and committed to an asylum when Giles was just three, but he was nevertheless a strong influence; Giles would later claim a preference for his father's architecture over that of his far more famous grandfather. Giles's own reputation was made when he was in his early twenties, after he won a competition to design a new Anglican cathedral for Liverpool in 1903. He had idly prepared the drawings from his home at 40 York Mansions in Battersea, with no real expectation of success having previously completed nothing larger than a pipe rack for his sister. At least that's what he told journalists after his design was unanimously selected by the board from 103 entries. The complicated design and construction of the cathedral would occupy the rest of his life; although consecrated in 1924

PREVIOUS SPREAD
One of Giles Gilbert Scott's initial sketches of his proposed brickwork exterior for Battersea Power Station. At this point, the chimneys are square. © RIBApix

(Scott was knighted soon after), it was not completed until 1978, eighteen years after his death.

While working on Liverpool Cathedral, Scott took on other commissions, many of them churches but also several notable secular buildings: Oxford's New Bodleian Library was one of his, as was London's understated Waterloo Bridge, built largely by women during the Second World War and, toward the end of his career, the stern but stylish Bankside Power Station on the Thames across from St Paul's Cathedral.

Perhaps Scott's most popular design was for the K2 kiosk, Britain's first red telephone box. Again, he won the commission through a competition, this one held in 1925. This distinctive bit of mass-produced, utilitarian street furniture illustrates many of the reasons that Scott was such a good choice for the LPC. The K2 was bold and distinctive without being showy. It was sturdy but also elegant thanks to subtle decorative mouldings, and the decoration wasn't superfluous: the Tudor crowns adorning the top of the kiosk, for example, were pierced to provide ventilation. Above all, his design referenced traditional British architecture – the domed top was most likely modelled on John Soane's 1816 self-designed mausoleum in St Pancras Gardens – and applied it to something that might otherwise have seemed intimidatingly modern; he made the unfamiliar somehow reassuring and ultimately much loved, a strategy that he would apply with great success at Battersea.

John Betjeman described Scott as "a jovial, generous man who looked more like a cheerful naval officer than an architect", and he was easily assimilated into the Battersea project when he was appointed towards the end of 1929. The LPC could not have asked for a better spokesperson: the esteemed architect would later proclaim that "power stations can be fine buildings"[1] adding that it just needed to be demonstrated and that, significantly, he understood the rationale behind the power station's controversial location. Years later when the construction of Bankside would bring this issue to the fore again he would tell *The Times*, "There is a tendency to classify power stations with factories and to locate them in industrial areas, but they differ from factories in one important respect: they are public utility undertakings, marketing their product in a localised and centralised market and the nearer they are to that market the more economically and efficiently they function."

The project architect up to this point was James Theodore Halliday of the Manchester-based practice Halliday & Agate. Halliday had been working with LPC engineer Leonard Pearce on improving the general appearance, ensuring there was no great disparity in the heights of the turbine hall and switch house. His greatest input would be on the interiors, as from this point on work on the exterior was taken over by Scott.

Scott precisely defined his role when he wrote to the engineers of a new power station on the River Lea in 1947. "I confine my work entirely to matters of appearance," he told them, "I prepare elevations, and when these are approved I do scale details and full-sizes, select the materials, visit the job occasionally to see that these materials are used in the right way, and inspect sample walling, etc. but I do not superintend the erection, nor transact the business side. All this is done by the promoters' architectural staff, or another architect, who also prepare the necessary working drawings embodying, of course, my details in them."[2]

Scott was no ideologue. He believed it idle to compare styles and say that one was better than another. The purpose of the building was foremost. This was key at a time when there was considerable conflict between traditionalists and modernists. For power stations, Scott favoured an almost austere art deco or expressionist design. This, along with his attention to materials, would come together at Bankside, where Scott's conviction that industrial buildings could be celebrated architectural constructions in their own right was to meet its full flowering, with Scott involved in the project from the start. By contrast, Battersea is a "compromise" according to Scott scholar Gavin Stamp, who has written extensively about both Battersea and Bankside.[3] That may be the case, but Battersea certainly isn't a fudge.

Scott's progress can be charted through the drawings he submitted, several of which focused on the area around the chimneys. The plan of the building had been set by Pearce and the demands of the groundbreaking gas-washing system with its elongated flue, so Scott could do nothing about the basic four-cornered design. Instead, he had to find a way to make the sheer mass of the building palatable to the public.

Although at this stage permission had only been granted for half of the power station – construction of the B Station would only get the go-ahead from the government when it was clear that the A Station was as non-polluting as promised – Scott always had in mind the completed building and his initial drawings featured all four chimneys. In his first designs these were square, like obelisks – four Cleopatra's Needles on top of a great brick box. This was rejected because the square chimneys would be too heavy for the foundations, which were already almost completed. So Scott made the chimneys cylindrical. Now the issue was how to make a pleasing transition from the square corner towers of the power station to the round chimney bases – a problem that has vexed architects since the Romans first began putting domes on buildings.

A sketch of a first solution, with the chimneys on a sort of rounded pediment, was published in *The Times* of 2nd April 1931 and it immediately drew a haughty response from art historian Herbert Furst: "A lamentable eyesore," he huffed. The chimneys, he wrote, were too apologetic, too small. "Their present height is wrong in relation to the building itself… the general effect now is that of elongated bottle-necks one associates with certain brands of sauce."

Possibly stung by having his work likened to a bottle of ketchup, Scott had another go and offered up a new design that saw the towers gradually step up like an Aztec pyramid from the top of the boiler house to the base of the chimneys. It is a simple, elegant solution with echoes of the prevailing art deco style.

The problem of the chimneys solved, Scott attended to the brickwork envelope wrapping around the steel building. This is arguably the building's triumph. As in a cathedral, the main turbine hall was a single vast space with no intermediary floors, so when it came to the facade Scott was free to ignore the horizontal and concentrate on the vertical. He scored the main frontage with tracks of raised and recessed brickwork running up the full height of the building, with more and deeper grooves crowning the top. The effect is like pilasters on a classical building but on a far grander scale; the chimneys above are familiar neo-classical columns. It is all reassuringly familiar but, at the same time, the size and the height is suggestive of the skyscraper architecture then going up in America (both the Chrysler and Empire State buildings were under construction at the same time as Battersea Power Station). In fact, with no windows and no prominently visible door – nothing to denote the human scale – it is hard to judge exactly the size of the building. It is a thrilling ensemble, and it set a standard for "brick cathedrals" that would be imitated for the coming decades.

Before construction could begin, the ground had to be drained and the entire area enclosed by concrete walls and steel sheet piling forty feet below the ground, with pumps employed on occasion to keep the Thames out. Digging of the foundations began in 1929 and erection of the steelwork commenced in October the following

THE BRICKWORK ENVELOPE

The interior of one of what initally were just two chimneys, big enough even at the narrowest point to accommodate a tube train. © Institution of Civil Engineers

year, but it was not until 23rd April – St George's Day – in 1931 that the foundation stone was laid. Herbert Morrison, Labour's minister for transport, was among those attending an unveiling ceremony that began with the reading of a transatlantic cable from Lord Bessborough, a former director of the London Power Company, now Governor General of Canada.

The building was steel-framed – in the main, steel was brought to Battersea by boat from Glasgow – and in-filled with Blockley bricks (the number most often given is six million) pointed in a special straw-coloured mortar. For the interiors a more standard Fletton brick was used, with a Midhurst White sand-brick for light wells and iron-hard Accrington engineering bricks in areas where acidity was high. Laying of the brickwork began in March 1931 while work continued on the superstructure, which was not completed until May 1933, at which point the chimneys could be added.

The idea was to construct these of pre-cast reinforced concrete blocks that could be slotted into place, a system used with success in France, but the London County Council was worried they would not stand up to high winds. Instead, gigantic reinforced-concrete chimneys were cast by LG Mouchel and Partners (a curious firm in that it can also claim to be the inventor and designer of the first football net in 1889, as well as curved concrete cooling towers and Earls Court Exhibition Centre). At their base, the chimneys had an internal diameter of just over twenty-eight feet, narrowing to twenty-two feet at the top – at their narrowest point the chimneys are still about twice the size of a Central Line tube tunnel. They went up at the rate of four feet per week until they reached a final height of 352 feet.[4] Initially they were painted buff but were repainted cream after the war, and remained that colour ever after. The building work was mainly undertaken by the contractors Mowlem and carried a total cost of £2,141,550 (£136.7m today, adjusted for inflation).

The completion of the A Station's two chimneys that year made it London's tallest structure, which it remained for eleven years until the erection of the TV mast at Crystal Palace. Although the building was not considered fully complete until 1935, it was able to commence the business of power production in June 1933, when station manager John Ambrose operated the switch that brought it into service.

It was acclaimed from the start. Even before the power station opened, a reporter from the *Daily Mail* was granted a preliminary nose around in 1932 and he subsequently waxed poetically about its "extraordinary mixture of massiveness, delicacy, industrial grimness, artistry, commercial expediency and beauty". The *Daily Herald* called it a "flaming altar of the modern temple of power", while another paper heralded it as "the miracle of Battersea". It was not just the newspapers: the government's First Commissioner of Works, William Ormsby-Gore, rather excitedly called it "one of the most excellent buildings that has ever been built by man". The objections of 1929 were seemingly forgotten and the London Power Company basked in the almost universal praise lavished upon its new flagship building. Even the much-feared smoke emitted from the chimneys was now deemed almost ornamental, like "sprays of ostrich feathers".[5]

Scott was a little uncomfortable with all this, particularly statements such as that made by the Royal Academy, which expressed the opinion that "the genius of Scott had invested [Battersea] with a real nobility of art". He wrote to *The Times* in 1934, almost apologetically, stating, "I do not think that public references to the Battersea Power Station do justice to Dr Pearce, the engineer-in-chief to the London Power Company and the designer of the station, and others who have worked with him. My name seems to be more prominently associated with this building than theirs… but my work was confined solely to appearance of the exterior. It is to draw attention to the work of Dr Pearce and those working under him, and also Messrs Halliday and Agate, who were responsible for the architectural features of the interior, that I write this letter."

Scott was quite right because the power station's interiors, which were largely unseen by the press and public, were every bit as glorious as the highly praised exteriors. The boiler house – which would become the eventual centre part of the building when the B Station was built – was the largest space at 494 feet long, 104 feet wide and 148 feet high. Echoing the exterior, it was lined by giant fluted pilasters and contained the control aisle, six Babcock

& Wilcox boilers (soon increased to nine), coal conveyers and coal bunkers, and the mechanical annex to the turbine house. The northern end was partitioned off for offices and toilets. The eastern exterior wall was lined with steel, a temporary arrangement while the LPC awaited permission to go ahead with the second half of the power station.

West of this was the grander turbine house, with its two chimneys up top either end. This grand hall had walls faced with terracotta slabs of grey-blue tint with a black dado. Floors were of precast terrazzo tiles matching the walls. The space was broken into bays, giving an almost ceremonial appearance, like a colonnade, and overlooked by two balconies. Even the generating units – initially two 69MW Metropolitan-Vickers British Thomson-Huston sets, later joined by an extra 105MW Metropolitan-Vickers unit, all spinning at 1,500 revolutions a minute – were carefully looked after. A former station manager remarks in *Landmark of London*, the CEGB's brief history of the building, that when he served at the station in its first twenty years these machines "were painted with cellulose paint" and then cleaned so thoroughly with rubbing compound they would be "glistening like a motor car".

The third element was the switch house, which is the (relatively) low-rise annex closest to the railway line into Victoria. This contained sixty-one sets of Metropolitan-Vickers 66,000-volt switchgear, massive circuit breakers that looked like something from an HG Wells story. The switch house floor could be divided into three by roller shutters that could be lowered in case of explosion. It also contained the elegant control room, the crown jewel of the power station. "Special attention has been paid to the construction and decoration of the control room," wrote LPC engineers Arthur Creswell Dean and Charles Seager Berry in a 1935 paper on the construction of the power station. It had six large steel-

THE GUTS OF THE THING

Although it was filled with massive generators, the gleaming turbine house appeared more like a science lab than an industrial plant. © Institution of Civil Engineers

framed double-glazed bay windows overlooking the turbine house. The walls were lined with a soft grey Napoleon marble with black Belgian marble facings. The switchboard was coloured to match the

The control room was an elegant vision of the future, marrying Jazz Age stylings (that fabulous steel-and-glass ceiling) with the apparatus of heavy industry. © RIBApix

walls. The floor was of teak blocks and a steel-and-glass ceiling light divided into eight bays ran the full length of the room. The control panel had a distinctive L-shape; the furniture had walnut veneer. It was highly technical and absurdly opulent: a vision of the future as it should be. This area was deemed so precious that the scientists who worked there were asked to wear felt overshoes.

Halliday also created a lavish director's entrance to the south of switch house, faced in grey and black marble and with two ornamental bronze doors depicting Power and Energy, purportedly copied by Halliday from Rene Paul Chambellan's bronze relief panels in the lobby of the Chanin Building in New York. The ambition of both Scott and Halliday – and the patronage of the LPC – came together to create something quite extraordinary, an instant landmark. In May 1939, a jury of sixty eminent personalities voted it the second most popular modern building in Britain (behind the Peter Jones department store on Sloane Square) in a poll conducted by the *Architects' Journal*. The actor Charles Laughton was one of those who placed the power station top, as did Kenneth Clark, director of the National Gallery. Battersea Power Station had arrived and it was quite incredible. Now it was time to put it to work.

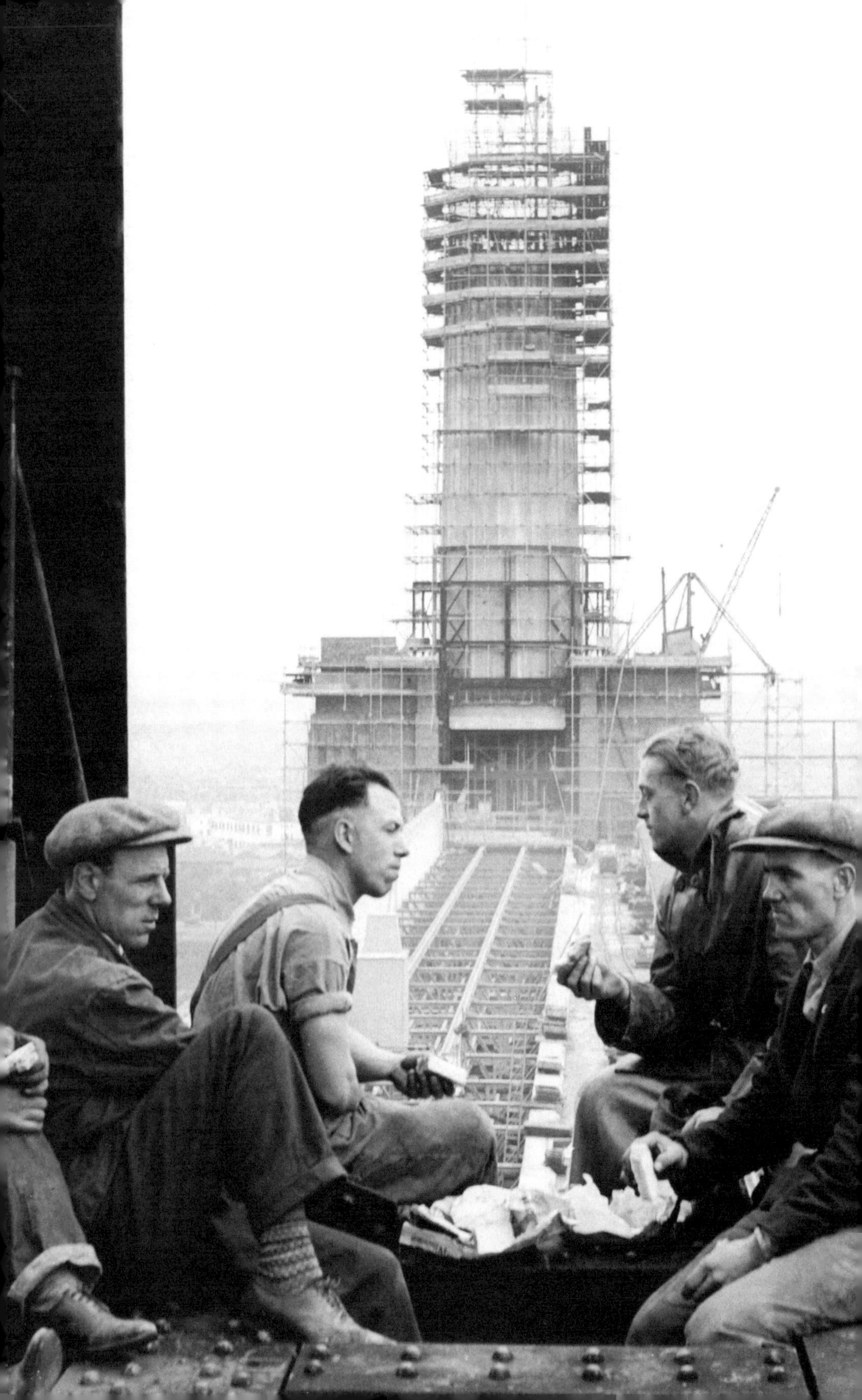

CHAPTER FOUR

NEW POWER GENERATION

Battersea survives the Blitz, the Big Freeze and blackouts but falters in the face of the nuclear threat

IT WAS A BRAVE OR FOOLISH PERSON who stood between a British family and their Sunday dinner in the 1930s, so little wonder that the newspapers found a common focus for their stories when London was hit by a power cut on 29th July 1934. "Grid Failure Spoils Sunday Dinners," the *Daily Mirror* announced, while the *Western Morning News* went with "Consternation in the Kitchen". The outage struck at 11.45am and caused a huge blackout extending as far as Peterborough, Maidenhead, Yarmouth and Brighton, an area that included all of London and the Home Counties. It lasted between fifteen minutes and two hours depending on where you were. "Church organs, electric clocks, tramcars and trolley buses, traffic signals, railways and – the cooking of Sunday dinners were affected," reported the *Western Morning News*. "Many who had no alternative made their meal off sandwiches and cold viands."

The blackout was estimated to have affected around thirteen-and-a half million people over an area covering 12,000 square miles. It could have been worse as at this time only fifty percent of Britain was connected to an electricity supply and gas ovens were still dominant. All the same, some saw the power outage as a horrifying vision of the uncertainties of a modern world in which everybody and everything became reliant on electricity. Even time would be scrambled: "From one point at the corner of Jermyn Street it was possible to see four clocks, their fingers pointed to 11.27, 3.17, 3.45, 3.55," reported the *Western Morning News*. Some columnists worried what this meant for the country should a power station become the target of enemy action in a future war – a showdown with Hitler's Germany was already a looming prospect. The finger of blame was pointed squarely at Battersea Power Station, which had been built to ensure just such a blackout did not occur.

The problem was identified as a breakdown of one of the turbines at Deptford West (the 1929 successor to Ferranti's original Deptford Power Station), the knock-on effect of which was an overload on Battersea, where one of the station's two generators was off-line for repairs. There was a certain irony here, in that the very system Battersea had been designed to support had resulted in the biggest electricity failure in British history.

In January 1935, the recently knighted Sir Francis Fladgate wrote to his old enemy *The Times* boasting that since the construction of Battersea, "five steam stations in various parts of London have been scrapped". The burden

PREVIOUS SPREAD
Workers take a lunch break during the construction of the A Station in July 1932. The steel framework was designed and built by Arrol & Co of Glasgow.
© Getty Images

was now being carried by super stations such as Battersea, many built in a string along the Thames, producing power for what was being called the National Grid – 4,075 miles of transmission lines that would carry electricity around Britain on upwards of 27,000 newly erected pylons. (The arrival of the pylons in the English landscape was greeted with more hostility than even that which had been directed at Battersea, although it also inspired some beautiful imagery from poet Stephen Spender who described them as "bare like nude giant girls that have no secret".)[1]

Battersea's A Station went into operation in June 1933, although this first phase was not fully completed until 1935. © Historic England

The intention was to bring together the country's most efficient stations in a single transmission grid that ensured no power generated would go to waste. It was more economical to transmit power around the country than have local municipalities construct their own power stations. On top of which, the interconnected stations could take the strain should any problems occur with a single station. And although this had backfired rather embarrassingly in 1934 it was to prove successful for the remainder of Battersea Power Station's working life.

Power generation had begun in June 1933 with two 69MW generators – already among the biggest in use in the country – and a third on the way, a behemoth of 105MW that after its installation in September 1935 would remain the largest in the country until 1956.

At this point, it might be worth a brief explanation of how a power station like this worked. Battersea was coal fired; the coal initially came from Barry in Wales, selected because of its low sulphur content, although later coal from the north-east was used. Some came by road and occasionally by rail, but the majority came via the Thames on a specially built fleet of colliers, with collapsible masts and funnels for passing beneath bridges, earning them the nickname "flat-irons", or "flatties". They sat so low in the water that the feet of the crew were almost always wet.[2]

Although the boats had been modified, they still needed to time their fully laden trips upriver for when the tide was out and the clearance under the bridges was at its greatest. The first flattie, named *Alexander Kennedy*, was launched in July 1932 and by 1954 there were twenty-six such vessels. They also served the power station at Fulham – not to be confused with its neighbour at Lots Road. The power station at Fulham was built in 1936 and had four chimneys all in a row so that it appeared like an ocean liner; it was demolished in the 1980s to make way for a Sainsbury's store.

HOW IT WORKED

The coal was offloaded by cranes, each one of which could lift five tonnes of coal at a time and a combined 150 tonnes per hour: even so, the unloading of just a single collier could take seven hours. The coal was deposited on conveyer belts that carried it to a vast bunker that would eventually be able to hold 75,000 to 85,000 tonnes. This was enough for several months' use as the A Station only burnt around 4,000 tonnes a week (this rose to 10,000 tonnes when the B Station was completed).

The wharf at Battersea was one of the busiest, messiest, noisiest parts of the station, but even here everything was ultra-modern; for instance, when the coal dropped from the conveyer belt into a hopper, it was automatically weighed and recorded. From the bunker, the coal was taken by conveyer belts to the furnaces through several feeding points – twenty per boiler – so it was evenly distributed. The furnaces were mechanically stoked and heated six boilers (later rising to nine), which could turn 250,000lb of water into steam at a pressure of 625lb per square inch. This drove the giant blades of the turbines that in turn rotated a shaft at high speed. The shaft was connected to a generator containing magnets that span at 1,500 revolutions per minute within wire coils to produce the electricity. This was generated at 11,000 volts and then stepped up to 66,000 volts before passing through transformers to match the voltage required for different needs: from 33,000 volts for heavy industry to 240 volts for domestic use. The electricity left the station in seven 66,000-volt cables and eight 22,000-volt cables.

Having done its job, the steam was cooled using water from the Thames and turned back into water itself. This was channelled back to the boiler where it could be heated into steam to start the process all over again. The smoke from the furnaces went out of the chimneys at the rate of twenty million cubic feet an hour via the gas-washing flues.

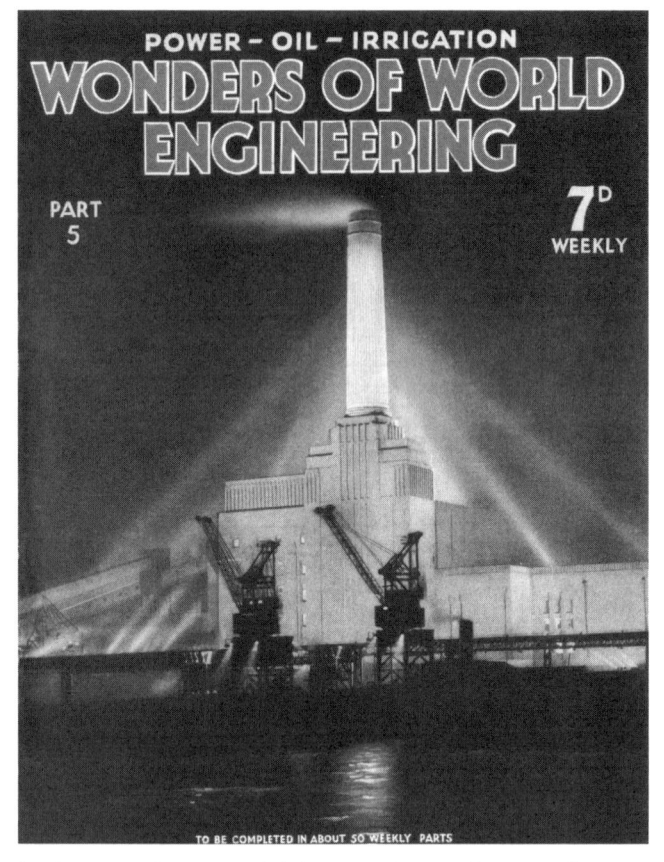

Looking more like a giant lighthouse or beacon, Battersea Power Station graces the cover of a 1937 engineering magazine.

In a 1937 issue of a magazine called *Wonders of World Engineering*,[3] writer David Masters rhapsodised over the workings of Battersea: "The heat in the furnace is so intense and the incandescence is so bright that those who tend the fires dare not look at them with the naked eye. To look into a furnace resembles looking into the heart of the sun." Furnace workers sheltered behind shields inset with strips of purple glass for viewing.

Masters thought the turbine hall looked like an "ultra-modern restaurant" complete with labourers using electric washers and scrubbers to ensure the room remained spotless. He was in awe of the turbines that "spin day and night to supply the thousand and one requirements of the modern age". All this power, he marvelled, was controlled by "switches of a magnitude that it is difficult for the average man to comprehend". These switches, which turned on and off the power, were so big – each taller than a man – that they could only be opened and closed by two travelling cranes.

Among the responsibilities of the station workers was monitoring the weather forecasts, because this would give an idea of the amount of electricity that would be required over the course of a day; for every degree of temperature below 45ºF, an additional output of 1,000kW was required. The control room also housed the control board containing dozens of dials and diagrammatic plans showing the exact state of each circuit, which switches were live and which were earthed. It had two telegraphs like those in a ship that the duty officers used to communicate orders to the men at the turbines.

Masters was taken by the men who operated the power station: "The quiet competence displayed about the power house is impressive. Something of the efficiency of the machines they control seems to inspire the men. It is similar to the spirit that inspires the crew of a battleship. Officers are always on duty night and day. They sit at desks with their log sheets before them recording the performance of the machines under their control."

The article concluded with Masters describing how one side of the power station was covered with "acres and acres" of black-painted corrugated iron: "Battersea Power Station, as it stands, is only half a dream come true. Not until all that corrugated iron has been stripped away and another building of the same size has been joined to it, with two more gigantic chimneys pointing to heaven, will the whole dream be realised."

Construction of the B Station began that same year, 1937, and continued as Britain went to war in 1939. As conceived, it was the mirror image of the A Station, only now with modifications, some brought about by improvements in engineering, others as a result of war shortages. The latter meant that the quality of the B Station interiors was utilitarian compared to what had come before; the rooms were less decorative and lit throughout by electric lights rather than skylights.[4] A new boiler design meant that the boiler house roof of B had to be built fifteen feet higher than that of A, while in the flue linings, steel replaced bricks when it was discovered the gas-washing process was harming the walls and chimneys.

Battersea's third chimney – the one on the north-east corner – was up by 1941, by which time a defence regulation had been introduced to switch off the gas-washing processes after RAF pilots reported how they could always locate the centre of London by the distinctive white clouds hanging above the power station. The concern was that Luftwaffe bombers would do the same. Gas-washing had never been the trouble-free solution the London Power Company had hoped for. From the very first days of Battersea A, it had been noted that in certain atmospheric conditions, the river-cooled chimney gases would sink to the ground so the streets around Battersea smelt faintly of sulphur. Another unforeseen outcome of gas-washing was that the excess water that was being returned to the Thames was highly acidic. When it was finally turned off for good in 1974 the impact on the Thames was dramatic – afterwards workers from the station could wade into the river at low tide to catch eel and dace using bacon fat from the staff canteen as bait.

The demands of the war were such that not only was gas-washing turned off, but pollution was actively encouraged. In 1940, the minister for home security had insisted that Battersea and other power stations should increase the amount of smoke they produced, "to intensify the general haze in the areas concerned with a view to hindering attacks of hostile aircraft".[5]

THE B STATION

The steel frame goes up for the tower that would serve as the base for the third chimney. Construction on the B Station kicked off in 1937 and continued through World War II, albeit at a reduced pace. © Institution of Civil Engineers

Despite the precautions, the power station was hit by a 500lb bomb on the very first night of the Blitz, 7th September 1940. It failed to explode but still badly damaged the switch house. On shift that evening was Arthur Palmer, soon to become Labour MP for

Wimbledon; he would later recall, "A surprising feature was how a large power station could swallow up bombs fairly easily without being put out of action. Everything depended on where the bomb fell… it put the control room out of action but because it was the control room alone it was possible for emergency connections to be made and the station put into action again in a reasonably short period." Also victims of enemy action were the flatties, with four sunk during the war including the *Alexander Kennedy*, the first to be launched.

All the while, Battersea continued to produce electricity for the munitions factories to the west of London. A fourth turbine, of 100MW, was added in 1941, initially connected to the A Station boilers while work continued on the B Station.

As the bombs continued to fall, Battersea was used for more than just providing cloud cover and generating electricity. Reacting to the very real threat of invasion by Germany, the Bank of England decided it needed to destroy its reserves of banknotes and sent them to Battersea to be burned. The bank insisted on throwing the bundles of notes into the furnaces itself but faced with the blasting heat bank staff didn't throw the bundles in far enough. The next day the power station workers came in to find the ash bunker full of pound and ten-shilling notes.

In the immediate post-war period, the still incomplete, three-chimneyed power station was needed more than ever. Snow began to fall on 23rd January 1947, marking the start of what quickly became known as the Big Freeze, Britain's worst winter for years. Coal supplies had yet to be fully replenished and the power station only had ten days' stock, which was far short of the usual four to six weeks' surplus. Now, the vicious weather had closed the mines, snowed in the trains and the collier fleet from the north-east was frozen in harbour.

By 7th February electricity was being strictly rationed: there was no power between nine in the morning and midday, and between two and four in the afternoon for homes across the country. The writer Christopher Isherwood, making a visit to London from his adopted home in America, recorded how many locals "stared longingly at my new overcoat. With coal strictly rationed, gas reduced to a blue ghost and electricity often cut off altogether, everybody in England was shivering."[6]

Kew Observatory recorded no sunshine at all from 2nd to 22nd February and the rationing of electricity continued until May. This was an inauspicious start to a new chapter in Battersea's life as at this time both coal-mining and electricity were undergoing nationalisation under the guidance of Herbert Morrison (grandfather of Peter Mandelson). In 1948 Battersea ceased to be a privately owned operation and was brought under the control of the newly formed government-run British Electricity Authority, renamed the Central Electricity Authority in 1955 and then the Central Electricity Generating Board (CEGB) in 1957.

Work on the B Station was on hold at this point but it got underway again in 1951. Leonard Pearce, the original designer of Battersea, had died in 1947 and the task of completion fell to the BEA and its contractor Taylor Woodrow. Technology had changed considerably since construction had begun on the second-phase building and this presented difficulties, particularly with the new pulverised fuel boilers, which needed to be modified to fit inside the already finished boiler house creating operational difficulties that would recur over the next thirty years. As one station manager told the authors of *Landmark of London*: "The modern idea is to design your plant first and then get the architect to provide a pleasant-looking building to cover it. With Battersea the cover was designed first and you had to squeeze the plant in and then run it."[7]

NEW POWER GENERATION

Battersea as it was for the fourteen years from 1941 and 1955, with an asymmetrical and visually unpleasing three chimneys. © Historic England

After eight years with two chimneys and fourteen years with three, it was only now, in 1955, that the fourth chimney went up. Battersea Power Station was finally complete in its full, intended, symmetrical splendour.

London itself was undergoing great changes as the city was rebuilt after the war. Battersea played its part in this. Pimlico's post-war Churchill Gardens estate of 2,000 homes, twenty shops, a church and pub was connected directly to the power station – as was the neighbouring private Dolphin Square complex – by a tunnel under the Thames, through which hot water was pumped to provide heating. The scheme was one of the first of its kind in the UK and the first in London. It wasn't entirely successful as the excess from Battersea's main generators was insufficient, so two additional small turbo-alternators had to be installed. Years later, when the power station was taken out of use, the boilers had to be maintained to keep the residents of Churchill Gardens warm.

As Britain moved into the 1960s, most homes had fridges, irons and television sets, while electric cookers and electric heating were also growing in popularity. This was the peak of Battersea's existence, when it provided power for one fifth of London, not to mention employment for almost one thousand workers. The heat radiating from its boilers also made the building attractive to the 200 or so stray cats that were reckoned to occupy it according to *New Scientist*.[8]

If this was a golden age for Battersea it did not last long. The coal-powered station had started to age even before it was complete. Construction had taken twenty-two years, and technologies and thinking had changed in that time. As early as 1952, one future station manager was reported to have declined a job at Battersea saying, "I'm not a martyr." When he was given the job anyway, he recalls his heart sinking as he began his first day: "My God," he said, "what have I done?"[9]

Battersea was in danger of being rendered obsolete by the system it had been built to support. The success of the National Grid meant the original rationale for choosing a central London site for a power station no longer stood: it was now cheaper to transport electricity by cable than it was to supply the station with coal. Added to which, Britain was entering the nuclear age, opening its first nuclear power station at Windscale in Cumberland in 1956. Now better known as Sellafield, it had been built to explore the potential of creating an atomic bomb in 1941 but was later converted into the world's first industrial-scale nuclear power station. At the opening ceremony, attended by the Queen, Conservative politician Rab Butler, the Lord Privy Seal, predicted that by 1965, every new power station would be an atomic one.[10]

Even architects were turning against the building: Robert Furneaux Jordan, writing in *The Architectural Journal* in 1952, called Battersea "the largest, last and worst manifestation of the disastrous process that began at the Renaissance with the divorce of structure and design". Just as George Gilbert Scott had used a Gothic hotel to hide a "fine train shed", he argued, his grandson had used "ten million bricks arranged in Gothic flutings" to hide some "fine machinery". Jordan preferred the new power stations, believing them "healthier, more virile, more economic, less pompous".

In the nuclear age, few buildings were as dated as a coal-fired power station, and this became particularly apparent after London experienced the choking crisis of smog in 1953. The gas-washed smoke from Battersea was not to blame but it was still seen as part of the problem. *Evening News* cartoonist Joseph Lee, who had regularly, and it seemed fondly, featured Battersea Power Station as the location for his whimsical one-panel sketches, even took a swipe, drawing a majestic Battersea against grim, grey skies, fourth chimney clad in scaffolding. The accompanying caption read, "… and that's the fourth and final chimney to Battersea's great power station, 337 feet high and fitted with the latest scientific smoke-cleansing and grit-arresting devices… You'd see 'em quite clearly if it wasn't for the smog."

An aside in Bill Naughton's 1963 London novel *Alfie* ran with the theme: "The wind was blowing from the west, so that you didn't get the smoke from Battersea Power Station. 'Washed' smoke they call it – but have you ever tasted it?" In a similar vein, the back cover blurb of the paperback edition of Nell Dunn's grimy tales of south London, *Up the Junction*, read, "Innocence in Battersea lasts as long as the flower remains unsooted by the power station." Both *Alfie* and *Up the Junction* were made into films and you can perhaps trace the changing perceptions of Battersea through its appearances

Battersea Park in 1973, with the looming chimneys of the power station as a constant reminder that despite the greenery, this was no country idyll but urban central London. © Historic England

on screen. Alfred Hitchcock, never slow to recognise a memorable location when he saw one, used the original two-chimneyed station in the opening scene of 1936's *Sabotage* as the subject of an attack by an enemy agent – an echo of the very fears expressed in Battersea's early years. The plot was rehashed in 1951's *High Treason*, a superior bit of anti-Communist propaganda masquerading as noirish thriller, which followed a group of saboteurs who planned to destroy the power station in the first stage of a plot to take over the UK. In the final shoot-out, policemen and spies exchange gunfire amid the cacophonous hiss and clang of the turbine hall, while in the serene calm of a London office the plot's architect discusses the nature and meaning of power with a Scotland Yard detective.

In 1955's *The Quatermass Experiment*, Hammer films had Battersea saving the world when its current was used to electrocute a shape-shifting parasitical alien attempting to destroy Westminster Abbey. However, by 1965 – a couple of years after the Great Train Robbers staged a full-scale dress rehearsal for their stick-up in the neighbouring railway yard – Battersea was being depicted in a less glamorous fashion. Captioned "A Well-Known Power Station", it appears in Dick Lester's Beatles romp *Help!* where it is shown blowing a fuse at a critical juncture, allowing the Fabs to escape their bolthole in Buckingham Palace ("A Well-Known Palace"), but doing little for Battersea's reputation as a working power station. Things were taken even further in 1967's satirical *Smashing Time*, when the restaurant at the top of the Post Office Tower starts to revolve so fast it causes the power station to explode, London's brash newest icon annihilating a venerable predecessor – a metaphor for the 1960s if ever there was. The cycle of destruction had begun in November 1964, when two of Battersea's chimneys were smashed in the *Doctor Who* episodes "The Dalek Invasion of Earth".

The cinematic catastrophes may have been inspired by a real breakdown, only Battersea's second of note but a particularly unfortunate one in the circumstances. It happened on 20th April 1964, the night that BBC2 was supposed to launch. A turbine fire twenty-five minutes before airtime saw the power station shut down, causing widespread blackouts across west London, including at the BBC's Lime Grove studios. The debut of the nation's second TV channel had to be postponed until the following day. The kerfuffle was great – a kangaroo the BBC had hired to act as mascot had a panic attack in the blacked-out studio – and Battersea's reputation was hugely damaged. A few days later *New Scientist* was moved to comment that "to economists, town planner and those with common sense, the case for the disestablishment of Battersea Power Station must now by overwhelming. Equipment which was the most modern of its kind in the 1930s cannot now be economic. It is a blot on the landscape…"[11]

But Battersea was not yet done. While the creaking A Station was decommissioned in March 1975, the B Station continued to operate. Then, in December 1976, the building experienced one of its most extraordinary moments since the war, one that cemented its place in popular culture and possibly helped ensure its survival long after the furnaces had burnt out. For this, it had to thank a pig called Algie. But unlike most pigs, Algie could fly.

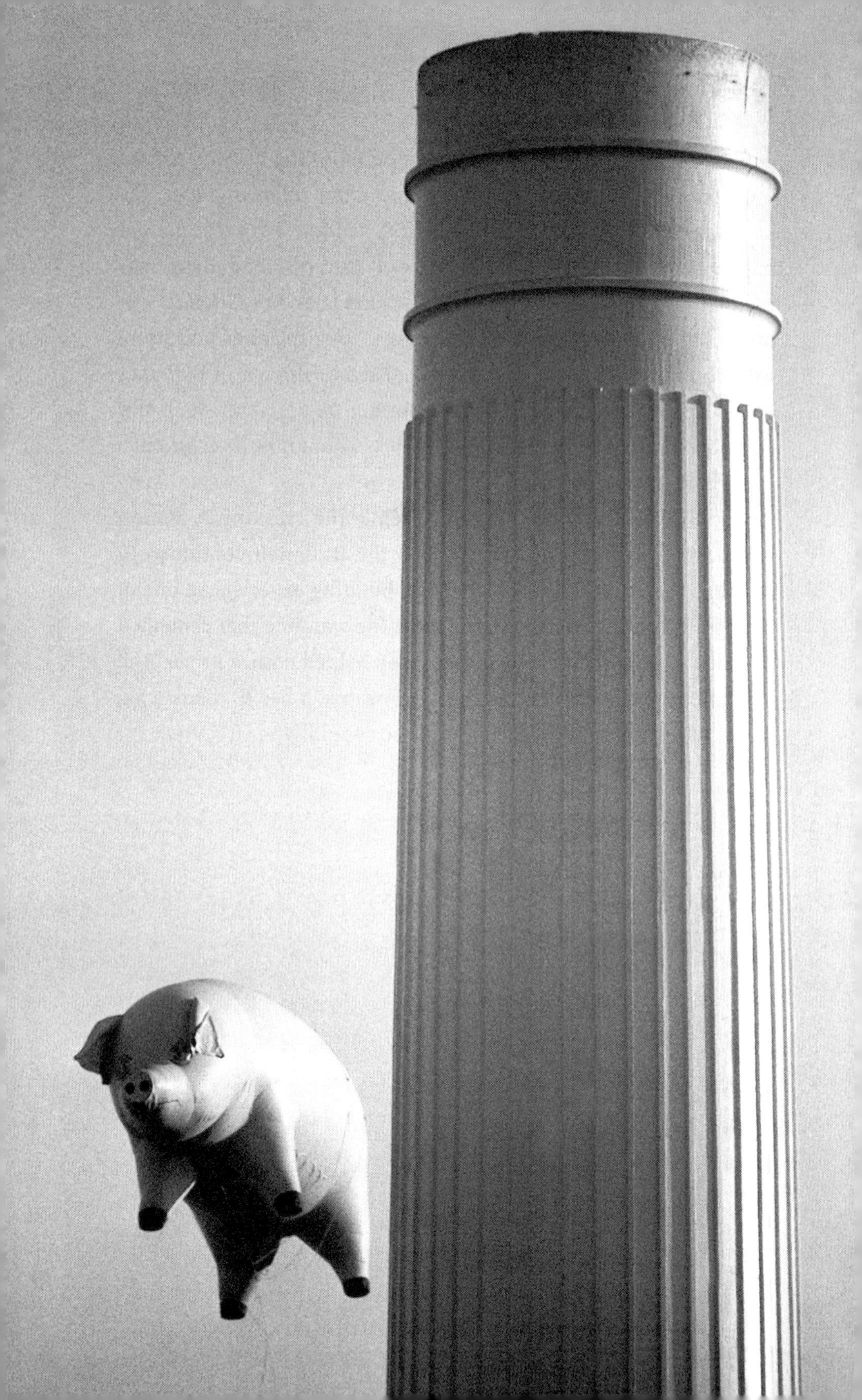

CHAPTER FIVE

PIGS MIGHT FLY

The power station plays second fiddle to an inflatable pig and as a result becomes more famous than ever

THERE IS AN ARRESTING SCENE in Alfonso Cuarón's 2006 science-fiction film *Children of Men*. Set in London in 2027 and based on a novel by PD James, the world is suffering an infertility crisis – nobody has been born for eighteen years – and civilisation is breaking down. Clive Owen, playing the furrow-browed hero Theo, takes a Rolls-Royce through grimy streets past several London landmarks – Big Ben, Admiralty Arch, St James's Park – before arriving at his destination. Battersea Power Station looms ahead, looking more like a fortress than ever. Theo's car passes through security gates and crosses a bridge towards its gargantuan entrance.

In this desolate future the power station is the Ark of the Arts and it is where Theo meets his cousin Nigel, a man charged with gathering together the world's artistic masterpieces – the two embrace beside Michelango's "David" and dine under Picasso's "Guernica" before continuing the conversation in front of a glass wall beyond which the chimneys of Battersea loom large.

Location manager Michael Sharp was in the early stages of scouting locations for *Children of Men* when he went to visit friends on the shoot for another dystopian movie, *V for Vendetta*, in Westminster. They were using Battersea Power Station as a unit base, so Sharp parked his car and then took in the surroundings. "I was looking at Battersea and like many people I was fond of it," he says.[1] "But I also thought it would work for *Children of Men*. We wanted strong images that had to represent London but not cheesy London. Using somewhere like Battersea meant there was no question of where you were, it was London but proper London, authentic London."

Sharp discussed the idea with Cuarón, who approved. "It's such a bold statement of a building, there aren't many buildings of that scale around, particularly in brick," says Sharp. "It's a great beast that dominates everything around it and you cannot imagine it not being there." As pre-production progressed, the film-makers decided to reimagine the power station as a storehouse of cultural treasures. "The building itself is a piece of art, internationally recognised, so this seemed the right place for the collector, this man accumulating all the world's art," says Sharp.

Theo's visit to the Ark is scored by King Crimson's "The Court of the Crimson King", but homage is being paid to another great British band of the progressive era. While Theo and Nigel talk about art and immortality, a huge

PREVIOUS SPREAD
Algie the pig tethered beside one of Battersea's chimney stacks in early December 1976 during the photo shoot for the cover of the Pink Floyd album *Animals*. © Alamy

THE ARK OF THE ARTS

For the 2006 film *Children of Men*, Battersea was reimagined as a secure repository for the world's art treasures. Digital artist Neil Miller "futurised" Giles Gilbert Scott's architecture and added the bridge. © Universal Studios LLC/neilmillervfx.com

pink pig can be seen floating mockingly outside the window behind them, with the chimneys in the background. This is Algie, a pig created by rock band Pink Floyd as a cover star, stage prop and gas-filled metaphor.

Battersea Power Station was already a national landmark when Pink Floyd put Algie on the cover of their 1977 album *Animals*. But the resulting piece of art, showing a moodily lit power station against dramatic London skies – with a small incongruous pig hovering between the two southern chimneys – took the building's fame to another level. It may even have helped pave the way for the power station's later elevation to listed-building status as it transformed Battersea from a purely London landmark to a piece of rock iconography familiar to millions all over the world.

After Algie, the pig and the power station became intimately connected. The pair have been referenced in all manner of ways, from computer games (1984's Spectrum classic *Jet Set Willy*) to the 2012 Olympic opening ceremony. When the makers of *The Simpsons Movie* wanted to promote the launch of the film in 2007, they did so by flying their own "Spider Pig" above Battersea. But when *Children of Men* digitally refloated Algie it was more than just a knowing allusion to a world-famous album cover. Director Cuarón was evoking all sorts of associations, including the relationship between greed and power, and the moral fable that is George Orwell's *Animal Farm*. It is the same ground Roger Waters was treading nearly forty years previously.

It was Waters, the driving force behind Pink Floyd in the 1970s, who came up with the cover concept for *Animals*. The execution was by Hipgnosis, who did all of Pink Floyd's artwork between 1968 and 1979. They were a design agency formed by Aubrey Powell and Storm Thorgerson, a combustible pair who had grown up in Cambridge with Waters and Syd Barrett, two of Floyd's founder members. Hipgnosis was highly regarded among musicians for its imaginative concepts and attention to detail, even if record labels sometimes balked at the costs or were baffled by covers like *Atom Heart Mother*, done for Floyd, which was just a photograph of a cow in a field, no band name, no album title. But bands trusted Thorgerson for his ability to create truly memorable imagery, such as the mysterious prism for *Dark Side of the Moon*, which would become something of an emblem for Pink Floyd.

At Waters' request, Hipgnosis had already knocked up one idea for *Animals*, which featured a small child clutching a teddy bear at an open bedroom door, watching his parents furiously copulating. Waters wasn't convinced and went away to have a think. "Roger was living in Battersea and he invited me round for tea," says Aubrey Powell when we meet in his flat, coincidentally just across the river from the power station.[2] "I went to the flat and he said, 'Look out the window, what can you see?' and I said, 'Battersea Power Station.' He said, 'Isn't it absolutely fucking amazing? I'd like to use it on the next album cover.'"

Waters told Powell that he wanted to fly an inflatable pig above the power station. "I thought it was interesting but I wasn't quite sure where he was coming from. He said he wasn't sure either but we should go and have a look." The pair drove to the power station and explored, Powell taking photographs to get an idea of the landscape. After consideration, they decided they wanted the pig between two chimneys and Powell set about getting permission.

This was surprisingly easily achieved. The power station management had long accepted that their building had a burgeoning secondary career in modelling and film, and now it was becoming a fashionable accessory in the music business. In 1965 it had appeared with The Beatles in *Help!* then eight years later The Who included a photograph of it in a booklet to accompany their Mod rock opera *Quadrophenia*. Freak rockers Junior's Eyes, who backed David Bowie on *Space Oddity*, called their only album *Battersea Power Station*. In 1971, Slade recorded a promo for single "Get Down and Get With It" on Battersea's roof. If the power station could survive Noddy Holder's mutton chops and throaty yodel, what threat did a pig-shaped balloon present?

Pink Floyd had experimented with inflatables at gigs before, notably a giant octopus floated on a lake in Crystal Palace Park in 1971. That had been made by Australian artist Jeffrey Shaw and his colleague from the Netherlands, Theo Botschuijver. To make the pig, Waters turned again to Botschuijver. The plan was for the pig to be photographed on the album cover and then taken on the subsequent tour, so Botschuijver had to create something that would stand up to scrutiny. After visiting local farms, he began making models. "The danger I noticed straightaway was that it could look like a Walt

Disney figure," he says over the line from the Netherlands.[3] "Pigs are usually portrayed as friendly, chubby, cartoonesque animals but [Roger] wanted a realistic pig, more aggressive." The final pig did look pretty fearsome, with black rings around narrowed eyes, a sneery wrinkled snout and two fearsome tusks poking from a downturned mouth.

It was manufactured in Germany by a company called Ballonfabrik with a little reluctance: "They didn't like my pig," Botschuijver says. "I had a lot of trouble convincing them this was the pig the band wanted." After some persuasion, the company delivered what was required, a mean-looking porker about fifty-five foot long and made out of a thin, rubberised cotton.

The shoot was scheduled for Thursday 2nd December 1976. Hipgnosis was after the full package: photographs for the album's covers, front and back, and inner sleeve, which could also be used on badges and posters, plus footage for a promotional film. Aubrey Powell had engaged around a dozen photographers, chosen for their range of styles. The principal pair were Howard Bartrop and Dennis Waugh, who were given plum positions in front of the power station on the southern side – Waugh on the railway sidings and Bartrop, who had taken several cover photographs for Hipgnosis, slightly elevated on the balcony of some flats. "Howard had the prime position, he had the whole landscape while other people were doing reportage, wandering around shooting on the ground," says Rob Brimson, a Hipgnosis photographer.[4] Another photographer, Robert Ellis, was positioned on the roof, while Brimson was supposed to be aboard a helicopter, which was waiting at the nearby Battersea Heliport on standby. Waugh appreciated the chance to get close to the power station. "Growing up in New Zealand, I was brought up on images of London and one thing I remember is the disappointment at how small everything really was," he says. "Battersea was different."[5]

A MEAN-LOOKING PORKER

On the railway bridge, Powell had painted the word "Animals": the intention was to get a photograph with this in the foreground so the album title would be incorporated into the urban landscape. Powell ended up cropping it out of the final image but for years afterwards the fading graffiti could still be made out.

On the bitterly cold morning of the shoot the photographers, band, the pig – now christened Algie – and its handlers assembled at the power station. Champagne – pink of course – was served to toast the big event. There was a sense of expectation in the air. But Algie would not perform. Botschuijver explains: "Gas when it expands

The pig was called Algie, short presumably for Algernon, and with tusks and narrowed eyes it was a mean-looking beast, but he was actually a she, a sow. © Theo Botschuijver

gets quite cold and freezes in the bottle and none comes out. So we couldn't inflate it, it didn't work. We parked it by the power station half-inflated and decided to come back next morning."

The next day they made a second attempt. Robert Ellis, an experienced rock photographer, took his position on the power station's roof. "I've no idea why I was there, other than perhaps they took pity on me and gave me a cosy spot on a freezing cold morning," he says.[6] "Up there it was just warm steam blowing about in the cold wind like from a smoke machine on some giant rock stage. The main thing was dirt, coal dust, and getting up there was a long and difficult climb. I had to go round the back by the Thames, clambering over piles of coal to get to iron rings set in the walls and then up into the loading bays, across the vast area over more heaps of coal to get to a stone staircase up through several floors until a last set of iron steps leading to a hatch in the roof and out into the open air."

With everybody in place, the pig was inflated and was soon airborne, rubbing against one of the chimneys. "The thing was anchored to a winch on a truck," says Botschuijver, who was monitoring progress. "Somebody walked past with a camera and wanted a picture so he asked for it to go higher and the guy from Germany loosened the winch and it started to unwind. He jerked the brake and I heard – ding! The ring broke and the pig flew away."

Down on the railway tracks, Dennis Waugh was watching the pig's ascent. "I remember thinking, that's rather high and then… fuck me, they've lost it!" Brimson was waiting for the pig to take to the air before heading off to board the helicopter: "It was amazing how fast it went," he says. "Everybody watched it go and there was absolute panic." Howard Bartrop was just worried that he'd missed his shot: "I remember seeing it go and thinking I was in such trouble because it was now out of frame and definitely not between the two chimneys," he says. "That was the brief, to get it between the chimneys. But the pig didn't want to play."[7]

First to react were the band themselves. "Pink Floyd ran away," says Powell. "They laughed, jumped in their cars and drove off while we all stood around wondering what to do." Powell was worried the pig would fly into the Heathrow flight path and contacted the police. Botschuijver snatched some photographs for posterity and then diligently covered his own backside. "This was the first time I had lost an inflatable," he says. "I scouted the terrain to find the metal ring that broke, which I found and put in an envelope. Then I went to the telephone and called the nearest lawyer and made a statement that it was my design but the execution was German."

Brimson was sent to the helipad. "The pilot was ready to go and we were going to pile in, work out where the wind was blowing and chase the fucker, but it was already gone. We'd lost the pig."

Powell admits being terrified. "Storm and I hustled off to our studio in Denmark Street where we immediately put it out on radio that anybody who saw this pig should get in touch," he says. "Airline pilots were reporting seeing it at 30,000 feet and it was a real danger. They had to shut down Heathrow. If it happened today I'd be in prison. The RAF sent up fighter jets to try and shoot it down. I was freaking out, I thought I'd be responsible for an airliner crash."

The pig's escape was gleefully reported by the press, with some of the more cynical wondering whether the whole thing was perhaps an elaborate publicity stunt, something Botschuijver and Powell are at pains to deny. Later that evening, Powell was waiting with a policeman for news when he took a phone call. "This man asked if we were the people looking for a pink pig, because the bloody thing was in his field frightening his cows."

The gas had contracted in the evening air and the pig had crash-landed in a field in Kent, where it bounced around in the mud, semi-

According to Botschuijver and Brimson, at the request of the Civil Aviation Authority, a marksman was present on the first day of the shoot ready to take down the pig if it broke loose. He failed to turn up on the second day when Algie escaped.

inflated. A road crew was despatched to haul it back to London. "It was slightly damaged but we got it back and did cleaning and repairs," says Botschuijver. Would it be third time lucky?

The shoot had already taken up far more time and money than Hipgnosis had planned, so the number of photographers was halved for the third day of shooting. This time the pig took flight without any mishap and the photographers had their moment. The helicopter was also let loose, with cameraman Nigel Lesmoir-Gordon capturing some wonderful film of the pig floating above the station. Brimson was aboard taking stills and worried he was "going to chuck up over London" as the helicopter spiralled round the smoking chimneys. (Only two chimneys were smoking as the A Station had been taken out of service the previous year.)

Which brings us to the cover shot itself. Three principal witnesses each remember this being taken on a different day. For Powell, it was the very first day – the day of the non-inflating pig – when "it was the most spectacular and romantic day lighting wise, it was Turneresque, amazing clouds, a really extraordinary early winter day". Brimson believes the shot came on the second day, shortly after the pig had escaped. And Howard Bartrop, who took the photograph, remembers it happening on the final day.

What everybody agrees on is that while the power station looked splendid in Bartrop's photo, it didn't feature a pig. "The best shot was from the first day, with this unbelievably dramatic sky," insists Powell. "It looked incredible but the pig wasn't there. On the third day, there was the perfect image of the pig between the stacks, so we stripped the pig from the third day and put it in the picture from the first day."

Having shot six or seven photographs over the course of the three days, Bartrop's recollection is that he was packing up to go home on the final day when the sun suddenly reappeared. "Occasionally there's a gap on the horizon between the cloud base and the horizon itself not much bigger than the disc of the sun, and that's the exact space the sun was in," he says. "I ran like hell back up the stairs and got into position. I knew it looked fantastic but I had no idea whether they wanted something so classical. I had a feeling that somebody underneath with an ultra-wide angle getting the two chimneys with the pig coming up from the bottom would be the strongest image. But in the end it became more of a portrait of the building than of the pig."

The question remains: why Battersea and why a pig? At the time, Waters was evasive, telling a London radio station only, "I like the four phallic towers and the idea of power I find appealing in a strange sort of way." But in 2008, he opened up more fully to *Rolling Stone*[8] explaining that he chose the power station because, he said, he'd always loved it as a piece of architecture. He also ascribed a certain symbolism to it: "There were four bits to it, representing the four members of the band. But it was upside down, so it was like a tortoise on its back, not going anywhere, really." It is a recollection perhaps tempered by hindsight: Waters left the band in the 1980s and then spent much of his solo career in a monumental huff that his old friends could carry on without him.

And the pig? Aubrey Powell offers this: "You need to put this in the context of the time. Pigs were policeman in the Sixties and Seventies. The pig was a symbol, a way for Roger to bash people he didn't like. The pig was a way to put down 'The Man'. It was like the power station was this immense factory, filled with drones, worker bees, with the pig over it, this figure of hate. It's an extraordinarily powerful and potent image."

"People see it as a fun image," says Rob Brimson, "but I always saw it as profoundly disturbing and making a very strong comment on the relationship between power, in this case electrical power, and the fat pig."

The pig went on tour with the band and the metaphor became even more macabre. Theo Botschuijver was asked to add searchlights for eyes and a panel in its belly so its guts could spill out. (A request to wreathe the pig with the smell of cooking bacon could not be fulfilled.) When Waters left Floyd he took Algie with him and used it in his solo shows. His former band mates, who continued to record and perform as Pink Floyd, had their own pig made, adding conspicuous testicles to differentiate it from Waters' sow.

Despite all the complications, Hipgnosis was not done with the power station. Brimson recalls shooting two further covers inside the building: one of the turbine hall for rock band UFO (*Lights Out*, 1977) and another for Hawkwind (*Quark, Strangeness and Calm*, 1977) in the control room. And, of course, post-*Animals* other musicians would continue to channel its dramatic form: The Jam filmed the video for "News of the World" on the roof, and it featured in videos by artists as diverse as Bill Wyman and Hanson. It appeared on the back cover of Morrissey's 1990 album *Bona Drag* and inside Muse's *The Resistance* in 2009. It inspired a song, "Battersea Odyssey", by Super Furry Animals in 2007.

Even Pink Floyd renewed its acquaintance, returning in 2011 to celebrate the 35th anniversary of *Animals*, when an inflatable pig was once again hoisted up between the chimneys.[9] This time it was not Algie, who by now was no longer airworthy and had been retired to a barn in Suffolk.

"When I look back at all the aggravation, we could have just taken the photo of the pig in the studio," says Powell. "But we believed everything should be done for real. That was always what we did and the experience was part of the whole process. We wanted a living sculpture, a one-off moment. It became a very important symbol for Pink Floyd, and the association of Battersea Power Station became cemented with the band. But it wasn't a publicity stunt, it was a pain in the arse."

TRANSFER BUS SECTION 2-3
MAIN BUS SECTION 2-3
GENERATOR 2
DIRECT COUPLED EXCITER
STANDB
No2

CHAPTER SIX

POWERING DOWN

As Battersea becomes obsolete the question arises of what to do with it, and everyone and his dog has a bright idea

FOR WORKERS AT BATTERSEA POWER STATION, Algie's adventure was just another day at the office. Photographers and film crews were becoming increasingly regular visitors as the Central Electricity Generating Board decided to get as much use as possible out of a building that was nearing the end of its life. *New Scientist* reflected the new reality in a November 1982 issue, reporting that "one Friday in late September the only work for the station's 300-odd staff was as extras, looking on while John Cleese chased naked ladies through the coal yards in a scene for the next Monty Python film".

POWERING DOWN

For Richard Lester's *Superman III*, film-makers spent a week in the coal yard working on a scene involving Christopher Reeve crushing a lump of coal into a diamond. It took ages, the power station didn't feature and the station workers were always getting told off as one or other of them inadvertently popped into shot.[1]

More excitement surrounded the visit of punk-pop singer Toyah Willcox, who it was rumoured was going to ride naked on a white horse through the coal yard. "So we all went out there to watch," recalls maintenance worker Terry Smith, "but she never turned up." The video for "Brave New World" was eventually shot at the power station with Willcox on a white horse but fully clothed, dosed with brandy and with none of the workers present.[2]

There were fewer workers every year by this time. The A Station had closed in 1975. Its turbines were shut down on 17th March by retired station manager John Ambrose, the man who as charge engineer had brought the first set into service in 1933. It was gradually stripped of machinery, while its glorious control room was preserved for events (including CEGB meetings) and filming. "It had reached the end of its life, but it was sad as it was a bit of history," says Peter Hill, who managed the maintenance team. "It had seen so much work and still looked amazing, all this brass and marble, so artistic. There was a party when it closed."

I interview Hill at Flanagan's, an Irish pub on Battersea Park Road opposite the power station where he still occasionally meets former workmates from the power station. There are three colleagues with him on the evening we meet – Dave Hislop, Terry Smith and Terry Whatley – who all worked as part of Hill's maintenance crew. In the 1970s, the pub was one of the favourite after-work haunts for power station workers. Back then it was called the Old Red

PREVIOUS SPREAD
One of the control rooms at Battersea was the setting for a fashion shoot for the boutique Mr Freedom of Kensington Church Street at the beginning of the 1970s. © Chris Richardson

House, presumably in homage to the lively Georgian tavern that once made Battersea Fields such a happy hunting ground for London's young squires.

When Hill began at Battersea in 1971, the station employed nearly 900 people, many of whom lived locally and worked in the dirty, noisy parts such as the coal store or boiler hall. The station manager sat at the top of the pile, while the charge engineers had the important job of monitoring the controls and ensuring the station could supply the necessary amount of power to what was now called the Super Grid, an update of the pre-war National Grid. With the closure of Battersea A, the CEGB had wanted to reduce staff to 300 but union intervention ensured this was achieved through a gradual process of natural wastage rather than dramatic job loss. Like most industries of the era, Battersea was unionised but rarely went on strike, although it had been picketed during the miners' strike of 1974; the miners even got hold of a boat, which they used to turn back the flatties delivering coal to Battersea by river. "We took them sandwiches," remembers Dave Hislop, a scaffolder at the station in the 1970s.

Everybody knew the days of the centrally located coal-fired power stations were drawing to a close. "Every year there'd be a list of power stations due to come out of service and every year Battersea would move nearer the top," says Hislop. The demise of the B Station was slowed by the 1973 oil crisis, which made most of the CEGB's oil-fired stations uneconomical and kept Battersea busy.

Hill and his colleagues were all in their twenties at the time and the power station provided them not just with employment but also a social life. A freestanding building in the yard housed a canteen and recreation room; food was subsidised – "They wanted to fatten us up," chuckles Hill – and there were clubs for just about everything, including football, fishing and photography. Evidence of team spirit

A white-jacketed engineer keeps a lonely vigil in one of the turbine halls on a Christmas Day in the mid 1950s. © bridgetbishop.co.uk

is there in the achievements of Battersea's first-aiders who came top in national competitions nine times in eighteen years. The in-house fire team was also a serious affair, with workers given half days off in which to practise.

"It was the sort of environment where you had to look out for each other," says Hislop. "As maintenance workers, we worked all over the power station, wherever we were needed and it was very hot, very noisy and very dirty. You had all the noise from the pipes, the steam. It was always clanging and hissing." Before the implementation of the Health and Safety at Work Act of 1974 workers did not necessarily have helmets or earplugs and had to fall back on stuffing their ears with cotton wool. Unsurprisingly, many former workers have since experienced problems with their ears (and lungs – the building contained massive amounts of asbestos).

Fittingly, given that it was something of an anachronism in so many ways, the power station was operating much as it had since the 1930s. Although coal was no longer sourced from Wales, it still arrived by boat along the Thames. It was now bought on the international market from wherever was cheapest and transported to England via Rotterdam.

The river remained essential to Battersea's function. One of Hislop's jobs was to go down to the wharf and check the huge intake pipe through which the water from the Thames entered the power station. All kinds of things could get caught in the mouth of the pipe. "You'd go down to see what was blocking it and sometimes there'd be a corpse," he says.

Even the practice of using Battersea's furnaces to dispose of sensitive matter continued. During the war it had been Bank of England currency supplies but in the 1970s it was confidential files and documents from the US Embassy on Grosvenor Square. "They'd come down and get rid of all this confidential material," says Whatley. "They'd turn up with guards carrying guns." This unorthodox use of the power station is confirmed in the CEGB's own *Landmark of London* publication, which describes the memo-burning as part of Battersea's "routine operation".

Battersea was special in other ways too. "It was the only power station to have a chauffeur," says Hill. "It was for the station manager. It would pick him up at Waterloo and take him to Battersea, and also to Bankside for CEGB meetings."

Battersea was the bigger station but Bankside was more modern. Replacing an old coal-fired station that had stood on the site since 1891, it was oil-fired and so required no dirty coaling jetties or bunkers. Although also designed by Giles Gilbert Scott, the presence of St Paul's Cathedral just across the river from Bankside had forced the architect to deliver a design that was less obtrusive. He settled on a single, centrally placed chimney that was square to fit better with the surrounding architecture and which was kept to a modest height. It began operating in 1952 and became the flagship operation for the CEGB.

In October 1978, Battersea's stock plummeted when a fire took out No 4 turbine, leaving it sufficiently badly damaged that it had to be decommissioned. "That was a real nail in the coffin," says Terry Whatley, "as it left Battersea with only two generating sets and they weren't in great condition."

As the power station limped towards its final reckoning, Wandsworth Council began to think about what to do with it – or, more accurately, the land that would remain after the power station was closed and, presumably, knocked down. The CEGB too were contemplating their options and had already fielded "hundreds of enquiries" from parties interested in the site. The power station's future was to be the subject of regular meetings at Wandsworth Town Hall, right up until 14th October 1980, when the sudden and surprise announcement was made by the Secretary of State for the Environment Michael Heseltine that Battersea Power Station was to be given Grade II listed-building status. This was an acknowledgement that the power station was of national interest and could not now be demolished at the end of its working life. As Delcia Keate, senior designation advisor at English Heritage explains: "It was added to the National Heritage List for England in recognition of its powerful scale, celebrated silhouette, and that, as a power station it was the first to rationalise large-scale distribution of power. The building is a masterpiece of industrial design. It is one of London's most prominent landmarks and one of a few with a genuine claim to the title 'iconic'."[3]

Had the CEGB decided to knock down the defunct A Station, even just its two chimneys, at any time after it went out of service in 1975, as it could quite easily have done, the listing would never have been entertained. The CEGB's lethargy was a lucky escape for preservationists.

At Wandsworth Council and at the CEGB, the listing was not received with enthusiasm. Martin Johnson was chairman of Wandsworth's technical services committee, whose responsibilities included planning. "Before the power station closed I was in weekly discussions with officers about how the site might be used," he says. "Then out of the blue one Monday morning Mr Heseltine listed it. There was no consultation, no prior discussion – I think I would have been aware of any. That was unusual. When other places get listed, it's usually been spoken about for years. There was none of that with the power station."[4]

There was good reason for Heseltine's haste. When Battersea was listed it was alongside a dozen other 20th-century buildings, including the art deco Hoover factory on Western Avenue and the Gillette factory on the Great West Road. This was a rapid response to the destruction of the Firestone factory, also on the Great West Road. Built in 1928, the factory was one of the finest industrial buildings in London, styled along the lines of a sleek colonnaded ancient Egyptian temple. When it closed in 1979 the twenty-eight-acre site was purchased by Trafalgar House PLC. Almost immediately, there was local concern that the building would be demolished, and the company was told by the Department of the Environment that an emergency "spot listing" was being considered. Trafalgar, who also owned the Ritz Hotel and the *Daily Express* newspaper, acted swiftly. Before a civil servant could sign an order the developers sent in the bulldozers. The factory was reduced to rubble over the August Bank Holiday weekend. Trafalgar had freed itself from any commitment to maintain the factory's architectural features by simply obliterating them. The episode inspired the founding of The Thirties Society (now the Twentieth Century Society) with its remit to safeguard the heritage of architecture and design in Britain from 1914 onwards. Newspaper columnist Simon Jenkins wrote in its first journal, "I can recall few buildings of the last decade whose destruction has produced more spontaneous outrage from laymen." Stung by this experience, they switched focus to buildings that faced a similar threat, while Heseltine promised it would not be allowed to happen again.

Contrary to Johnson's recollections, at least two campaign groups – the aforementioned Thirties Society and another preservation society, SAVE Britain's Heritage – had already been lobbying for Battersea's protection. But things moved swiftly after Firestone. When Heseltine announced the listing of Battersea it came just six weeks after that August Bank Holiday. Speaking at the AGM of the Victorian Society in October 1980, Heseltine said: "I have no intention of standing by while buildings of the inter-war period are destroyed without very careful consideration being given to the possibility of preserving them." (As Battersea Power Station later revealed its considerable challenges to developers, word went round that Heseltine had listed Battersea purely to spite Margaret Thatcher, who was said to loathe the building. This is categorically denied by a number of Wandsworth councillors but it is too delicious a tale not to repeat here.)

The listing of Battersea was to have dramatic repercussions over the following decades and something of this was grasped immediately. By this time, the power station's two remaining turbines were rarely in use and then mainly to continue heating the Churchill Gardens Estate and Dolphin Square in Pimlico. In November 1980, *The Times*' London Diary pointed out that with the power station expected to end "its noble life" in a year or two, an alternative use was required. A prize of £10 was offered to the reader "who comes up with the most practicable suggestion for the building's future use". This whimsical competition had been prompted by the comments of Michael Montague, chairman of the English Tourist Board. "I must say that I fail to see what on earth we can do with it," he was quoted as saying. "There may be good reasons for listing it, which I am not qualified to assess. But those who want to list buildings in which they see some tourist potential should proceed cautiously." Would the decision to list Battersea, asked the Diary's editor Alan Hamilton, leave "the Secretary of State... having to remove certain sticky substances from his handsome features?"

The Times had already addressed this issue on 18th October in a prescient leader published a few days after Heseltine's announcement. While acknowledging that Battersea had a "place in the affections of many who care nothing about architecture" and "was the supreme embodiment of thirtyish ideas about cathedrals of industry", it argued that "listing cannot usually avert the fate of a building which is obstinately unamenable to current use". The writer continued, "Battersea is a challenge to the imagination. An aeronautical museum, like the impressive Air and Space Museum in Washington, perhaps hung with Spitfires and Swordfishes – or even Concorde, pointing skywards?" This was also the suggestion of architectural historian Gavin Stamp in *The Spectator* on 20th September 1980. Thus began what was to become one of London's most popular party games of the 1980s and beyond: trying to work out what on earth to do with Battersea Power Station.

In fairness to Giles Gilbert Scott, he had considered this very issue before his death in February 1960: he thought Battersea should be turned into an industrial museum. When *The Times*' London Diary reported back on 27th November 1980, Hamilton could announce a "heavy mailbag of ideas from the serious to the silly… One fact emerges clearly: Londoners love the majestic old upturned dining table." Among the respondents were Alan Beith, the Liberal chief whip and MP for Berwick-upon-Tweed, who would stand for leadership against Paddy Ashdown in 1988. Beith was one of several correspondents to suggest it should be converted to nuclear power. Others believed it would make a fine new home for Westminster or the European Parliament – the chimneys could be used, someone pointed out, to "carry away the hot air". Other suggestions included flats for the elderly, a church ("Many overseas visitors already think it is"), or somewhere to hide the EEC grain mountain. Some credit is due to Mr Cawkell of Kentish Town who felt the power station should simply be left to stand as it was: "Let it just be," he wrote. "An elegant piece of industrial art that gives delight to see."

The two most popular ideas were to turn it into a museum – either one for aircraft as mooted by *The Times* and Stamp, or as overspill for London's existing museums – or to use it as some kind of sports centre. The most detailed proposal came from Bernard Dembo of Maidenhead, who earned *The Times*' prize of a tenner for a concept involving filling the boiler room and turbine halls with a swimming pool, squash courts, tennis courts, a rollerskating rink, an athletics track and skateboarding facilities, with the facility to cover the lot with artificial turf for football, hockey and cricket. On the upper floors would be nightclubs, restaurants and discos. Dembo is therefore the first in a long list of people to make a bit of money by thinking up unworkable alternative uses for Battersea Power Station.

A CHALLENGE TO THE IMAGINATION

Away from the main halls Battersea was a rabbit warren of tunnels, cable flats, passageways and basements. © bridgetbishop.co.uk

As all this was going on, plans along similar lines were being prepared by Marcus Binney, chairman of pressure group SAVE Britain's Heritage, who was working on a scheme for a combined sports centre and exhibition hall. In 1981, Binney's proposals were published in a booklet, *The Colossus of Battersea*, co-authored with Gavin Stamp, who had previously written about Battersea in his 1979 book *Temples of Power*. With input from architects Martin Richardson and Graham Morrison, *The Colossus of Battersea* was intended to kick-start discussion on how Battersea Power Station could be retained and given a new lease of life. It was a publication that would have longstanding consequences.

SAVE presented its case clearly in the introduction: "Monumental though Battersea Power Station certainly is, it cannot realistically be preserved simply as an industrial monument. It is also far too large to become an industrial museum. What is needed is a commercially viable mixture of uses which will attract the investment necessary to finance purchase, repair, conversion and continuing maintenance." Its proposal was to turn Battersea into a leisure complex centred on a major indoor sports arena for athletics (seating 8,000), tennis (seating 10,000) and boxing (seating 11,500), which could also be used for pop concerts and conferences. Below the arena would be an ice-skating rink and below that two levels of parking. One of the two flanking turbine halls would be used for tennis, badminton, basketball, volleyball, five-a-side-football and gymnastics, with additional space constructed for twenty squash courts, archery and a shooting range. Leftover space would be used as overspill for the Science Museum and as recording and film studios, as well as offices or shops.

SAVE also proposed the conversion of the coal store into a covered Olympic swimming pool and turning the power station's offices, canteen and social room into workshops for craft and light industry. The integrity of the building's heritage would be upheld as much as possible, including the retention of "features of interest in terms of industrial archaeology" such as the coal crane and jetty, and the huge cranes and gantries in the turbine hall.

SAVE knew this wasn't going to be easy. "Considerable sections of brickwork are in need of remedial treatment," it admitted but argued that they were not intimidatingly large when measured against the potential space available within the building. The problem of the awkward location ("at once central and isolated") was acknowledged and the solution offered of 1,350 car parking spaces on the ground floor, as well as a pedestrian footbridge to

Battersea Park train station and a subterranean tunnel into the park itself. The biggest stumbling block was the price. In 1980, the CEGB had estimated that repairs would cost around £700,000 – this, SAVE pointed out, was considerably less than the amount it would cost to demolish the thing and the bill for conversion could be set against the potential income from the completed development. Almost as an afterthought, SAVE added that the space near the railway into Victoria could be used for housing, perhaps 400 units, capped at eight storeys high. No more would be needed because few would ever want to live in the shadow of a former power station next to a railway line on the wrong side of the river.

It was a neat and sympathetic package and it was granted planning permission by Wandsworth in April 1982 – you do not have to own land to get outline planning permission, and developers sometimes get planning before they make a purchase so they can get a better idea of the value of the land.

The notion of the power station as a place of leisure would now become embedded into Battersea's brickwork for the next three decades. By SAVE's own admission it would become the basis of many future planning applications and proposals. The publication therefore had a mixed legacy. It focused minds, showing there was great potential for the building if it was developed cleverly, but it also narrowed options, as stakeholders became obsessed with the idea of using it for leisure purposes.

Conservative-led Wandsworth Council was particularly keen on this as it was thought this would be the best way to bring jobs into the area – in the 1980s unemployment was perhaps the single biggest issue facing the Conservative government. When Wandsworth's technical services committee prepared a brief with the CEGB creating parameters for the power station's future in 1983, employment was one of seven primary objectives. "The plan for it was to generate jobs," says Ravi Govindia, who as a Wandsworth councillor helped create the Battersea Power Station Development Brief, published in September 1983.[5] "That was the big drive and that's why we went for something leisure based. There was a desire to have a non-industrial use, a new use, and leisure seemed the obvious fit." Retail and office usages were explicitly ruled out as Wandsworth was concerned with protecting the nearby town centre at Clapham Junction. Not for the last time, the issue of Battersea's future fell victim to a political lack of foresight that focused on satisfying immediate public-image problems at the expense of long-term benefits.

There was also at this time a counter proposal to use the power station for refuse burning, submitted by the Lesser Group in June 1982. This was also approved by Wandsworth in November of that year and we shall return to it in the next chapter. Meanwhile, the debate continued in the press, much of it inspired by Gavin Stamp's eulogy to the power station published in *The Times* in April 1983 under the headline "What Shall we Do with this Cathedral of Power?" Again, readers were quick to make suggestions. Charles Marsden-Smedley thought it could be used as the centrepiece of an exposition along the lines of the 1951 Festival of Britain; Martin Tod thought it should be an "awe-inspiring mosque"; spoilsport Sylvia Sobernheim suggested its "looming ugliness" should be demolished.

The smartest response came from Raymond Apthorpe, a professor of developmental studies based in The Hague. He argued that development of the power station had to go hand-in-hand with that of the surrounding area, otherwise it would just be a "monstrous curiosity". If Battersea was to become a "meaningful landmark" it needed to serve as a "physical focal point" for a regeneration scheme with "river, road, rail and cycle access, linked in some way with Battersea Park". The alternative was that Battersea would become "a well preserved relic, with all the energy gone out of it".

CLOSURE

As the talk continued, the end of the power station's working life drew nearer. (Sister station Bankside had already shut down in 1981, a victim of the global oil crisis.) In the summer of 1982, the heating of the Churchill Gardens Estate was transferred to a new, replacement plant. Battersea was now operating only on standby, ready to fill in when other stations were closed for maintenance or repair. The few staff that remained were kept busy polishing the control panels. Even the stray cats had abandoned the building, admittedly having been encouraged to do so by a CEGB extermination programme.

The life had virtually been extinguished from Battersea. When in 1982 the Monty Python team came to film scenes for *The Meaning of Life* they had to bring their own generators. By now Terry Smith had been moved to another substation, where one of his jobs was to break up a diesel turbine that was no longer needed. "Then at the very last minute, they said this spare turbine had to be sent to Battersea," he says. This was on the orders of Walter Marshall, chairman of the CEGB, who realised that with Battersea barely functioning he had no way to power the lights for the gatherings he liked to hold in the control room. The new turbine was installed so Marshall could carry on entertaining the big wigs.

Marshall would soon play a prominent role in the miners' strike, by which time Battersea was no longer in service – handy timing for a government that was desperately trying to reduce national reliance upon coal ahead of this pivotal confrontation. Battersea B ceased to produce electricity on 25th January 1983 at 6.21pm and the great brass doors were closed for the last time, without ceremony, on 31st October 1983. After fifty years of service the great polluter was silenced. Now things would really get dirty.

JOHN COLLINS
BIG DIPPER
ROTOR-DROMES
MAX MYERS
PRESENTS THE
ROTOR
ROTOR
THE WORLD'S GREATEST SENSATION

CHAPTER SEVEN

A CUNNING PLAN

A competition is held to find a developer for the power station and although the entries are underwhelming, sparks are soon flying

CAST
John Broome Chairman of the Alton Towers theme park and Trentham Gardens, both in Staffordshire, with ambitious plans to extend his operations to a third site
Alf Dubs Czech-born Labour politician who became MP for Battersea; now Lord Dubs of the House of Lords
Martin Johnson Chairman of the technical services committee at Wandsworth Council and part of the judging panel for the CEGB's competition to find a developer for Battersea
Peter Legge Head of a Dublin-based architectural practice that up to this time had specialised in pharmaceutical plants
Mark Leslie Cambridge and Harvard-educated architect, and London-based employee of Peter Legge Associates
David Roche Low-key property developer and distant relative of Mark Leslie, brought in to form a consortium to bid on the power station

A CUNNING PLAN

THE SECOND ACT in the life of Battersea Power Station began with a small announcement in *The Times*. It was placed by the CEGB on 19th October 1983 and invited "development teams interested in purchasing the site to enter a competition for the reuse and rehabilitation of Battersea Power Station". Entrants were to enclose a cheque for £25 with their application form. The competition was to be managed by the giant construction firm Taylor Woodrow and the closing date for registration was 9th January 1984. When the competition concluded, a brash schoolteacher-turned-entrepreneur called John Broome would be clutching the keys to one of London's greatest architectural assets.

The CEGB felt it had been dealt a rum hand by Heseltine. Instead of a valuable slice of land it could flog off for a tidy profit it was now saddled with a great white elephant. It was at a loss to know what to do and hoped that a competition might result in an as-yet-unconsidered solution. Or it might prove the opposite: that there was nothing that could be done with Battersea at all, which would be an even more welcome result.

Andrew Derbyshire was the CEGB member with responsibility for architectural matters and it was he who proposed the competition. He was convinced it would demonstrate that there was nothing that could be done with the building and that the only sensible course would be demolition.[1]

It didn't quite work out that way.

Mark Leslie saw the announcement in *The Times*. At the time, Leslie was the one-man London office of Peter Legge Associates, an architectural practice based in Ireland that built hi-tech pharmaceutical plants. Leslie had been born in London in 1952 and studied architecture at Cambridge and Harvard before going to work for Peter Legge

PREVIOUS SPREAD
The Battersea Park funfair was part of the 1951 Festival of Britain. Visited by a young Mark Leslie, it inspired his vision for a new use for the neighbouring power station. © TopFoto

in Ireland. In 1982, Leslie's wife was posted to the Irish Embassy in London and Legge agreed Leslie could move with her to see if he could drum up work for the company in London.

"Everybody in the world had an opinion on what to do with the building," says Leslie, who now runs Martello Media in Dublin, a firm that specialises in immersive educational experiences in museums and galleries. "My idea was that it would make a fabulous technology theme park."[2]

One of his primary inspirations was the funfair that had stood in Battersea Park between 1951 and 1974. This was originally part of the 1951 Festival of Britain, which had its main presence on the South Bank. Battersea's more frivolous sideshow carried an echo of the old pleasure gardens on Battersea Fields around the Red House – and also, unwittingly, realised something of the spirit of the unbuilt Dream City of 1907. The funfair occupied the centre of the park and was based around a Grand Vista and Fountain Lake, designed by cartoonist and stage designer Osbert Lancaster and artist John Piper. It was a considerable success, drawing more than eight million visitors and outlasting other Festival attractions.[3]

However, by the 1970s annual visitor numbers were barely above a million. The end was signalled on 30th May 1972, when a three-car train on the Big Dipper became detached from the drive chain and hurtled backwards down the track. Five children were killed and thirteen injured. It remains the world's worst rollercoaster tragedy. The funfair's reputation never recovered and it closed in 1974. An attempt to revive it failed in 1975, when Wandsworth rejected a planning application by EMI and Trust Houses Forte to create a Disneyland-style theme park called Magic World. The design work had been done by a Texan company called Leisure and Recreation Concepts (LARC), which built theme parks in the United States – LARC would re-enter the Battersea story quite soon.

Like many Londoners, Mark Leslie had visited the funfair as a child. He was excited by the idea of restoring something like it to Battersea, but with a theme relevant to London and the power station. "What was Britain's essential contribution to the world?" he recalls asking himself. "Well, it was the first industrial superpower and there was a great story to be told there. London was home to a scientific revolution, the country of Boyle and Newton, steam and electricity, and in these great halls at Battersea Power Station you could put something that was a whole lot more fun than the Science Museum but a whole lot more educational than Disneyland."

Leslie envisaged a fusion of Battersea's twin spirits of industry and recreation. Intrigued, Peter Legge gave him the go-ahead and Leslie set about designing an attraction that would use amusement park rides to tell the story of science and technology "from Newton to the present day". Leslie still has some of the original concept drawings and they give a sense of the ambition and imagination of this slightly insane project: a model of an R100 airship and a Spitfire hang from the ceiling of one turbine hall, while the boiler room is taken up by a Blitz ride: "You'd be on a rollercoaster that started in a tube station, taking you into the sky through barrage balloons and searchlights," explains Leslie.

The experience was to be divided into the Age of Steam, the Age of Electricity and the Space Age. Within this loose timeframe there was a Victorian waterfront and Dickensian street; there were to be recreations of Pepys' and Shakespeare's London. Other areas are labelled HG Wells, Jack the Ripper and "Industrial Revolution horrors". There would be reconstructions of London architecture including the Euston Arch and Crystal Palace, with a full-scale model of Brunel's *Great Eastern* boat docked on the riverfront. Some of the power station's original equipment would be retained. Crucially, says Leslie, the site would have been developed incrementally.

MARK LESLIE'S SCHEME

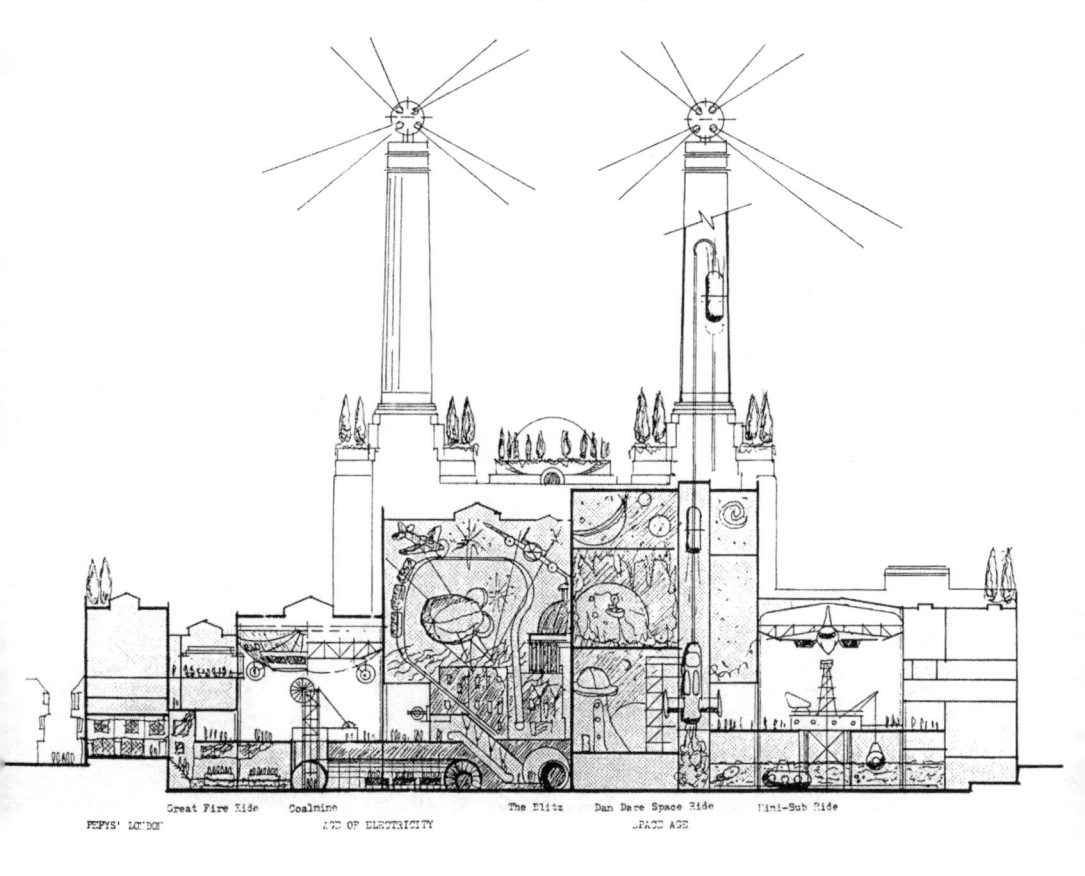

A cross section of Mark Leslie's loose science and technology-based scheme for the power station with labels indicating areas devoted to Pepys' London, the Great Fire, the Blitz, a Dan Dare space ride and a mini-sub ride. © Mark Leslie

"My idea was to seal the building up and use the space around the power station to make a really big outdoor theme park and then slowly add to it," he says. "I felt the profits from a theme park by the river would pay for the rest. We would open the control room to the public and then keep adding indoor rides as we had the money. We wanted to keep at least one turbine hall in place and put in a glass wall that you could see the turbines through."

Leslie had his scheme but needed the cash to make it happen. The CEGB's competition was for a funded scheme, which meant submissions needed to come from a developer rather than an

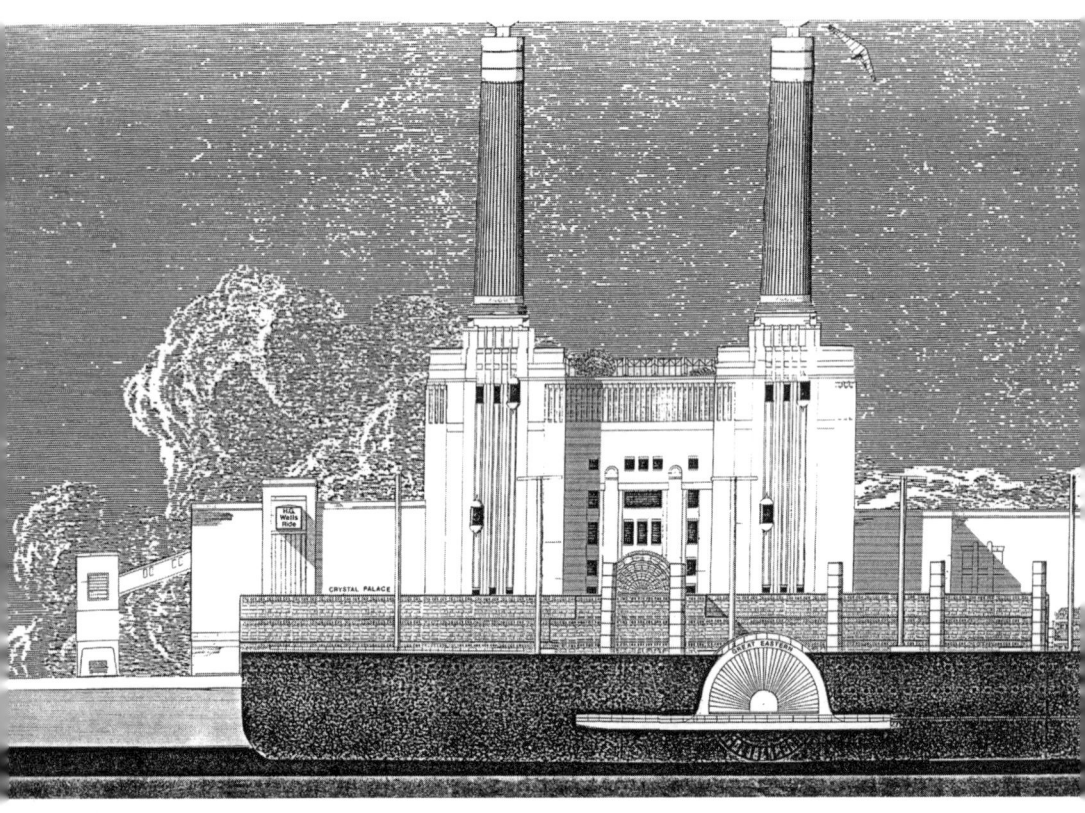

One of Leslie's more fabulous ideas was to have a specially commissioned full-scale replica of Brunel's revolutionary but ill-fated iron sailing steam ship, the SS *Great Eastern*, moored on the Thames in front of the power station. © Mark Leslie

architect. Theoretically, this would weed out any impractical ideas.

Fortunately, Leslie had somebody he could call. "I approached a distant relative by marriage, David Roche, who ran a company called Roche Leisure," says Leslie. "He jumped at the idea. He thought it would be fabulous. But he needed to put together a consortium."

By Roche's own admission, Roche Leisure was a small development company with a varied portfolio: a hotel in Scotland, an industrial estate in Lancashire, several offices in London. "The basic object of the exercise was to do quite a lot of research and to win a competition," says Roche, when we meet at his mews house in central London.[4]

Roche had no great affection for the building – "It's just a shed with some chimneys," he says – but nevertheless he saw potential and so he set about building a consortium. Touche Ross and Morgan Grenfell were brought in to help with financing, Gouldens were the solicitors and Mowlem was charged with construction. Mowlem had been the construction firm that had built the power station back in the 1930s and Roche thought they might have some of the original drawings. "Which they did," he says. "Somewhere. We never actually found them." Roche even got Marcus Binney's SAVE to support Leslie's scheme, which was a canny piece of politics. "I brought him on board to give the impression I cared," says Roche. But something was still missing.

"I needed a funfair operator," says Roche. "I talked to Walter Goldsmith, director general of the Institute of Directors and he told me I had to speak to somebody serious, like Alton Towers. He introduced me to John Broome. That was probably my biggest mistake of the whole enterprise."

John Broome was born in 1943 near Chester. He followed his father, a headmaster, into the teaching profession but always had an eye for a deal: he claimed that when he was sixteen he won a house at public auction for £2,000 even though he only had £122 in his savings account, something that earned him a thrashing from his father but "taught him the folly of approaching business with a cavalier attitude".[5]

In 1973, he married Jane Bagshaw, whose father owned Alton Towers, then a stately home with a sideline in fairground rides. Broome took over the site's model railway and then gradually increased his involvement and the number of rides until in 1980 he relaunched Alton Towers as a full-blown theme park. He introduced attention-grabbing rides, such as the £1.25m Corkscrew, the UK's first double-loop rollercoaster, followed by a £2.25m log flume and the £2m Black Hole space ride. Alton Towers became – according to Broome – the most popular paid attraction in the country outside London, and certainly one of the most talked about.

An active Tory and wholehearted admirer of Margaret Thatcher, Broome was emblematic of the high-flying 1980s, an entrepreneur in a hurry. In 1982, he purchased Trentham Gardens near Stoke, with ambitious plans to turn that into a theme park modelled loosely on Florida's Wet 'n' Wild park, focusing on sports facilities, but with a conference centre and hotel. This £20m development, he assured the press, would lead to 1,500 jobs, adding that he was on the look-out for a third project for his burgeoning empire.

Even so, Broome seemed to be less than enthusiastic when Roche met him at Trentham Gardens. "Broome was non-committal," says Roche. Leslie says much the same: "We got a frosty reception. He thought it was a stupid idea. A theme park had to be outdoors in the country. Nobody had ever done an indoor one before."

Broome, though, was more interested than he made out. "The problem he had was that having heard our idea he wanted to do it himself, but the competition had closed, he couldn't enter on his own," says Roche. "So he had to join my consortium."

At this point, things began to get messy. As Broome increased his involvement he approached LARC, the Texan firm that had been involved in the failed attempt to revive Battersea Funfair in 1975 and which had designed some of the attractions at Alton Towers. The Texans presented him with a version of the Mark Leslie scheme that took a more general view of British history, without the specific focus on science, industry and technology. "Mark's very bright," says Roche. "His original theme, which I suppose happened in the Millennium Dome, was more intellectual and participatory with a science angle. As Broome got involved he brought in LARC and Mark was no longer in the picture, but he remained part of the consortium as he was on the entry form. But he was more or less put to one side.

"I didn't like either idea," he adds. "To me it was a shopping centre."

Roche's big plan was to place enough rides inside the power station and on the surrounding land to satisfy Wandsworth Council and the CEGB that they were creating a leisure space, and to fill the rest of the site with shops. "We'd win the competition on the basis it was a theme park as that is jolly nice and makes people comfortable and is exciting. But to make money it had to be a retail destination." He likens his plan to the Metro Centre, the vast shopping centre that opened in Gateshead in the north-east in 1986.

This was scarcely ideal. As the consortium prepared to meet the CEGB's competition board, three leading representatives had entirely different notions of what their scheme should be.

Lord Ezra, chairman of the National Coal Board until 1982, headed the judging panel, which consisted of notables including President of the Royal Academy Sir Hugh Casson, Sir Robert Lawrence of the British Railways Board, editor of the *Evening Standard* Louis Kirby, chief executive of the London Docklands Development Corporation Reginald War and Andrew Derbyshire of the CEGB. Wandsworth was represented in the shape of councillor Stuart Hercock and chairman of the technical services committee Martin Johnson.

"I think I was one of the only ones without a title," says Johnson, who recalls that all he received for his service on the board was a commemorative CEGB fruit bowl. "I was rather proud to be representing the local interest as what always struck me was how little they knew about the site. They weren't selected because of any connection with Battersea and Wandsworth, it was all about their reputations."[6]

One person raising objections was the local MP, Labour's Alf Dubs. Born in Prague, Dubs arrived in England in 1939 on the Kindertransport, the rescue mission that saved 10,000 Jewish children from the Nazis. He became MP for Battersea South in 1979 and after his old constituency was abolished, stood and won the seat for Battersea in 1983. Dubs was often at odds with Wandsworth's Conservative council, led from 1983 until 1992 by Paul Beresford, a committed Thatcherite who was revolutionising council services and espousing the power of the market in a way that would have considerable impact on Battersea Power Station.

"I remember Alf Dubs criticising the set-up at one point because there was no local connection and he had to retract that and apologise when he found out I was involved," says Johnson. "But I was the only local representative [there was actually also councillor Stuart Hercock], and looking back that was quite wrong and wouldn't happen now. Now you'd have many more representatives from the community."

As well as noting the lack of local representation, Dubs would also write to the CEGB with his concerns. "I asked them to put in a clause that if the winning consortium did not go ahead with the scheme the building would revert to the public sector, which they declined," he says.[7] Dubs – now Lord Dubs – was concerned that the CEGB, facing privatisation, was about to dispose of a public building in undue haste. "I don't blame them for getting rid of it because times had moved on but I do blame them for disposing of such a valuable iconic asset without giving it any thought. They had a responsibility not just for an iconic building but also the public purse. They were just giving away a valuable asset."

This was not a concern in the boardroom near Bank, in the City, where the judging panel met. As well as the main competition, it also had to consider a "community" competition, which asked

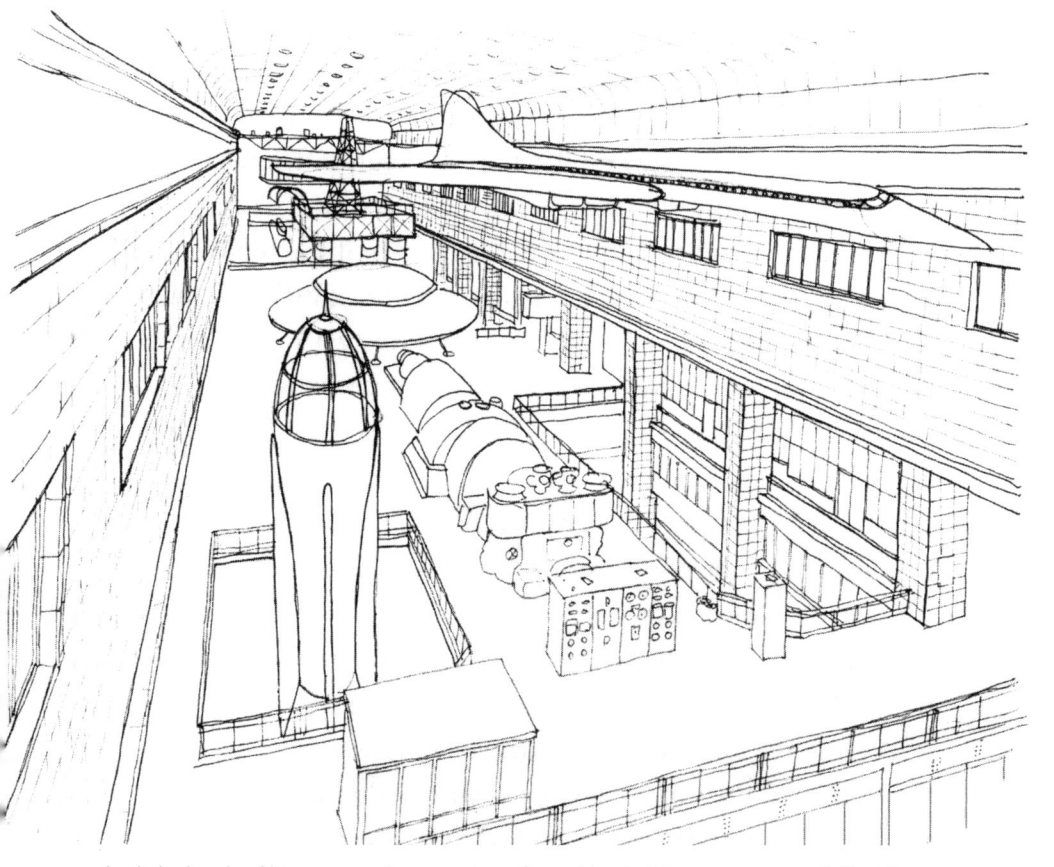

Leslie's sketch of his proposed conversion of a turbine hall into a space-age hall with Concorde hung from the ceiling and miscellaneous bits of rocketry. © Mark Leslie

locals to send their own ideas. Some of these were exhibited at the Arts Centre in Battersea in November 1983. "This wasn't taken all that seriously," says Johnson. "One of the community entries was that the working class of Battersea should be invited to jump down the chimneys for the entertainment of Hooray Henrys." Johnson feels this reflected great cynicism among elements of the local community, who believed that the CEGB's panel weren't really interested in local concerns. Right from the start, the circumstances surrounding the redevelopment of the power station were causing local unrest.

In fact, the CEGB had roped in some serious advisors. The architect Sir Hugh Wilson was asked to analyse the technical and financial feasibility of all the entries, and there was also expert testimony from engineers WG Curtin & Partners and Rendel, Palmer & Tritton, quantity surveyors Wakeman Trower & Partners, and County Bank, a subsidiary of National Westminster. Roche recalls lots of correspondence and discussion after the initial presentation. "It went on for some time and the questions got more and more difficult. Most of the questions were about accounting and we were able to answer them based on a set of numbers I did with the chief accountant at Alton Towers." He describes the meetings with the CEGB as like playing a tennis match where you couldn't see your opponent, with the result you never knew what sort of question was going to be lobbed at you.

The committee's queries related to several criteria that had to be met by the successful bidder. These included the financial viability of the scheme and the amount the bidders were prepared to pay the CEGB for the power station, as well as the scheme's benefit to the local community, prospects for job creation and contribution to the riverfront. The proposal also needed to meet the approval of Wandsworth Council.

Seven completed submissions met the 9th January 1984 deadline and were shortlisted for consideration. All went on public display between 5th April and 8th May. They were a mixed bunch but of uniformly dubious architectural merit thanks to the developer-led nature of the competition. One scheme had a six-floor shopping centre in the central boiler house, with an exhibition space in one turbine hall and a sports centre in the other, and a marina on the river. Another proposed to turn the power station into an enormous conference centre with two halls seating 9,000, and with the land around filled with exhibition spaces, hotels and offices. A third was similar to the SAVE scheme, with the boiler house used for sport and entertainment, a swimming pool in one of the turbine halls and a considerable amount – too much it turned out – of retail filling in the gaps. The fourth scheme was to turn the boiler house into a 2,600-seat theatre "capable of staging Busby Berkeley-scale shows", with TV studios, an ice rink, restaurants, tennis courts, squash courts and a gym taking up the rest of the room.

These were all fairly routine but the three other schemes were of greater interest. There was one plan to turn the whole thing into a combination of luxury flats, hotels and retail, with a marina made out of the flooded coal store and a helipad placed on nearby land. It is an early example of the sort of luxury development that now dominates London. In fact, this idea would, essentially, be resuscitated in Rafael Viñoly's 2010 Battersea masterplan, only on a much grander scale. Back in 1984, this scheme was rejected by the panel for falling "substantially outside the brief" by giving nothing back to the local community. This is extraordinary in retrospect – that even in the hyper-capitalist climate of 1984, deep in the Thatcherite heartland of Wandsworth, the sort of luxury flats that now dominate the Battersea waterfront were considered socially unacceptable.

A second noteworthy scheme was to adapt the power station into a refuse-burning plant. This had first been proposed in June 1982, even before the CEGB competition was conceived. The idea was that the power station would be used to burn 500,000 tonnes of rubbish per year, generating 40MW of electricity. It would require some reconstruction work – essentially, the installation of a large ramp to the south so lorries could drive straight into the building and dump their rubbish. The two surviving turbines in Battersea B would be restored to use, as would one of the chimneys. There were problems – for one thing, the insertion of a ramp would require listed building consent and there were also concerns about whether the dilapidated brickwork would receive the renovation it clearly needed. But there was also a pleasing symmetry to this, as it would see the building returned to industrial use.

This plan had been granted planning permission by Wandsworth in 1982 but it now had to win the CEGB competition so the developers could earn the right to actually buy the power station. There was another obstacle. As this project was related to London's infrastructure, the Greater London Council also had to grant approval. As it happens, they were not keen. Simon Turney, the chairman of the GLC's public services committee, told *The Times* in 1983 that using Battersea for waste-burning would be too expensive and represented "an under-utilisation of these important and extensive premises, and would not provide employment opportunities commensurate with its size and potential". The GLC then spent three years mulling over the idea before finally saying no, by which time any decision had long been rendered irrelevant.

The final scheme was from the Roche consortium. Unsurprisingly, given the behind-the-scenes schisms, the plan submitted for public exhibition was a bit vague. When it first entered the competition, Roche's team had presented Mark Leslie's drawings but as the conversation with the CEGB continued, LARC's ideas had begun to take precedence.

LARC's owner Michael Jenkins had considerable expertise in theme parks but less appreciation for the subtleties of British history. "The Americans saw it as Beefeaters, buses and the *Queen Mary*," says Leslie. "They decided that Britain's great contribution to the world was the British Empire, so they designed a whole theme park, in parallel and unbeknownst to us, on the theme of Empire. They'd never heard of the Industrial Revolution, they thought America had invented everything. Except they were struggling to find anything

SLAVERY, MASSACRES AND SODOMY

to celebrate in the Empire that wasn't contentious. They could have a cracking theme park on the horrors of Empire – slavery, massacres, sodomy – but the bankers would have hated it."

For the CEGB board, the specific content was secondary to the general concept, and the idea of a giant indoor funfair by the Thames was an appealing one. "It was the most futuristic proposal," says Johnson, who doesn't recall the particulars of the scheme – whether it was science-themed or based around the Empire – just that it had lots of rides. This was ideal for Roche, still trying to sneak in his shopping centre under the cloak of the Broome/Leslie/LARC theme park. "There was a willingness to embrace this," says Roche. "The razzmatazz was about bringing a bit of America to Britain, where things were still rather dull. Ours was the only scheme with a real element of entertainment and that came from Broome, make no mistake. It wouldn't have won without him."

There was one other out-of-competition scheme pitched into the ring. This was an unofficial, semi-serious suggestion by Cedric Price, the architect who had helped Lord Snowdon design the London Zoo aviary in 1961 and who spent much of his career inventing whimsical structures that could never be built. When they were built, he often wanted them knocked down again so the space could be reused. In 1999 he campaigned successfully against the listing of his own arts centre in Kentish Town as he felt something better could be put in its place. Price, one of his obituaries noted, was the only architect to also be a fully-qualified member of the National Institute of Demolition Contractors. He was outspoken and eccentric but he could be prescient: his 1984 idea for developing the South Bank, for example, included "a great wheel-like structure of observation cars".

Price had once proposed that the best thing to be done with York Minster would be to knock it down, so it was no surprise that his idea for Battersea Power Station would be devoid of sentimentality.

A CUNNING PLAN

Cedric Price's endearingly barmy idea of floating the power station's four chimneys above the streets of Battersea. © Cedric Price fonds, Collection Centre Canadien d'Architecture/Canadian Centre for Architecture, Montréal

In March 1984, he told *The Times* that given the expense of refurbishment the building should be demolished, leaving only the four chimneys and overhead masonry as a "natural hazard," supported by steelwork. The space underneath, he suggested, could be used for housing. He produced some rather surreal illustrations of the concept published in *Building Design* in April 1984, which showed the roof and chimneys of the power station floating ominously above the streets of Battersea. He called it "The Bathat". If nothing else, it recognised that for most people by far the most significant thing about the building was its chimneys.

With the shortlist announced – to a generally unimpressed reception from the trade press – the judges considered their options. Given the brief, the only viable schemes were Roche's, the conference centre, the refuse-burning centre and the Busby Berkeley theatre. With the Roche Consortium scheme promising, rather imaginatively, to provide up to 6,500 jobs, and Roche massively downplaying his retail ambitions, it was a clear frontrunner, even as *Building* magazine highlighted the sharp disconnect between the building's history and the twee, pre-industrial theme park proposed.

The competition brief had also asked the entrants how much they would be prepared to pay the CEGB for the power station and surrounding fifteen acres of land. The Roche consortium's offer was £1.5m, conditional on all asbestos being removed from the building. Given that asbestos-removal would cost the CEGB an estimated £4m, it effectively meant that it was paying somebody to take the building off its hands.

Concerns about financial viability removed both the conference centre and Busby Berkeley theatre schemes, and with four of the others ruled out for not satisfying elements of the brief this left just the Roche consortium and waste-burning schemes in contention. The committee was siding toward the former. There were reservations, but the scheme ticked enough boxes for the CEGB to argue it had done its best to find a workable project even if few were entirely convinced by its appearance. Andrew Derbyshire would write in his assessor's report that the panel had "some sympathy with those members of the public who used words like kitsch, gimmicky and tasteless" but that they trusted the scheme's promoters knew their business and were giving the public what it wanted.

A week before the winner was to be announced at a press conference in July 1984, David Roche was told the decision was in the consortium's favour. "It was a great moment and I called the rest of the consortium and told them we'd won. It was a big secret and we all kept to the embargo," he remembers. "Except Broome."

Legge, Leslie and Roche all tell the same story: the day before the official press conference to announce the winner, John Broome went on TV and told everybody that he had won.

"The board were livid," says Roche. "It was a pre-emptive takeover of the consortium."

On 3rd July 1984, *The Times* reported, "It will be announced today… [the competition] has been won by the Alton Towers company." The story was full of fluff about Alton Towers, with no mention of Roche, let alone Legge or Leslie. Later that day, the official announcement was made in a CEGB press conference held in Battersea Power Station's control room. The accompanying press release – supplied by Leslie – stated with impressive imprecision that the Roche & Co consortium would "create a theme park with a series of historical and futuristic attractions".

It had been an extraordinary piece of manoeuvring by Broome that had completely wrong-footed Roche, who had anticipated problems with their fragile alliance, but hadn't expected them to happen so swiftly or be exploited so ruthlessly. Now, with the weight of the Alton Towers brand behind him – not to mention the sympathies of both local and national government – Broome was able to turn the screw. "There was," says Roche with some understatement, "a furious row."

In the immediate aftermath, Roche says he was advised by the CEGB to sack Broome from the consortium but instead, fatally and despite his own fury, he tried to reach a compromise. "We were happy to let him be chairman of the consortium with all the publicity that came with that," says Roche. "But he wanted to own it and force me and Legge out. I was a small property man with a track record but I didn't have Alton Towers, so if there was an issue of shall we take it forward with Roche or take it forward with Alton Towers, the answer was blindingly obvious."

While Leslie and Legge took their grievances to the press, Roche was quietly negotiating an exit strategy. He offered to sell Broome his right to buy the power station for an undisclosed sum – "Enough to pay the school fees," he says, refusing now, even thirty years later, to reveal the exact figure. The deal was done "with a great deal of nervousness," says Roche. "At this stage there was absolutely no trust between the parties at all. The money had to be in the bank before I handed anything over. For a few weeks, I had the right to buy all of [Battersea] for £1.5m. Now, that wouldn't buy me a flat."

Leslie wanted to fight his corner, but was persuaded by his boss, Peter Legge, that the best thing would be to walk away. "I was furious," he says. "I wanted to do my scheme but Peter very wisely said we were on a hiding to nothing, a tiny firm from Ireland who nobody cared about." They eventually received enough money from Broome to cover their fees, and both men signed gagging orders.

Given Roche's lack of sympathy for the building, perhaps this was a lucky escape for Battersea Power Station. "It was always my view, from day one, that the only answer was to knock the fucker down," he says.

Just weeks after the competition to decide its future had concluded, Battersea Power Station was already on its second owner. David Roche was the first of several developers to pocket a tidy profit without having done all that much to earn it. "It was mega bullshit by lots of people including me," muses a philosophical Roche. "But the problem with bullshit is it can sometimes work but when it doesn't the whole thing falls apart."

MAIN ARENA

A magnificent Ice Rink in a natural island setting supported by extensive dancing fountains. Dual level viewing balconies throughout complex.

A fantasy atmosphere – English nostalgia combined with futuristic shows, rides and theatres.

CHAPTER EIGHT

THE BROOME YEARS

Broome's Battersea Leisure company and its plans to transform the power station into a peculiarly English Disneyland

CAST

Paul Beresford Conservative Party politician, practising dentist and the leader of Wandsworth Council from 1983 to 1992. Knighted in 1990 for services to inner city rehabilitation; currently MP for Mole Valley, Surrey
John Broome The new owner of Battersea Power Station, where he planned to emulate his theme park successes at Alton Towers
Paddy Browne Broome's project architect, from the firm Fitzroy Robinson Partnership
David Cooper Broome's solicitor, described in *The Independent* in 2006 as "Britain's most expensive solicitor"
John Gidman Broome's project manager from 1986 to 1988
Michael Jenkins Texan founder and president of Leisure and Recreation Concepts, Inc (LARC), designers of theme parks and other entertainment experiences
Martin Johnson Long-standing Wandsworth councillor
Gerald Jones Chief executive of Wandsworth Council and prior to his retirement in 2010 reported to be Britain's highest-paid town hall boss
Alex McCuaig Chairman and executive creative director of experiential design company MET Studio

THE BROOME YEARS

EVERYBODY WHO WORKED WITH JOHN BROOME at Battersea Power Station has a story about him but one of the best, or most telling, comes from John Gidman, who was Broome's project manager between 1986 and 1988: "One evening I was watching *Wogan* and Eddie 'the Eagle' Edwards was on," says Gidman, referring to England's popularly inept ski-jumper who competed in the 1988 Winter Olympics. "They asked him what it was like to be at the top of the ski jump looking down and he said, 'Well, it's not as frightening as the new ride at Alton Towers.' I said to Broome the next day, it was amazing, he mentioned Alton Towers. And Broome said, 'I know, it cost me two thousand quid for that.'"[1]

Broome was a showman, an expert at generating publicity. His greatest coup, by any standards, was getting Margaret Thatcher to visit Battersea in June 1988, where she wore a hard hat, fired a laser gun and listened to his bold announcement that the grand opening for his "colossal pleasure palace" would be on 21st May 1990, adding that it would open at 2.30pm sharp so don't be late, as anybody arriving at 2.35pm would miss out. When the allotted time came around, the only people present at the power station were members of a local pressure group. By then, the game was more or less up for Broome. As Eddie the Eagle had claimed, Alton Towers had some thrilling rides but there was nothing quite as giddy as the rise and fall of the developer John Broome.

Broome acquired the right to buy Battersea Power Station from David Roche towards the end of 1984 and by March of the following year he had set up a company, Battersea Leisure, to manage the project. At this point, Broome was still waiting for the CEGB to make good on its promise to remove the building's asbestos. While his theme-ride creators at LARC refined their plans in advance of a formal planning

PREVIOUS SPREAD
John Broome in July 1984 celebrating the Roche Consortium's winning bid. The art shows his plans for the turbine hall, which include an ice-skating rink.
© REX Shutterstock

application, Broome appointed an architect to oversee the work. Surprisingly, he plumped for the Fitzroy Robinson Partnership, a well-established firm of respectable British commercial architects best known for its work on City office blocks. In August 1985, Fitzroy Robinson's Paddy Browne joined the project, which the press was then costing at a total of £50m.

His role was to ensure that LARC's designs were consistent with the power station's Grade II-listing, and to make sure everything complied with existing planning legislation, building regulations and the terms of sale as laid down by the CEBG.

"My job was to make [the power station] into a usable structure, that was it in a nutshell," says Browne.[2] "We took the base scheme that LARC came up with and tried to make it real." As Browne explains it, this was far from straightforward. At Alton Towers a ride could be stuck in the middle of a field and embedded in concrete; at Battersea that same ride would be inside a giant brick-and-steel shed, where its movements could cause damaging vibrations and extreme noise. "People screaming is part of the experience," says Browne. "But we had to look at the acoustics of when it happened inside a brick structure."

Work on the planning application process progressed throughout 1985. An idea of the scheme as it stood at the end of that summer can be had from a four-page promotional broadsheet, entitled *Battersea Power House*, published by Battersea Leisure in September 1985. The front page was, excitingly, all about parking – actually a major concern of local residents. Sir Frederick Snow & Partners were Broome's traffic consultants and they returned with reassuring figures about visitor numbers and parking spaces, even if some of the overspill parking was as far away as Liverpool Street. There was also tantalising mention of an overhead rail-line, a monorail, which never seems to appear again. *Battersea Power House* also made

Published in September 1985, *Battersea Power House* was a four-page advertorial meant to alleviate local fears.

claims for the number of jobs that would be created: 4,500 at the power station itself and 1,500 in the surrounding area in catering, retail, maintenance and cleaning.

Most of the publication, though, was devoted to promoting the delights within the power station – "The centre is not just about having one million square feet of interior space, it's about fantasy and fun, enjoyment and learning, escapism and reality." Much of this would take place in the old boiler house, now divided into four galleries, each with its own entertainment theme. The ground floor was to be filled with a 160-foot ice-lake for skating with a giant waterfall. The first floor was for kids and proposed entertaining them with a Shadow Room, where children could cast shadows that remained on the wall, and a Gravitron, which was a flying saucer that simulated weightlessness, as well as a haunted theatre and puppet theatre. There was also a Power Play Area, which "uses many of the original power station pieces of equipment to create fun", something that sounds potentially risky.

The second floor was for "young adults", where they could watch glassblowers, wood carvers and leather workers – which makes you wonder if anyone involved with the scheme had ever met a young adult. There was also simulated golf and a host of other games, which the *Battersea Power House* names as Fascination, Skeeball, the Kentucky Derby, Shoot Away and the Water Race but otherwise offers no further information on what these might be. On the third floor were an "oriental restaurant" and an odd variety of shops, including one for music called the Mod Shop and another titled Movie Memorabilia. Finally, the top floor would feature a bonkers mix of a balloon ride, rides based on flight simulators and a disco.

The former coal yards and wharf were to be landscaped into every manner of garden imaginable – sculpture, rose, Japanese, rock, topiary, perennial – with a gazebo, pagoda, lily pond, wishing well and dancing fountain for good measure.

The brochure also contained a huge advert for Alton Towers and the copious illustrations included photographs of existing theme parks, including Alton Towers. In these visualisations, the massive boiler house looks very much like a shopping centre, with shops, restaurants and entertainment spaces spread around the walls, leaving the vast central space open to the roof: the balconies on each floor are in a bizarre neo-colonial style. There are many attractions named on the floorplan but not described, including a Victorian shoppe, Granny's kitchen, "patents for progress exhibit", "tobacco shop and exhibit" and "2010 arcade". In one corner of the ground floor, sandwiched between an art exposition and "water wall" is a tiny "history of Battersea" space.

"Well what do you think?" the editorial asked. "A derelict industrial monument, or a 21st-century power house of fun?"

The promotional material makes plain this is not an attempt to tailor a theme park towards the specific needs and history of its location, but simply a plan to stick Alton Towers inside an old building close to the centre of London. There is no trace of LARC's proposed British Empire theme, let alone Leslie's science and technology concept. This massive disconnect between the reality of the power station and the vision of its contents is made explicit by a front-page illustration that depicts the ice-lake and surrounding terraces but which doesn't include any indication of the walls or roof of the power station. It looks like it is located out in the open. It is also notable how few rides there actually are; it is, as Roche always insisted it should be, effectively a shopping centre, with a handful of rides around the edges. Perhaps this was the only way Battersea Leisure would hit its promised employment targets.

Those targets were already raising eyebrows. The numbers did not seem to add up. Multiply £3.50 by three million [the stated admission price and projected number of admissions] and you have an income of £10.5m. Now multiply 4,500 employees by a base annual salary of £5,000 and you have £22.5m.[3] Expenditure eclipses income by £12m a year and that is before you even consider the cost of refurbishment of the building and subsequent development.

LARC's drawings were reviewed by the architects at Fitzroy Robinson and submitted to Wandsworth at the end of 1985. The council reported back the following February expressing reservations about parking, the nature and number of jobs that would be generated, and the proposed removal of the wharfside

As far as the visuals went, the Broome scheme, designed by Texan firm LARC and the UK's Fitzroy Robinson architectural practice, made no reference to the fact this was a development inside a former power station.

cranes and conveyer belts. Nevertheless, outline permission was granted, despite the presence of local protestors outside the town hall wearing Mickey Mouse ears.

Planning permission was granted on 6th May 1986, two days before the local elections, with listed building consent following on 5th June 1986. "We got planning consent at the last hour before the local elections when there was a fear Wandsworth could go the other way, to Labour," recalls David Cooper, Broome's solicitor and later one of the most successful planning lawyers in the country.[4] "We needed the Section 52 agreement and the execution of British Rail. We had to go to British Rail's office at Euston at the last minute to get their massive seal on the form before it was too late."

Section 52 agreements were the additional obligations demanded by the local council (these were replaced by Section 106 agreements). In this case, as part of the planning permission, Battersea Leisure was required to create a public riverside walk and there were specific stipulations on parking, limitations on the size and type of retail, a crèche had to be created for employees and a community building of some unspecified type would be constructed.

Browne's immediate problem was to tackle the specific problems thrown up by the incongruity of installing a theme park inside a power station, which weren't just limited to noise and movement. "We wanted people to have an adventure but we didn't want to forget our responsibilities," he says. "The building code of the time didn't cope with a building of that nature. One of the problems was energy. According to regulation, we needed to insulate the building but then with the rides and the amount of people inside, it would generate so much heat you'd have to double or treble the amount of air conditioning. It made no sense. Fire was another problem. There were no planning regulations suitable for the size. We also employed a behavioural psychologist. He looked at how people would behave in this environment, where they would go and how they would respond to announcements." Browne was also asked by Broome to look into putting two helipads on the site, for the helicopter Broome had on permanent hire, which he used to get between Alton Towers and Battersea.

To find solutions, Browne was sent across the Atlantic, where big schemes were more commonplace. In Baltimore, the Pratt Street Power Plant was the subject of a development by Six Flags to turn it into a theme park, and this was investigated by Browne (the development subsequently failed). He also looked at hyper-sized shopping centres in Florida and Texas, and at the West Edmonton Mall in Canada, one of the largest in world. "Yes it was vast, it even had a zoo in the middle of it, but it was only on two levels and the power station was five," says Browne. "That made a significant difference. It was flat rather than high. It was a good experience, useful in some ways, but Broome was wrong in thinking we could learn from it."

Realising that Broome might need to be told things he didn't want to hear, Browne suggested he appoint a project manager. One of the firms he suggested was Woolf, with whom he had worked previously on a project constructing office space above Blackfriars station. Broome got in touch and John Gidman and his boss, David Woolf, agreed to meet Broome at his home in Cheshire. "I asked David what we would charge for fees, so we did some sums on a piece of paper," says Gidman. "When we got there, Broome wasn't around, he was out buying this 2,000-acre site next door for the shooting rights."

Woolf and Gidman had agreed they wouldn't take a contract worth less than £1m. "Paddy had talked us through it," says Gidman. "We knew it was quite a hefty demolition job. It required taking out the boilers and the hoppers in the guts of the building and then putting in rides and attractions. Broome sat down and David told him our fees would be a million. Broome said he could only pay £950,000. I said to David, 'Don't do it, let's go.' David said he wouldn't move from £990,000 and Broome said 'It's a deal.' We shook hands and walked out. We worked out we'd be making something like £18,000 a month. We went outside, drove down the gravel driveway, parked in a farmyard and threw our arms around each other. It was a cracking deal."

David Cooper, who was Broome's solicitor at the time, says this was typical of the way his erstwhile client conducted business. "Broome was his own worst enemy," he says. "He was a showman and gave the impression that he thought he could walk on water, and that his charm and charisma could see him through." It is a view echoed by Gerald Jones, chief executive of Wandsworth Council: "He was more like a circus magnate than a developer," he says. "He'd never been immersed in anything like this and seemed out of his depth. Alton Towers was the limit of his achievement."[5]

At this stage Broome's biggest problem was that Battersea Leisure did not own anything. The CEGB had agreed to hand over the power station after decontamination but when this might be was unclear. Fitzroy Robinson met the CEGB to discuss the progress of the asbestos-removal programme and found it was falling further and further behind schedule. Browne feels it simply hadn't been made a high enough priority by the CEGB. Because of this, Battersea Leisure was suffering a serious credibility problem in that Broome could not raise finance for land he still didn't officially own.

In November 1986, Fitzroy Robinson took the bold step of recommending that Battersea Leisure renegotiate the purchase and take on the power station asbestos and all. This was not straightforward: there had been an issue in 1983 about the way private contractors had handled asbestos removal during the development of Fulham Power Station, the upshot of which was that the CEGB had to guarantee in future it would strip power stations of asbestos itself before handing them over. But the CEGB was persuaded and Broome finally took ownership of the power station in March 1987, a month after receiving his CBE.

Decontamination and demolition would be a massive job. Ten firms tendered with Griffiths McGee securing the contract, worth £11.5m. Overall costs had risen dramatically to £135m, according to Wandsworth Council's progress report. Griffiths McGee began work on 30th March 1987. Over the next eighty-five weeks the contractor would remove 4,000 tonnes of asbestos-contaminated material, as well as thousands of tonnes of steel and concrete – "Enough to build three large London office buildings," according to Paddy Browne's briefing documents. Bits of Battersea Power Station were dispersed around Europe: steel was sold to Sweden and Spain to be used in construction, ship and car manufacturing, and for the production of white goods; around 150 tonnes of lead went to Ireland for housing; and 200 tonnes of brass went to Italy to make fittings. Browne even invited art students down to the site to select lumps of concrete and brickwork to use for sculptures.

Also happening at this time was the removal of the power station's west wall. The roof had been taken off the boiler house to allow machinery and steel to be removed, at which time it was discovered that the upper portion of the west wall had suffered extensive sulphur damage. It was decided to take it down, but only after Battersea Leisure gave a guarantee it would be rebuilt within two years. The company was asked to hand over £855,000 in escrow to cover this but did not and the wall was never replaced.

As work went on, further damage was discovered. Power stations deteriorate rapidly after closure as they cool, and this was compounded by leaking drainpipes and poor ventilation. Fitzroy Robinson reported damage to brickwork caused by a combination of chemicals and rainwater in a number of areas. With every discovery, the cost of the project increased

There were other problems. Project manager John Gidman, who was now working from offices inside the power station, found the drawings given to him by LARC were inadequate. "We wanted to get stuck in," says Gidman, "but there were no working drawings. All they were providing was an artist's impression. Lots of sketches, very pretty pictures, but nothing that could be turned into engineering drawings. I told them that might work in the States but not here."

Gidman went to Dallas to talk to LARC. "It was a thirty-six-hour trip," he says. "I got to Dallas and went to their offices. I was expecting to see about forty people and there were four of them. I came back to London and said we had to get some people involved. Broome didn't like it." LARC president Michael Jenkins insists that his company had "approximately sixty" people working on the project, including several in London.[6]

In a bid to bring things under control, Gidman lobbied for the appointment of MET Studio, an office of experiential designers specialised in creating immersive exhibits and interiors for galleries, museums and studios, led by a chap called Alex McCuaig. "We took Alex on," says Gidman. "We stuffed the offices full of designers so we could work on concepts that we could take out to the leisure industry – the people who make these rides – and get some decent material, together with a price tag."

Progress was slow and questions were being asked at Wandsworth Town Hall. Among those doing the asking was councillor Martin Johnson, who had sat on the judging panel for the CEGB competition. He was not impressed by Broome. "Periodically you'd discover he didn't actually have sufficient money to do whatever he was proposing," he says. "It just got crazier and crazier. I'd get phone calls over the weekend. That's not usual. He'd complain that the planning officers were trying to trip him up, wanting him to do this, that or the other, and it would cost him so much. He seemed to think he could circumvent the system."

Paul Beresford, leader of Wandsworth Council at the time, now affects a curiously detached view of the man his office had pinned so much hope on. "Broome would sell you a whole lot of fantastic schemes and ideas," he says.[7] "He would come into my office and we'd all sit there and try to keep our faces straight. He'd bring all these plans and drawings, and some models. You'd listen, wait for the dust to settle and then point out one or two small problems. He'd take that on board, run away and then come back four weeks later with yet another presentation, and we'd sit there and go through it all over again. He was so flamboyant about it. I don't think he appreciated that we had to expend a lot of energy simply trying not to laugh. One time, he took me on his helicopter up to Alton Towers. He stuck us on one of his rollercoasters and we were all strapped in and headed off into this black hole. It was very interesting but it didn't really contribute to anything."

Beresford seems not to have been a fan of the Broome scheme. "Have you been to Alton Towers?" he asks. "Do you really want Alton Towers in the middle of Battersea?" He does, however, betray a certain grudging admiration for the developer's chutzpah. "Only John Broome could have got Maggie there," he says.

According to councillor Martin Johnson, Broome frequently talked of his relationship with Thatcher. "He'd always drop into the conversation that he'd spoken to Maggie the other day. But it didn't get him anywhere. She was as straight as a die. She would never put any pressure on us to do anything. She was just there [at the launch] because she thought it was a good plan."

Broome had planned his scheme in stages and he gave gifts to selected parties as each stage was completed. "The first one was a print of the power station, which I've still got," says Johnson. "Mrs Thatcher would always get number one of whatever was being offered and I was always number ten."

For Thatcher's visit, John Gidman filled the offices with drawing boards and as many people as he could find. "Broome was all puffed up, the press were there and Maggie was shown around the offices to meet the people, half of whom had nothing to do with the project.

Then they let off these fireworks and Maggie's security people went mad." Fire engines were despatched. "I wouldn't have been surprised if he called the fire brigade himself," says Beresford. The day ended on Richard Branson's paddle steamer, going up and down the Thames with Broome holding court, informing Gidman that when The Battersea opened in two years' time he would have the royal family turning up en masse. (The development's name, incidentally, could have been a lot worse – also considered were Alton Towers II, Tower Inferno and South Chelsea Fun Palace.)[8]

The official launch was accompanied by a lavish book. "Only private enterprise could raise the money to take on a challenge like this, to restore [the power station] and give it a rebirth," Broome declaimed. The publication claimed that The Battersea would contain over 200 games, rides, shows, exhibits and attractions for the anticipated 33,831 visitors on an average peak day. Approximately fifty-two percent of available space would be given over to entertainment, with thirty-two percent of that on rides. Food and retail would take up another thirty-two percent. It would be open until 2am, 364 days a year. There would be car parking for 2,243 cars and seventy-eight coaches, and trains would arrive from Victoria every eight minutes on the company's own windowless "Battersea Bullet" trains, the first high-speed main-line electric train to be designed and ordered by any private company in the world. "You'd be processed at Victoria then get on this train, watching all these video screens that would tell you about the experience you were about to have, and then it would pull in after a mile and you'd reach the welcome area and get processed," says Gidman. "That was one idea. He was full of big ideas, I can't fault that."

Inside, the ice-skating lake was still there, as was the waterfall and a hot-air balloon ride to take visitors up to the roof and down again. But now the five galleries were to be themed on the continents:

Asia would include a Chinese Emporium, Poor Man's Market and Chinese restaurants, shops where you could purchase ivory from India, or watch Oriental jugglers, Indian magicians, Thai dancers and Chinese calligraphists; the African gallery would have Egyptian dancers, and the warriors and wildlife of the African bush; Europe encompassed an English village green – still with the glassblowers – and stalls at which visitors could buy French cheese, Dutch clogs, Italian pasta and castanets from Spain; the space devoted to America would have Canadian lumberjacks, Mississippi river boats and Mexican fiestas. Even at the time, this must have felt crass.

There were still plenty of rides, now including the Jumbo Jet Coaster, a super-speed rollercoaster incorporating special lighting, laser, music and fog effects, and the Runaway Train, a mine-train themed rollercoaster featuring dips, turns, hills, chasms, caves, waterfalls and tunnels.

An artist's impression of the Battersea Bullet, which was the high-speed train intended to shuttle visitors from mainline Victoria station to Broome's grand attraction. Why a high-speed service was needed for a journey of less than a mile was not explained.

On the ground, progress was minimal. Robert McAlpine was engaged as management contractor and piling had commenced in November 1988 but by the following March it had stopped as Broome sought refinancing. Costs had continued to escalate and Broome's complex funding seemed to echo the theming of his galleries, involving as it did multiple banks from around the world.

Project architect Paddy Browne first got wind that something might be wrong when artist Michael Warren approached him to say he hadn't been paid. Warren was the project's official artist and he had already completed more than one hundred oils and watercolours, one of which, entitled "Regeneration of the City" had been presented to Margaret Thatcher. Browne got the payment cleared but Warren's contract was abruptly terminated. "With hindsight, that was the first indication there were financial difficulties," says Browne. "Looking back I can see it was the beginning of the end."

Considerably more was owed to the main subcontractor, McAlpine, and there was also the matter of the unpaid bond to the council for the reconstruction of the west wall. In May 1989, Wandsworth noted that Battersea Leisure was reviewing costs and attempting to rearrange financing. Broome was now estimating his funding requirements to be in the region of £280m, but Alex McCuaig had taken a look at the numbers and come to the conclusion that there would be no change out of £400m. "LARC had been basing their figures on a theme park in an open space but at Battersea you have to bring stuff into the heart of London to a site that wasn't even that easy to get to. Then you had to restore the building and put on a new roof. It makes it five, six, seven times more expensive than a usual theme park." McCuaig presented this to John Gidman, who as project manager had the unenviable task of feeding it back to John Broome.[9]

When Broome received the news he wasn't happy. "Broome was

very much 'I'm the boss,' and what he said went. You had to be very sure of your ground if you questioned him, when giving costs and information," says Gidman. "But people like us weren't paid to say, 'Yes Mr Broome, no Mr Broome'. You've got to stick your head above the parapet, which he didn't like. Once he was hit with the real costs it all fell like a pack of cards."

"If he'd been given an accurate quote before he started and known what to expect then he might have been able to fund it properly," says McCuaig. Gidman is less sympathetic: "He was trying to bluster financial institutions and it was never going to work. But he seemed to think he was the king of the castle because he had the most successful amusement park in the country."

Broome's response was to fire Woolf and bring in new project managers, American firm Lehrer McGovern. "They walked around the site in their brand-new wellington boots and hard hats saying, 'We've got to get a handle on it,'" says Gidman, who remained on site for the handover.

MET Studio continued to work on designs as Broome chased new financing to cover costs that it seemed the project would never recoup. "It was a strange project because we were thinking that no matter what we designed, it would never happen," says McCuaig.

At one point, Warner Bros were said to be interested, so MET was asked to come up with rides based on characters from the studio's movies. This interest came via Michael Jenkins of LARC, who also introduced Broome to American mall developer Mel Simon of Simon Properties (Simon was also the producer of 1982 bawdy teen comedy *Porky's*). "Warner Bros was going to put in forty-five percent, Mel Simon was going to put in forty-five percent, and John Broome would be the figurehead and would have ten percent. LARC would complete the design and set up the management. Mel Simon and I went back to John Broome with the proposal that would have saved the project but John Broome rejected it because he wanted fifty-one percent."[10]

LARC would soon leave the project. With work having ground to a halt in February 1989, Broome began to blame the power station itself for the delays. He claimed that it had insufficient foundations, a remarkable allegation for a building that had stood without structural problems for more than fifty years.

"Of course there are foundations," says John Gidman. "There's no way you could hold up six million bricks without foundations." Paddy Browne says much the same: "The foundations were fine. There were some inadequacies given the proposed use but they were fine foundations." This is backed up by architects who worked on the site after Broome had departed.

Outwardly, Broome remained bullish: "We have a laid-back, mature, effective management team here that hits it right first time, strikes the button, makes no major mistakes and gets on with the job," he proclaimed in 1989, even as things began to unravel spectacularly.[11] In 1990 Britain entered a two-year period of recession, which would drastically affect property prices and make additional finance even harder to find. Broome went back to the drawing board. Paddy Browne and Fitzroy Robinson were kicked overboard as Broome turned to a new firm of architects, Renton Howard Wood Levine, to come up with an alternative scheme, briefly in partnership with developer Paul Bloomfield, known as "Boom Boom Bloomfield" following his involvement in schemes like Paternoster Square. With Battersea Leisure now renamed The Alton Group, planning permission was sought to turn the land around the power station – some of which Broome didn't actually own – into two million square feet of offices, plus 65,000 square feet of retail, a hotel, conference and exhibition centre, community facilities and car parking. The power station itself was to remain leisure based.

Coincidentally, at precisely the same time an alternative planning application was launched by another firm, the Business Design Centre, to turn the power station into a business centre. The scheme's architect was Maxwell Hutchinson, then president of RIBA, but it failed to meet Wandsworth's requirements.

Meanwhile, 21st May 1990 – announced by Broome two years previously as the date on which The Battersea would be open for business – came and went. On the day, the only people present outside the power station were members of the Battersea Power Station Community Group, a pressure group founded by local residents in October 1983. Vehemently critical of Broome and his scheme, the protestors held a spoof opening, mocking the developer and his equally reviled patron, Margaret Thatcher.

The last throw of the dice came that June, when a desperate Broome sold Alton Towers to Madam Tussauds for £60m to finance the new scheme. Paul Bloomfield had disappeared as rapidly as he had arrived, after disagreeing with Broome about the use of the power station: Bloomfield wanted to turn it into a conference centre, Broome wanted to retain it for leisure. Wandsworth – still waiting for Broome to pay the bond for the removal of the west wall – was not much impressed and its report of July 1990 was hugely critical of Broome's exploits thus far, insisting he "should be made to pay for damage done to the building and agreements broken". The council's planners slashed the floor space of his newly proposed office complex, blocked the exhibition centre and criticised the general over-development – the hotel, at twenty-two storeys, was clearly a non-starter given the location next to the power station – even if they accepted the new general concept.

Even Broome was now running out of gas. For this latest scheme to work, he needed to purchase the adjacent Battersea Wharf and he spent much of the next few years trying to raise finance

Issued in the wake of Margaret Thatcher's visit to launch the new development, *The Battersea* newsletter commits in print to not just an opening date but an opening time: 2.30pm on 21st May 1990.

in a miserable market. His search took him to Hong Kong and to Parkview International, a property development firm owned by the Hwang family. The Hwangs were not interested in Broome's scheme, but in 1993 agreed to purchase his debt of around £50m from the Bank of America for around £9.5m (this debt would get closer £70m when you included the money owed to McAlpine). And with that, John Broome was out of the picture.

Broome did not want to speak to me for this book, despite being initially keen. When I first contacted him with a request for an interview he seemed amenable and asked if I would forward a list of the specifics I would like to discuss. "I know I would be able to furnish you with highly interesting info if and when we meet," he wrote to me in July 2014. The list was duly submitted. That was as far as the conversation went.

Over the following eighteen months I attempted to contact Broome on numerous further occasions, directly, but also through his son Will and his PR John Williams of Mason Williams. Williams was optimistic Broome could be persuaded to at least talk on the phone but it never happened. After weeks of prevaricating, Williams sent an email explaining, "Unfortunately John does not have the time for an interview. He understands your desire to complete this section of the history of Battersea but it is a long time ago and he is completely involved in several new ventures in the UK and overseas. So looking forward rather than looking back."[12]

In the absence of an interview, Williams pointed me back to an article written by John Broome's son Will, posted in April 2014 on the website of the London-based events company he runs. In it, Broome Jr lauds his father's vision for Battersea and responds to some of the negative criticism it met with at the time and since. "Back in the 1980s things were cool," he writes. "Back then you could dream. And not only could you dream but you could also do things, which today would be ridiculed as 'not financially viable'." What his dad dreamt up, says Will, was something like "Disney, Westfield, ExCeL and Soho all rolled into one"… "Literally, better than Vegas." Why this "awesome idea" never came to be, he says, was down to the recession that hit in the late 1980s, during which the bottom fell out of the property market and the banks refused to lend money; less convincingly, he also recycles the story of the dodgy foundations.[13]

Will's evangelising of the Broome masterplan only serves to underline just how tacky and inappropriate the whole thing was but he does stake a good claim for the unacknowledged credit owed for the immense amount of restoration carried out on the power station. During his period of ownership, John Broome oversaw what was claimed to be the biggest asbestos-removal programme of all time, as well as the securing of the entire site, the underpinning of a million-square-foot building and the shoring up of the listed facade. Steve Kennard, one of the architects who would work on the building under its next owners, is in agreement on the value of the work: "It's massive what he did – take down one wall and the roof, and empty it of all the machinery. It was all good stuff if you were going to complete the scheme."

It is a shame that John Broome does not want to speak about his ten-year affair with the power station. He obviously believed in the project with a passion, although ultimately it was a passion that, according to his son Will, ended up costing him about £500m, his ownership of Alton Towers, a 200-acre country estate, a yacht, a helicopter, and several million pounds worth of art and antiques. Nobody likes to dwell on their failures but as John Williams pointed out in his email to me, Broome is hardly the only one that has gone bust over Battersea.

Perhaps everything might have been different if, as Alex McCuaig suggested, the project had been costed correctly in the first place but, even then, it seems highly unlikely finance would have been forthcoming because the figures just never added up. The revenue received over the turnstiles was never going to cover the expense of refurbishing, fitting out and running a theme park inside a listed power station. As Edward Lister, a later leader of Wandsworth Council, put it, "Broome's idea was totally unworkable but at the time it wasn't totally stupid when you couldn't think of anything else and there was no demand for housing. Because who wanted to live next to an old power station?"[14]

What is remarkable is that the business-savvy Tories at Wandsworth would put so much faith in Broome publicly, when privately they viewed him with scepticism. "He was such an emotional guy," says councillor Martin Johnson. "I remember him pleading with me about the hurdles he felt were being put in his way, 'I've known you know for six months Martin, please help me!' He was never going to be the character to develop this. He didn't have the money and he didn't have the professionalism. Was I convinced by him? Absolutely not. Successful developers don't behave like that. I assumed that if he bought it and couldn't do it, he'd sell it on quickly. I never imagined he'd become so emotionally involved."

Like many who would follow in his footsteps, Broome was seduced by the potential of the power station but incapable of realising his dreams for it. There is an irony to this, the brash, flamboyant Thatcherite brought down by a combination of his own ambition and a relic of the nationalised past. Beaten, Broome turned his attention to Carden Park in Cheshire, which he wanted to turn into a luxury hotel and golf course, offering shooting, fishing and horse-riding for corporate clients. He sold his home to try to meet the costs, but in October 1994 that project went into receivership, and Broome disappeared. Although he continued to work in property, he only returned to the public eye in September 2015 with the announcement of a plan to turn a Cornish theme park into a six-star resort, with rollercoasters, spa, accommodation and the largest tropical lake in Britain. This new scheme will purportedly provide 950 jobs and will be unlike anything Britain has ever seen before. This time, however, no precise opening date has been promised.

FUSED MAGAZINE

CHINA POWER STATION ISSUE
ART, ARCHITECTURE, MUSIC,
SOUND ART, DESIGN, LIFESTYLE
WWW.FUSEDMAGAZINE.COM
WWW.FUSEDMAGAZINE.COM/STORE

CHINA POWER STATION PART 1

CHAPTER NINE

THE PARKVIEW YEARS

Thirteen years of grand plans and bathos at the hands of Hong Kong developer Victor Hwang

CAST
Ron Arad Israeli industrial designer and architect
Cecil Balmond Designer and architect at Arup, who provided Parkview with its ultimate Battersea masterplan
CS Hwang Founder and patriarch of Hong Kong-based property development company Parkview
Victor Hwang One of five siblings involved in the family business but very much the driving force behind the development at Battersea
Gerald Jones Chief executive of Wandsworth Council
Steve Kennard In-house architect for Parkview
Edward Lister The leader of Wandsworth Council from 1992 to 2011; later deputy mayor at the Greater London Authority
Michael Roberts Former investment banker turned chief executive of Parkview
Neven Sidor Senior architect at Grimshaw Architects, one of several firms employed by Parkview during its ownership of the power station

THE PARKVIEW YEARS

THE PARKVIEW YEARS are summed up in a lavishly bound, oversized red book entitled *The Power Station Journal*. It was a custom-published parting gift from developer Victor Hwang to those who had worked on the Battersea Power Station project during the company's thirteen-year stewardship from 1993 to 2006. The book's pages are a celebration of imagination and vision, featuring a whole bunch of what-might-have-been images and illustrations. But the most telling item is found in a sealed envelope glued to the final page. Inside is a letter, dated December 2006. It is addressed "Dear comrades" and ends simply "Victor". In between Hwang writes, "We have fought many battles together. Along the way, we have seen many casualties (architects). We have fought these battles bravely and courageously, but the most heart-wrenching for me was to discover traitors from within."

Despite the fighting talk the letter offers a tacit acknowledgement that the war has been lost. Hwang is wistful: "And it seems right to also stop and ask oneself," he writes, "have we achieved anything?"

It is a question worth asking. Of all the missed opportunities in the recent history of Battersea Power Station, few stand out as painfully as the Parkview years. These were long, slow years of massive potential, horribly squandered. This was the time when something really could have happened, perhaps not a perfect something but all the same, an outcome that was preferable to what was to follow. This was a time of crazy ideas, when the paths of characters as varied as Samantha Fox, Michael Jackson and Noddy all briefly intersected with the power station.

That nothing happened – literally, nothing, not even a spade dug into the ground – was down partly to bad luck and poor timing, but mostly to the frantic inertia that afflicted Hwang. He splurged a small fortune on an ever-changing

PREVIOUS SPREAD
Souvenir issue of *Fused Magazine* accompanying the temporary use of three floors of the power station as a cavernous gallery for contemporary Chinese video and installation art.

carousel of architects and designers, who between them produced a bewildering array of schemes and plans that he briefly embraced before tossing away in favour of the next new big idea. His approach to architects seems to have been inspired by the Queen of Hearts ("Off with his head!") but those who worked with him insist that in Hwang the power station – the "beast", he affectionately calls it – had a champion, somebody who was sensitive to the building and its importance to London and Londoners. When he went, with him went London's best chance for a truly exciting rebirth of Battersea Power Station.

Victor Hwang was born in 1954 in Taiwan, the second of five siblings; like many Chinese, they would all adopt Western names, so along with Victor were George, Tony, Richard and Sally. Their father, Chou-Shiuan, owned a Hong Kong-based property development company called Chyau Fwu. In the 1980s, the firm's big project was Hong Kong Parkview, a huge high-end residential scheme of eighteen blocks. When that ran into financing problems, Hwang turned to Michael Roberts, a British investment banker who had worked in Hong Kong since the 1970s, having fled London's dismal weather and restrictive working practices. After the project was completed, Chyau Fwu was renamed Parkview International. Roberts would become the Hwangs' right-hand man on the Battersea Power Station project; he would also be one of those Victor Hwang would label a "traitor".

Victor was the family member most involved in Battersea. He moved to Britain when he was thirteen, attending Lindisfarne College, a private school in Wrexham that has since closed and, inevitably, been converted into luxury housing. "CS Hwang's sister was asked to come to England to select a school for the boys with the stipulation it had to be 200 miles from London's Chinatown, because if it was any closer they might have got up to mischief," says

Roberts, who has known the family for over thirty years. "That's why they ended up in North Wales."[1] Even so, Victor was not completely isolated from the fast life: he attended the Isle of Wight Festival in 1970 and spent time in London, where he first took notice of the giant power station beside the river in Battersea.

After school, he attended university in San Diego, then returned home expecting to breeze into an executive position at his father's firm. CS Hwang had other plans. "My father was a tough guy," says the publicity-shy Hwang, when we chat over Skype.[2] "He said, 'If you want to work for me, you work to my rules. Go and report to the site.' I asked him if there would be a position for me when I finished and he said only when people respected me. So I went from the bottom up. I worked on the construction site for two years. I majored in finance but I can go on site and tell if a bricklayer is doing something wrong."

By 1992, Victor and his brother George were heavily involved in the family business, although CS still called the shots. "The old man was a very sound guy but he didn't speak any English," says Roberts, "so meetings usually involved three of the four brothers, whoever was in Hong Kong at the time. George and Victor were nearly always there, Tony and Richard were younger and less prominent. But they did everything together, it was like a rolling board meeting and they were popping ideas out like a Catherine wheel." The one guiding factor was that everything they built had to be the best quality. In his parting letter, Victor would quote his father: "In everything you do, make a difference."

As his theme-park scheme threatened to collapse, John Broome flew into Hong Kong looking for cash. He spoke to CS Hwang. "Everybody in the UK comes out to Hong Kong when they want money for property," says Roberts. "Broome came and we talked to him but we didn't like his project. Funding for a gated attraction means the financier has to believe you'll get enough people through the doors to make the economics work. He couldn't raise money from anybody."

But CS Hwang could see potential. He'd made his fortune working "off centre" – that is developing cheaper land outside city centres. "Our family never had enough money to build in the centre," says Victor Hwang. "We always had to go off centre, and if you are building off centre you have to create something that has amazing architecture. That's what we always wanted, to build something special."

In Battersea, the Hwangs were presented with the rare opportunity to purchase several acres of land just outside central London with a landmark already in situ. "The land existed because of the power station," says Roberts. "But that's not what appealed: it was the land around it." In spring 1993, CS flew into London with Victor. "We landed at about 5am, drove round the site and decided to acquire the property," says Victor. "The decision was made and we closed the transaction within forty-eight hours."

Roberts, who was now working in London, got a phone call at 7am. "They said they wanted to buy. Today. And they bought it just like that. I think we paid the banks £9.5m, which sounds incredibly cheap, but you don't pick up something like that, a derelict power station, without inheriting problems. You are buying a licence to spend money."

Victor moved to London as the family representative and the company got to work. Wandsworth's chief executive Gerald Jones was worried from the off that Parkview had taken on a bigger challenge than it could handle. "When Broome left, all the problems were still there: the chimneys, the transport, the state of the infrastructure itself," he says. "Poor old Hwang bought it for £10m plus debts. I was worried when I heard he had a £50m mortgage from RBS and

THE PARKVIEW YEARS

Among the many uses Battersea was put to during the Parkview years was as a giant billboard, notably when in December 1994 advertising agency TBWA projected model Eva Herzigova in a Wonderbra onto the river-facing facade. © TopFoto

Michael Roberts said they'd already added another £10m. I could see they would be building up a pyramid of debt."

For the first eighteen months, Parkview tried to work out what it actually owned and then added to it by buying up adjacent plots of land. "Broome hadn't tidied everything up," explains Roberts. Hwang expanded the site from the fifteen acres acquired from Broome to around thirty-six acres through several different purchases. None of this was straightforward. As late as January 1996, three years after striking a deal, Parkview was still in court negotiating with Broome, while also duelling with McAlpine over the huge debt he'd passed on to them. The Hong Kong company finally took on the freehold later that year. The Hwangs also struggled to get their heads round the

HELLO BOYS!

City way of doing business. Hwang believes he was held to ransom by the National Grid, Thames Water and London Electricity, which, he claims, forced extraordinary concessions from Parkview in return for not blocking its plans. One dispute was only settled when a Parkview lawyer bumped into the chairman of the National Grid at a meeting of London beekeepers. As Sir Philip Dowson of engineering company Arup would later tell Hwang, to succeed in development in the UK, "you have to be part of the conspiracy".

And what of the power station in all this? While development was on hold, the company looked at exploiting other uses for its sizeable asset. In December 1994 traffic was stopped on the Chelsea Embankment across the river when Eva Herzigova's cleavage was projected onto the building's facade as part of Wonderbra's "Hello Boys!" advertising campaign. The headline-grabbing initiative also advertised the power station as a venue for hire. Battersea became available for filming, events and concerts at a price of around £1,500 a day. Some of those taking up the offer included Tori Amos, Texas and Hanson, all of whom shot music videos at the power station around this time.

For some, this was the demeaning abuse of a majestic industrial building, but at least it kept the power station in the public eye. Not that the newspapers were short of good Battersea stories. New investors were regularly reported to be taking an interest, although some of these were so unlikely it is hard to believe they were ever serious. On 12th January 1996, the *Catholic Herald* reported that the Holy Trinity Church at Brompton was considering turning the power station into a "religious theme park", tenuously noting that "the expanding population of the church includes former topless model Samantha Fox". At the other end of the scale and just a few weeks later, the *Mail on Sunday* reported on 28th January 1996 that Noddy and Big Ears were being touted as possible residents, with the Trocadero company of Leicester Square rumoured to be in talks to develop a Noddyland theme park inside the power station. Then in June 1997, *The Sunday Times* revealed that Michael Jackson had toured Battersea with a view to creating a "self-contained fantasy centre", in a joint venture with a Saudi prince. Nothing and nobody, it seemed, was too outlandish for Battersea.

Victor Hwang had plans of his own. These were being developed for him by the distinguished engineering and design firm of Ove Arup & Partners. Their scheme was for a development of 4.5 million square feet that included two hotels, two theatres, an exhibition pavilion, retail, offices and some housing. The power station itself was to become a gigantic cinema. "Essentially the thinking was this," says Roberts. "We had an iconic structure that would cost a substantial premium to stabilise and make publicly accessible. It had to be publicly accessible because if you have an iconic building you have to let people into it. So what can it be? It's not going to be a church or railway station, so you are down to museums, exhibition spaces and retail. The other options were a hotel and offices but there are statutory requirements for natural light." (The power station has almost no windows.) "So," continues Roberts, "you can only use it for things like cinemas and bowling alleys, where the light is controlled. In the end, it boiled down to a cinema, food, drink, and retail. It almost self-selected."

The principal attraction would be a thirty-two-screen, 8,000-seat cinema run by Warner Bros, the absurdly named "Power Plex", featuring stadium seating and digital sound in a variety of auditoriums ranging from 150 to 600 seats. Parkview had been shopping around for other potential partners and was able to announce as co-investors Andrew Lloyd Webber's Really Useful Company, British airports operator BAA and US-based property developers the Gordon Group. The Really Useful Group would create a theatre inside the boiler room, which would become a giant shopping/entertainment complex with a Roman hill-town theme. The whole thing would be roofed by an artificial sky much like the one at the Gordon Group's Caesar's Palace in Las Vegas. Most thrillingly, there would be rides up the chimneys, one would offer a leisurely climb, while another would go up like a rocket.

The Arup masterplan received outline planning permission from Wandsworth Council in May 1997. The Hwang family travelled from Hong Kong to celebrate. The following month, Warner Bros celebrated its own £35m stake in the project with a launch party at the power station for summer-blockbuster-that-wasn't *Batman & Robin*, attended by stars George Clooney, Arnold Schwarzenegger and Uma Thurman. Battersea was converted into Gotham City for the night, complete with a "Wayne Manor". To mark the event a time capsule containing artefacts from the film and personal contributions from some of the VIPs present was sunk into the foundations, to be opened in 2097.

Members of the Battersea Power Station Community Group were also there, wielding prescient placards that read, "Power Station – Another Disaster Movie". The BPSCG had been on Parkview's case from the start, occupying its Mayfair office and publically accusing the company of less than transparent practices. A couple of scandals would eventually emerge: the first involving the jailing of a Barclays banker for not declaring a £25,000 "thank you" payment from Victor Hwang made shortly after the bank had granted him a £6.4m loan, and the second involving charges of insider trading that resulted in a fine of £160,000 for CS Hwang.[3]

To get to this point Hwang had already flirted with two international firms of architects – John Portman & Associates and RHWL Architects – and now he would dally with a third. John Outram Associates (JOA), best known for the design of a temple-

The scheme devised by John Outram Associates included a huge, 700-room hotel within the power station, surrounded by a fluid network of streets and squares. To see the scheme in its full blaze of psychedelic colour, visit the architect's website. © JOA

like Pumping Station on the Isle of Dogs, was one of six practices that in April 1997 was invited to submit designs for a 350-bed hotel. At the same time, JOA was asked to provide an alternative masterplan to the one recently drawn up by Arup – it seems Victor was having second thoughts even as the Arup plan received planning consent. In six weeks JOA produced an intriguing, fluid-looking scheme that met with approval from Hwang and his advisors. But when told that Parkview's consultant partners would have the freedom to alter these design "in gross and in detail", JOA walked. "Parkview wants Battersea to be like Las Vegas – I want it to be something else," said Outram. "Las Vegas is just a hack reconstruction of anywhere else in the world. I don't want Battersea to be like that."[4]

Architectural direction of the masterplan now went to London-based MacCormac Jamieson Prichard, which was instructed to act alongside US leisure specialists Wimberly Allison Tong & Goo on the hotels, and Canadians Sceno Plus on the two theatres. By 1999, two of these firms had been discarded (Sceno survived until 2006) bringing to a total five architectural practices dumped by Parkview over six years. Victor Hwang was getting a reputation for consuming architects the way others have meals.

Frustrated by his inability to unearth the perfect scheme and to crack the UK system of business, Victor assembled a board of consultants capable of making introductions at the highest levels. This was made up of the "three sirs": Arup's Sir Philip Dowson, Sir Frank Lampl, chairman of construction group Bovis and Sir Jack Zunz, ex co-chairman of Arup. Around the same time, the highly respected Nicholas Grimshaw, architect of the Eurostar terminal at Waterloo, was brought in. It was a top team and the financial climate was right. Now, surely, things would start to move.

Not a chance.

Parkview's Michael Roberts insists there was plenty going on that was not necessarily visible to the querulous campaigners and public at large. "A huge amount of time was spent on transport," he says. "Whatever you build, the first objection is always traffic. So we spent years working on the transport. It's balls-aching, because you are dealing with people who do not have the same time pressures or the same interests."

For somewhere so central, Battersea Power Station is a strangely isolated site. It is served by one railway station and one road, with the river acting as a barrier to the north and a ring of semi-industrial sites to the south. This situation would change dramatically in 2008 – two years after Parkview had sold up – when it was announced the American Embassy would be moving into the neighbourhood, prompting massive investment in local infrastructure. The situation Roberts and Hwang had to deal with was very different. To reach their visitor targets, they had to get massive numbers of people onto the site. One solution was to build a footbridge across the Thames as a more pedestrian friendly alternative to Chelsea Bridge. There were schemes, which, typically, were on the zany side of practical: one idea was a "living bridge" with shops and restaurants; another was an S-shaped bridge. None ever went to planning.

While provision was made for some car parking, it was envisaged that most people would arrive by rail from Victoria, as Broome had planned. This soon fell apart. "Railtrack were always adamant it would be easy to put in a link to Victoria with a shuttle train," says Edward Lister, leader of Wandsworth Council at the time. "I think to an extent everybody was slightly led down the garden path by that. It was only when some detailed work took place that it became clear there wasn't space. There was a choke point on the line into Victoria and there were no spare platforms. It was a dead duck."[5]

"That was a bombshell," says Gerald Jones, Wandsworth's then-chief executive. "Nobody had asked the right questions but Hwang and Roberts were pretty thorough and looked into it. So they had to look at inferior options, such as increasing capacity at Battersea Park and Queenstown Road stations." After spending a fortune on feasibility studies Parkview opted to redevelop Battersea Park station. Network Rail, who had taken over from Railtrack, insisted that Parkview pay for the refurbishment, and also pay Network Rail £30m for the pleasure. At least it was a solution. Battersea Park was one stop to Victoria, one stop to Clapham Junction. "We could service the site with that but had to get visitors from the train station," says Roberts. "We looked at an overhead walkway, across the dog home to the plaza at the front of the power station. We spent a lot of time working on this and then got a letter from somebody in somewhere like Warrington complaining that the walkway was too close to gas holders. We had to take these objections seriously and were always aware of bad publicity as it attracted huge attention." Roberts says that when negotiating their first planning permission, they had to deal with more than 300 interest groups including the ever-watchful Battersea Power Station Community Group.

There was also English Heritage, about whom Hwang is particularly scathing. "The scale of this thing was completely out of their understanding," he says. "They were used to putting up plaques for dead people. I told them they could do as much preservation as they wanted, but if you can't make the power station into a goose that lays a golden egg, it's only a question of time before it comes down. What we wanted was something for tomorrow and all they cared about was something for yesterday."

Other hold-ups were almost farcical. In 2001, a pair of peregrine falcons was discovered nesting in the north-west chimney, where restoration work was taking place. As these were at the time the only breeding pair in London, work was halted while a special 150-foot tower was built for the birds – one that they, naturally, showed little interest in inhabiting. Then the chimneys themselves became a concern. Parkview were adamant they needed to be replaced and commissioned experts who agreed; the BPSCG engaged its own experts who said the opposite. As far as the community group was concerned, removal of the chimneys would pave the way for getting the power station delisted and then bulldozed. It argued they could be renovated rather than restored and lobbied Wandsworth to ensure Parkview dealt with them one by one, not take them all down at the same time, leaving the building chimney-less and vulnerable.

Hwang saw this as an opportunity for a bit of grand theatre. "Victor decided to make it a spectacular event," says Michael Roberts. "The idea was to pre-cast the new chimneys on the ground, which makes more sense than building them in situ. You'd saw the old one off, get a bloody great crane to hold it and then almost the next day lift the next one in place. As a bit of engineering it was fascinating. We got a price for it, which was something like £12m." As with many of the other problems related to the deterioration of the building's structure, Parkview never got round to restoring or replacing the chimneys. That's partly because once they began there was no going back, and the overall cost of restoring the fabric of the power station now stood at around £70m.

The other headache for Roberts was basic logistics. "You had to get power and water to the site, you had to take sewage away, and you needed gas and telecoms," he says. "That's a lot of infrastructure. We looked into various ways of making it all energy efficient and decided to build a combined power and water recycling plant that would fit neatly in the old coal bunker on the docks. We even got a wonderful dowser, George Applegate, to dowse a couple of boreholes so we could have our own water."

In a bid to show Wandsworth what was possible, Parkview offered to take some senior figures from the council on a tour of landmark developments around the world. "We were very uncomfortable about the hospitality but ground our poor bastards down so they stayed in the cheapest hotels," says council chief exec Gerald Jones. "They were on very limited expenses and kept receipts for everything, and we read the riot act to them before they went out."

Parkview's in-house architect Steve Kennard believes the trip had value. "Wherever you look around the world, there are much bigger projects going on than we have in London, and this gave them a reference point of scale and ambition," he says. "We went to Hong Kong, which is 25 years ahead of London. We went to LA, Las Vegas, Minneapolis and Edmonton. We saw that everything had been done before, and when we returned they knew that any problem in Battersea had been solved elsewhere."[6]

Every problem, that is, but Victor himself.

Parkview received detailed planning consent in August 2000. At this point, the job of conceptualising the project had fallen to Simon Beames, a senior associate with Grimshaw Architects, who had formerly worked for Norman Foster. He had feverishly worked up plans for an entertainment centre, which would include a permanent base in the boiler house for the Cirque du Soleil. This had come about through a relationship Hwang had developed with the Canadian circus group after seeing their shows in Las Vegas. In collaboration with Cirque du Soleil founder Guy Laliberté, Hwang hatched a plan to create a permanent theatre for the troupe in London, so they could stage more elaborate shows than was possible when they moved from site to site. To celebrate the arrangement,

A hotel by Arup with external landscaped staircase curves up towards the power station remodelled by Grimshaw Architects to accommodate a cinema multiplex and a permanent home for Cirque du Soleil. © Grimshaw Architects

Cirque du Soleil raised a big-top tent beside the power station in December 2000 where it presented a three-week run of its latest show, *Quidam*.

Another intriguing – or ludicrous, depending on your perspective – idea involved creating a thrill ride in one of the chimneys, with a capsule that would shoot up, pop out the top and then plummet back down. One of the other chimneys would be a "one-table restaurant": diners would take their seats at the table at ground level, then the platform on which table and chairs were set would rise up the chimney to emerge at the top into a weather-dome (it would have been quite literally London's first "pop-up" restaurant). A stair would connect with a lower level, where there would be a kitchen and waiters to serve the meal. Each of the four daily slots – breakfast, lunch, afternoon tea and dinner – would be auctioned off for what would be marketed as the city's most exclusive restaurant.

Beames also proposed installing a boating lake on the roof but, true to form, Hwang lost interest. "Victor just wasn't satisfied with the level of design," says Roberts. Beames – who would go on to do concept design for the conservation of the *Cutty Sark* in Greenwich – was replaced by his colleague Neven Sidor. "It was difficult for Simon," says Sidor.[7] "He worked on [Battersea] for ages and was then told another team at Grimshaw was going to rip up everything he'd done." But for Hwang, there was always a new idea around the corner. He had the resources to indulge himself and he did.

If John Broome's schemes had been about delivering cheap thrills and jobs during the miserable mid-1980s, by the time of the millennium London had entered into a revitalised era of *grands projets*, notably the Millennium Dome, Millennium Bridge, the Great Court at the British Museum and Tate Modern. Even that long-neglected masterpiece by Giles Gilbert Scott's grandfather, the high gothic Midland Hotel, was finally getting a makeover as St Pancras was made the new terminus for the high-speed Eurostar rail link to Paris, Brussels and beyond. London was suddenly the coolest city in Europe and its economy was booming. In this climate, Battersea's proposed transformation into an ambitious, imaginative and inclusive leisure, shopping and cultural centre on the banks of the Thames chimed perfectly with the times.

So while Wandsworth Council was exasperated by the lack of tangible progress, there was still hope that Parkview would deliver. "Victor was very engaging and enthusiastic, and deeply committed. Plus he had the resources – planning applications and top end architects don't come cheap," says Ravi Govindia, then a Wandsworth councillor, later council leader. "There was a constant

The final scheme produced by Grimshaw in its seven-year relationship with Parkview is the one architect Neven Sidor is most proud of. The boiler house has clear views up to all four iconic chimneys. Escalators carry visitors up to the roof level where there are external "grazing plateaus". © Grimshaw Architects

stream of things he wanted to change or finesse. There were time limits on planning permission but it was difficult to turn him down because he always had a very good rationale." Evidence of the close working relationship between Hwang and the council came when Ian Thompson, Wandsworth's planner, took a consultancy role at

Parkview shortly after leaving his position at the council.

The constant churn was not without ramifications. Each new architect brought new ideas that invariably had implications for the rest of the site, causing the overall masterplan to be redrawn. It also meant the loss of potential partners as one by one Warner Bros, Lloyd Webber's Really Useful Group and Cirque du Soleil (after doing a second winter season at the power station) all pulled out when agreements couldn't be reached. Still Hwang remained unsatisfied.

"Victor was always driving towards getting a set of designs that were like the Taj Mahal," says Roberts. "As an ambition, it's to be applauded but it's impossible to achieve. In property development, you have to draw a line and be aware that when you complete a project in three or four years it will already be out of date. You can't ever be the latest thing but if you are quality then people will come to you for years. But if you can't freeze it, it can't be built."

In 2002, Hwang found his newest latest fad in Hyde Park. Every year since 2000, the Serpentine Gallery has commissioned a leading contemporary architect to design a temporary summer pavilion to stand outside the gallery; in 2002 this was a mad affair of connected triangle and trapezoids by Toyo Ito and Cecil Balmond, with its engineering rooted in a branch of geometry known as "fractals". Hwang was so taken by the pavilion he bought it and plonked it outside the power station where it served as his marketing suite. After inviting Balmond to the Parkview offices to explain the concept to his team, he took his boldest step yet: he asked Balmond to oversee the latest masterplan.

"He wanted something radical," says Balmond, who was then deputy chairman at Arup.[8] "I said are you sure? I gave him two plans: one was an extension of the existing plan and the other was more radical, fully 3D. I had to present that in Hong Kong to the father, who was still deciding things at that point. It was a big meeting, with thirty people. The father then asked to be excused and he, George and Victor went away into a huddle and came back half an hour later. Victor said, 'My father says we should trust you.'"

Sidor says, "Victor was usually suspicious of the establishment but Cecil he trusted because he was also an outsider, and he became a confidante and taste advisor. They were like the court and the architects had to take them their ideas. Steve Kennard was an important intermediary between the real world and Victor.

Basically, after the meeting, Steve would clarify what he thought Victor had decided."

While Sidor got on with designing the power station, Balmond inspected the site, seeking inspiration. "I stood on the main road looking at this monster and suddenly I saw the bottom drop out and the ground just emptied between us and I thought, that's it, I need to create that," he says. "That was the breakthrough. I wanted to undermine the mass of the power station. Too many of the masterplans respected the power station; I wanted to invade it, undermine it, literally pull the ground from beneath it."

This he did by surrounding the power station with five buildings, each a dramatic bit of architecture contributed by a different design practice: there was UNStudio from Holland; John Portman & Associates from the United States; Stirling Prize nominees Benson & Forsyth; Arup Associates; and Balmond's own Advanced Geometry Unit. Between them they would be contributing a 360-room hotel with roof-top walkway; two unconventional office buildings called the Twist and the Weave; a residential block of 750 apartments; and a 4,000-seat glass theatre based on Balmond's impossible-to-describe fractal system of architecture. The site would be illuminated by lighting artist Keiichi Tahara, and landscaped by West 8 and Gustafson Porter.

"The theatre would have been a special building for London," says Balmond. "It was the heart of the scheme, in fractal 3D form made out of glass with the podium in the roof. This would have been the most expensive and ambitious part of the project. My fundamental plan was to reject the north and open up the south, I took that as the front and I wanted to animate that. I saw it as an urban carpet to the south and an urban balcony to the north."

Inside the power station, Sidor was still grappling with the biggest problem of all, namely, the voluminous size of the internal space.

Cecil Balmond's masterplan for the site involved a "three-dimensional reorganisation of the landscape", burrowing down to create a spiralling realm of subterranean spaces that flowered into dramatic buildings above ground. © Balmond Studio

"You could fit Trafalgar Square and St Paul's Cathedral inside, that's how big it is," Hwang would tell *The Guardian* in 2005. Someone had worked out for him that it had enough floor space to seat two-and-a-half million people for dinner and you could accelerate a sports car inside from nought to sixty without hitting the walls. Sidor wanted to embrace the space. "The brickwork is the most dramatic feature especially with the roof off, so you can see the chimneys. But English Heritage wanted the roof back on so we found a scheme with a see-through roof. The crucial thing was that you would see the chimneys from inside, then you can appreciate the grandeur of the whole place."

It is around this time that Ron Arad was invited on board. Arad, an Israeli industrial designer and architect, was asked by Hwang to present something utterly unique for the power station and given almost no restrictions in terms of brief or budget. Arad proposed a rooftop hotel filling the space between the four chimneys. It would have shuttle pods to transport guests from the lobby to forty-four double-height suites, most of which would be 150 square feet, and they would be the most expensive in London. In his drawings it looks like a space-port dropped on top of the power station. It was to be called the "Upper World". Sidor says he and Arad "slugged it out" for control of the roof but Hwang liked craziness and Sidor believes his own designs were not crazy enough. "He needed a bit of *Mad Max* in there," Sidor told *Icon* magazine in 2014.[9] Hwang was actually a science-fiction fan: his December 2006 letter to his colleagues concludes with the Trekkie salute, "Live long and prosper".

Down below roof level, the main bulk of the boiler house was to be filled with retail, a 3,200-seat cinema and space for exhibitions. Hwang wanted the director of the Serpentine Gallery Julia Peyton-Jones to curate the space. This part of the plan went into action almost immediately, when in October 2006 the Serpentine held an exhibition of contemporary Chinese art inside the empty hulk of Battersea. Visitors carefully picked their way through dark and derelict rooms with pooled rainwater on the floor to view video art of toiling workers in a lightbulb factory and a long wall made of 100,000 rotting apples crammed inside wire cages (either a sly comment on cultural decay or a terrible waste of fruit).

Planning permission was acquired – including for the six-acre roof garden designed by Victor's daughter, Vicky, that would be both "living garden and art space curated in tune with the seasons". This was 2005 and Hwang now had a big decision to make: press the button and get on with it or get out. Cecil Balmond felt sure the button would be pressed: "Victor sanctioned phase one, he was beginning to spend serious money. It was happening."

Except it wasn't.

In September 2004 CS Hwang had died. This had devastating repercussions for the power station as it exploded the family company into five: four brothers and a sister. Any progress needed all parties to agree but, according to Michael Roberts, Victor's brothers did not believe in the project to the extent that they would put their individual fortunes at stake.

Roberts was already concerned with the financial feasibility of the scheme. The plan was to complete construction in three years, but he felt it would take five. With such a heavy focus on retail – and not big, established chains but smaller, quirky, boutiques – it was proving difficult to find clients who could commit so far ahead of completion, making it hard to raise the necessary finance. An additional problem was the stipulation that the power station was fixed first, meaning it was impossible to get value from the site until several hundred million pounds had been spent on making good the structure. More residential blocks might have eased the burden on retail, but Wandsworth Council had strict limits on this (something that would change dramatically within a few years). Roberts could only see things going in one direction.

"If the whole scheme was going to cost a billion, that means we're spending £330m a year. That's £25m a month, £6m a week. How can you cover that expenditure? I didn't see how the gap between the construction time frame and the need to sign up tenants could be squared. It was these three things – the exploded balance sheet, the real construction time frame and the demands of the financiers. I couldn't see how we could bridge the funding gap. Despite every fibre of me not wanting to let it go, it had become inevitable."

Roberts began to guide Hwang towards the idea of selling. "Victor hated it," says Roberts, who began to put out feelers, hoping to find a buyer happy to take on the Parkview scheme. Then, abruptly,

BETRAYAL

Roberts left the company in 2006. Hwang believed Roberts was talking to potential buyers behind his back, with a view to securing himself a position with the new owners after any takeover. Roberts was a "traitor".

Roberts denies the charge, saying only that one unsuccessful bidder approached him with a view to adding him to their team should they acquire the property. "There was no attempt at a management buyout but there was one bidder who wanted to take the management with them. They wanted to secure that knowledge – including me. It's interesting how these things become reinterpreted as a management buyout. There was no such thing."

Hwang was certainly hurt. "There was a falling out with Michael Roberts," he admits. "Michael had been working with me for twenty years and at the end, well, if you read my letter I say this was the saddest part for me. He was my right-hand man, I never expected he would betray what we were trying to do, betray the family. He was trying to sell to somebody else, be part of their deal and sell us out. That hurt. I don't mind if the new buyers wanted to take my team, but I wanted him to come clean, talk to me. He tried to do the deal, sell me out. You shouldn't do that to somebody you've worked with for more than twenty years."

"Victor had invested so much emotionally so to have it taken away, I was made the scapegoat," counters Roberts. "I actually think he had a nervous breakdown. He was in a bad shape. It was the end of a dream. The pressure you are under, you have said so many things to so many people, and there is that great loss of face, which is important to most people not just the Chinese. If you say you are going to do something and then you don't – well, we know what that is like and nobody likes it."

Loss of face or not, Hwang submitted to the inevitable and accepted that he was going to have to sell. It was a decision that stunned some of those working on the project – Cecil Balmond says it took him a year to get over it – but Hwang is now more phlegmatic. "In many ways, we were very romantic with the power station," he says. "It's a great property, the sort that doesn't come along very often, and it would have been a shame to do anything but the best. We always wanted something unusual. In the end we did get planning permission for something pretty fantastic but it didn't stack up financially. You can only do a project like this once in your life, and if you can't leave a legacy why bother?"

For critics, this was a farce. The Battersea Power Station Community Group labelled what had happened as nothing less than a "scam". Parkview, it pointed out, had bought the site for a pittance and then loaded up on debt to acquire more land. It had paid fortunes to architects, planners, advisors and consultants, and ultimately pocketed a tidy profit while achieving nothing in terms of jobs, housing or economic regeneration. Added to which, the building was in a far worse state than when Hwang had bought it.

Those with whom Victor Hwang worked closely remain adamant that he was serious, just chronically averse to committing. "Victor would get terribly excited about something and then get bored again and want something new," says Neven Sidor of Grimshaw Architects. "You had to keep entertaining him. You'd think you had an idea and now it was time to develop it, whereas Victor would be thinking, 'You showed me this last time.' You would tell him it was time to get going on it, but he wouldn't listen." Sidor describes an environment in which ideas were constantly tossed into the ring, fooled around with for a while, then tossed out again. At one time or another, he says, Battersea could have been a mega casino, a horse-racing track, a gigantic circus ring. "Victor wants to extract the best he can from the designer to make the maximum project for the best value," says Cecil Balmond, mastermind of the final masterplan for

Parkview. "It's a value proposition. It's not the cost, it's am I getting the best I can for that cost?"

To some extent Hwang was insulated from financial reality by his family's wealth and by the land's increasing value. Nothing got done, because there was no need for anything to get done. The longer he delayed the more valuable the land became, especially if it came with planning consent. The flipside was that he was able to pursue ideas of imagination and scale that give a tantalising glimpse of what the power station might have offered London. His plans placed the power station as the centrepiece of a genuine public space, with parks, theatres, conference centres, exhibition spaces and shops, whereas a more commercial developer would have filled it with offices and houses.

As Parkview departed the scene, a last lingering sense of idealism went with it. And as huge changes began to sweep through the Battersea area, the power station would come to embody a new type of development for London, one that only had one objective in mind: making money, and lots of it.

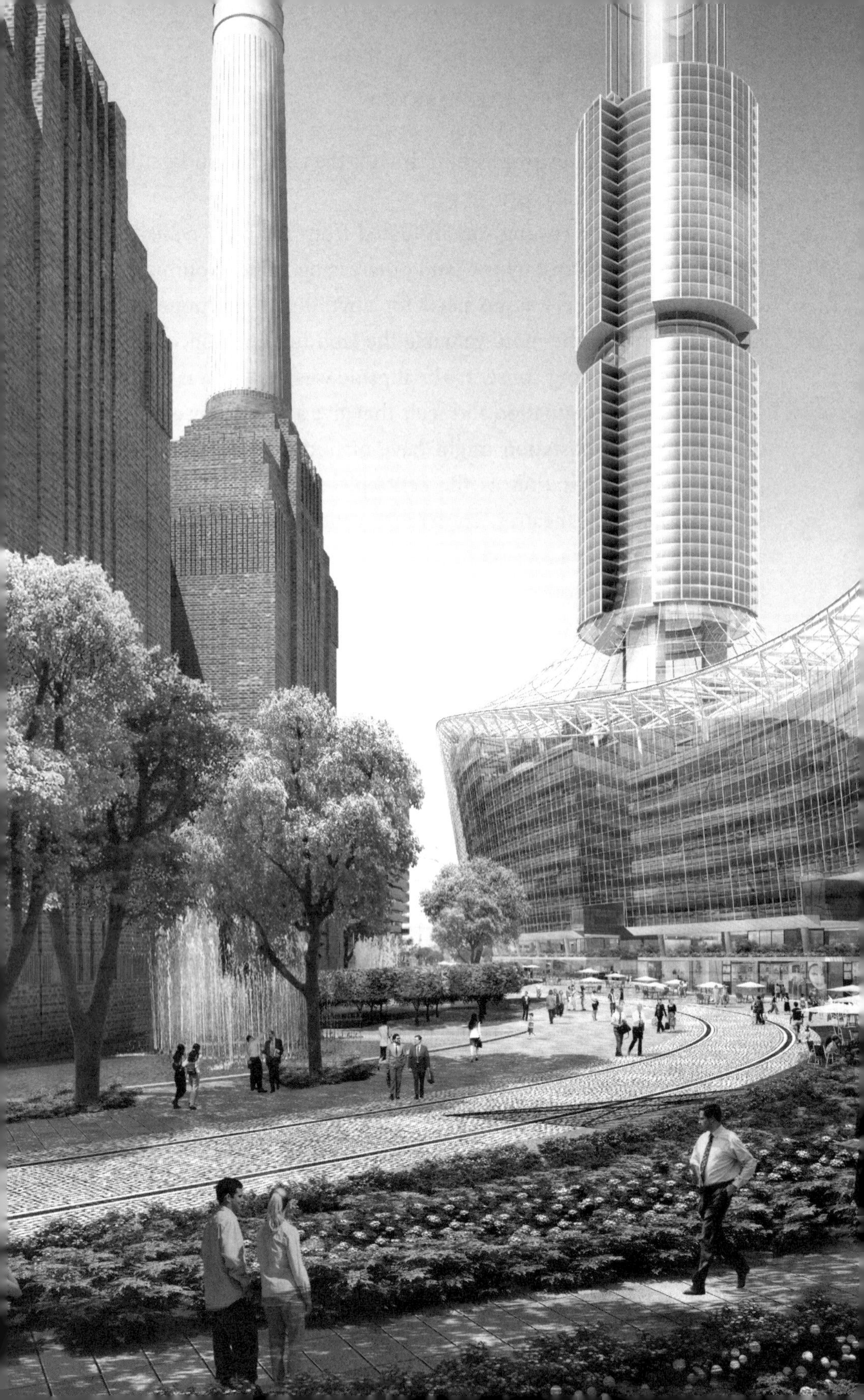

CHAPTER TEN

THE TREASURY YEARS

A pair of wild Celtic Tigers bite off considerably more than they can chew

CAST
Roman Abramovich Russian owner of Chelsea FC
Richard Barrett Irish developer and co-founder of Treasury Holdings
Paul Beresford Former leader of Wandsworth Council
Terry Farrell English architect
Ravi Govindia The leader of Wandsworth Council from 2011
Martin Johnson Long-standing councillor at Wandsworth
Gerald Jones Chief executive of Wandsworth Council
Edward Lister The leader of Wandsworth Council from 1992 to 2011; later deputy mayor at the Greater London Authority
Johnny Ronan Irish developer and co-founder of Treasury Holdings
Neven Sidor Partner at Grimshaw Architects
Rob Tincknell Treasury Holdings' man on the ground at the power station
Richard Tracey Former Conservative MP who worked for Parkview and Treasury Holdings subsidiary REO
Rafael Viñoly Uruguayan architect and creator of the Battersea Power Station masterplan

183

THE TREASURY YEARS

AFTER THE RESTRAINED PERSONALITY and slow-moving plans of Victor Hwang, the power station's new owners offered a culture shock to Wandsworth's punch-drunk planners. Irish outfit Treasury Holdings, which completed a deal worth £400m in November 2006, was run by two partners. Richard Barrett was quiet enough, a poet and angler who had trained in law and largely kept himself to himself, but the other, Johnny Ronan, was something else. A whirlwind with long hair that had a thick grey streak and was swept into a ponytail, he was nicknamed "the Buccaneer" and his high-living exploits involving cars, money and women were already rich pickings for Irish tabloids.

Barrett came from a traditionally wealthy family, while Ronan's dad was a pig farmer who had gone on to make millions in property, but they worked superbly as a team, charming planners and architects over long lunches where the most fiercely argued issue of the day was usually the wine list. Yet beneath the bluster and bonhomie they were shrewd and unsentimental, quick to spot an opportunity and wring it dry. They worked fast too, moving swiftly to get things done and acting boldly to realise their shared vision.

Where Victor Hwang had dwelled on problems and obstacles, Ronan and Barrett charged at them head on. Neither dilettantes nor chancers, they were property pros. "I had one fabulous lunch with Ronan and Barrett," says Gerald Jones, who was Wandsworth's chief executive at the time. "Ronan was the playboy type. He was an Irish charmer and used to things happening. He knew the right people. He was a showman but he had a grip on how to make things work. He managed a flock of consultants who did things for him. The other guy was a puzzle. He didn't say much but they had worked together on lots of schemes and made a fortune together."[1]

PREVIOUS SPREAD
New owners, Treasury Holdings, would rip up everything Parkview had done and implement a wholly new, aggressively commercial vision.
© Rafael Viñoly Architects

Ronan and Barrett had met at private school and then gone into business after meeting while independently working on the same property deal. Barrett was a barrister and Ronan an accountant, and they shared duties as their company, Treasury Holdings, spread from Ireland to China. Barrett tended to manage the finances and legal issues while Ronan worked on the developments. An early attempt to buy the Millennium Dome fell through at the last moment in 2001. The following year they began to eye up another London landmark. Rob Tincknell had just joined the company as development director when he was asked by Barrett to scout out a property that might come on the market. "He told me it was Battersea Power Station," says Tincknell. "I thought that was really ambitious but I went ahead and did a preliminary appraisal."[2]

A London move was logical, almost overdue, given that in the early years of the new millennium land in Ireland could be sold at nearly £20m an acre and Battersea could be purchased for half that. Ireland was on the rise and Irish developers had filled their pockets with free money from banks. London was about to experience a similar boom.

Everybody knew Parkview was in trouble; Irish property developers Ballymore had already been in negotiations with the Hong Kong outfit at the start of 2006, discussing a possible injection of £400m into Battersea to take it forward as a co-development. That had fallen through because Ballymore wanted to expand the residential side of the project, something Victor Hwang had been firmly against. Treasury remained watching from the wings. In a colourful contribution to a book about Irish property success published in 2008, Richard Barrett wrote, "The site lay tantalisingly waiting for a saviour, legs akimbo, breasts appetisingly on openish display. We laid in patient wait, hoping for the right moment, which eventually arrived."[3]

When Barrett charmed Hwang into the sale of Battersea over the course of an epic seven-hour lunch later that year, he was careful to assure the Hong Konger that his company would be executing Parkview's plan. The Irish pair's real intentions were very different.

"Treasury said they would build [according to] our planning permission," says Hwang. "Richard Barrett seemed to have the know-how and the muscle to build a developed plan. They told me they'd build this scheme and after thirteen years it seemed crazy not to do it after all the hurdles we'd jumped through."[4]

A very senior member of the Treasury team who did not wish to be named for this book says that in private, the Irish were appalled by the Parkview mixed-use scheme of fancy buildings covering a mere 4.5 million square feet. They did not believe it was viable, or came close to maximising the potential profits for the site. "They had buildings that were costing £1,000 a square foot to build and would only be worth £700 a square foot when completed," says Tincknell.

Treasury felt it was time for something drastic. If Battersea was going to work, it needed to become much bigger and the residential element needed to be vastly increased. The plan the Irish conceived was a dense, 8.25 million square feet residential-led scheme dominated by a huge tower that reared over the power station. Speaking to me in 2014, Hwang obviously feels he was misled by Treasury. He calls the Irish scheme "a tragedy", before going on to say, "I wouldn't put our name to something like that. That is not how our family would do it. Our values aren't like that. You could do a development like that anywhere, but London is not just anywhere."

It was indeed very different. It may even have been a tragedy. But if the power station was to survive, it may have been precisely what was needed because Wandsworth Council, for the first time since Battersea was shut down, was beginning to seriously ponder the reality of demolition. There was a growing opinion that its time was up, best summed up by architecture critic Rowan Moore writing in *The Guardian* that Battersea was like "a malodorous parent who refuses to do the decent thing and die, so that his heirs can put a Bulthaup kitchen in the family home".

When interviewing those who have worked on Battersea, the subject of demolition usually comes up. Often, the interviewee will test the ground first to see whether there is an openness to the issue being discussed, before they eventually come out and say it. "Would the CEGB have been better off just knocking it down and selling an empty site?" asks Michael Roberts, former CEO of Parkview, after three hours of conversation. "The presence of this building has stopped the redevelopment. It's a derelict power station and they normally get knocked down. How important is heritage?" According to Roberts, the site would be worth hundreds of millions of pounds more without the building.[5]

Martin Johnson, the senior Wandsworth councillor who was on the judging panel for the CEGB competition won by David Roche, grew up in Battersea. He has no love for the power station. "I remember it belching out smoke and spoiling the park," he says. "When you were a kid in the park you liked to imagine you were out in the country, but you could never do that in Battersea Park because you had this huge building looming over you."[6]

Some at Wandsworth talk, almost regretfully, about how sentiment towards the power station has changed. As Johnson sees it, "At the start, locals shrugged their shoulders and said knock it down, but the longer it was there and in the news, the more people warmed to the idea of keeping it. I thought it was ugly but you couldn't possibly say that or you'd be lynched by the locals."

Paul Beresford, Conservative leader of Wandsworth council in the 1980s, had to walk this tightrope, balancing personal distaste, or at least indifference, towards the structure and political frustration at the continuing delays against the feelings of Londoners who loved the power station. "When it was being built, nobody wanted it," he says. "Then when it was being knocked down, everybody changed sides. Then it was listed but all the contents had gone. All we had was a shell. We had to spend a lot of money on steel to stop it falling down. I've never prayed for an earthquake so much, but we knew we had to keep the damn thing up."[7]

Wandsworth, then, remained just about committed to the idea of saving the power station even if it sometimes went against its better judgement. There was, says chief executive Gerald Jones, "no political appetite" for delisting and demolition. That would be a long hard battle, pitting the council against public opinion and the heritage industry, particularly after the power station was upgraded to a II* listing in 2007. And Wandsworth's will was never tested. None of the owners ever raised the issue of demolition. Broome and Hwang were both prepared to work with the building, believing the difficulty of conversion was more than offset by its international reputation as a ready-made brand. But as Parkview's plans continued to stall that belief began to waver.

Right at the end of the Parkview era, a consortium fronted by former Conservative minister David Mellor arrived at Wandsworth Town Hall to discuss the power station. According to Jones, they had "clearly done their homework" and thought the numbers did not add up. "They said Hwang's cost estimates were built on sand and only amounted to a third of the real costs," says Jones. "They said the only solution was to pull it down."

Mellor was briefly Secretary of State for National Heritage in the early 1990s, when his responsibilities included ensuring the fabric of the power station was maintained. The Battersea Power Station Community Group had at one point hung a giant banner on the roofless ruin reading "Mellor Act!", to some publicity but no avail,

Mellor being otherwise occupied by the dramatic fall-out from his career-defining tabloid sex scandal.

By 2006, Mellor had moved into property development and investment, running his own company and acting as a partner in several others. Getting wind that Parkview were looking to sell, he set up a meeting. "Mellor said we had to apply for planning consent to delist," says Jones. "It wasn't viable if you had to spend £500m on the building and transportation before you could spend anything on the actual development." Jones began to wonder whether Mellor was right. "I always had these suspicions that it would end up getting pulled down," he says. "I remember the meeting with Mellor and thinking he was right, Hwang would never make it work and maybe it needed to be demolished. Maybe it was time to face it."

Although Mellor's consortium failed to wrest the power station from Parkview, they did provoke a change of thinking at Wandsworth. Planners became more flexible. The Mellor group had told the council that if the power station was not knocked down, the density of the project had to be doubled and the amount of residential development had to be greatly increased. Not only that but a significant number of the residential units would need to be sold ahead of refurbishment to raise the cash needed to repair the power station. "One of the things Wandsworth did wrong was that they insisted as a condition of planning that the building was weatherproofed and the chimneys fixed before any residential could be developed," says Jones. "In other words, they had to fix the heritage problems before milking the site for money."

Spooked by Parkview's failure and the Mellor meeting, Wandsworth significantly revised its expectations. Now the council was saying if a developer fixed up one wing of the power station they would be permitted to sell 600 residential units. By the time Treasury took possession this had relaxed still further with new planning regulations allowing for more residential to be released much earlier in the process. Treasury confirm this, saying that – with one notable exception – Wandsworth gave them pretty much anything they asked for. "They were very commercial," says Tincknell. "They are a development borough, you can talk to them about planning and phasing, and they understand. We told them that if they wanted the project to happen, they needed to let us sell some residential units before work began on the power station."

With Wandsworth's objections melting away, the Irish looked to build hard and high against the power station. Originally, any new building had not been allowed to go higher than the top of the turbine halls; by the time Treasury Holdings had finished, they had permission to build all the way up to the base of the chimneys. Although a senior member of the Treasury team insists that they never expressed any desire at any point to pursue demolition, the Irish instead chose to push to the limit what Wandsworth and English Heritage deemed acceptable, thereby threatening the integrity of the power station if not its actual structure.

Barrett and Ronan financed and managed the power station development through their Real Estate Opportunities (REO) arm, a listed company of which Treasury owned sixty-seven percent. "Our objective was to get the biggest planning consent we could to create value and use that to find financial backing," says Tincknell, who was based in China but was brought back to the UK to run Battersea. Treasury's scheme would be dense but it also had to appeal to planners and an increasingly sceptical public. The solution was to hold a limited design competition, essentially inviting three major architectural firms to pitch for business.

In April 2007 it was announced that Uruguayan architect Rafael Viñoly had been chosen ahead of Foster + Partners and SOM. Viñoly was immediately appointed to create a new £4bn masterplan that would include 3,200 apartments. This was a radical shift: in 1984, a residential scheme had been entered in the CEGB's original competition but rejected because in including housing it was deemed counter to the needs of Wandsworth. Now, with the council at the end of its tether and London's property market in overdrive, residential was all the rage. Tincknell started work in London on 4th January 2008. "There were three of us: me, a site maintenance guy and somebody involved in community liaison." The team soon grew, another appointment was Ronan's son, John, and they began to execute Viñoly's masterplan, which had originally been sketched at a dinner with Ronan on the back of a napkin.

"Treasury came along and said all Victor Hwang's crosses and weaves were unbuildable because they were unfinanceable, which didn't surprise me," says Ravi Govindia, leader of Wandsworth Council from 2011.[8] "They said the location lent itself to more intensive use. The model had worked elsewhere and they were prepared to work within the framework of what we wanted with the power station. There would be significant commercial and retail space, but not a supermarket, so it wouldn't interfere with our existing town centres."

Wandsworth was concerned that a large retail element would adversely affect nearby high streets. This was something that went all the way back to their original planning brief of 1983 – indeed it was one of the few principle elements still remaining that the council adhered to. REO would later drive a bus through that when they discovered that each year around £3.8bn was being spent by people from Wandsworth outside the borough because Wandsworth itself didn't have sufficient retail options. "That translates to about three million square feet of retail space needed to capture that spend," says Tincknell. "They began to see they could actually do with a new town centre."

The Viñoly masterplan was unveiled with pomp in June 2008. Its most eye-catching feature was a gigantic 980-foot "eco-tower", a sort of transparent chimney, plonked unceremoniously to the south-east of the power station. REO claimed it would have the largest solar-driven natural ventilation system ever conceived, one that would eliminate the need for air-conditioning in the residential and commercial spaces in the building.[9] Viñoly, favouring the sort of fluted language adored by international architects, announced grandly, "The visual presence of this near transparent marker on the skyline defines a new opportunity area signalling London's commitment to innovation and sustainability."

REO claimed the tower was essential, not just to help pay for the power station but also to ensure the development was carbon neutral. This was deemed important, as it came during a brief period when green issues had serious traction in the press. Politicians were falling over themselves to declare themselves greener than Kermit, to the extent that incoming prime minister David Cameron had excitedly told the press he was installing a £3,000 wind turbine on his roof, which he had to remove within days as he hadn't managed to put it in the right place.

Viñoly's tower might have been green, but it looked appalling and clearly was not transparent enough. London's outspoken new mayor Boris Johnson described it as an "inverted toilet-roll holder" and the ever-vigilant Battersea Power Station Community Group quickly worked out that it would have a significant impact on views of the Houses of Parliament as seen from the South Bank, ruining photo opportunities for tourists, a story quickly picked up by the press. After that intervention, the tower was never likely to get permission from Wandsworth, but it was a smart way of testing the water, allowing REO to get a handle on what it could get away with. It also drew public attention from the rest of the scheme, which was

THE VIÑOLY MASTERPLAN

Previous schemes always deferred to the power station, but Viñoly's masterplan centred on an extraordinary new chimney three times as high as Battersea's four stacks, with a glass veil sweeping out to encompass the new development. © Rafael Viñoly Architects

almost twice the size of Parkview's and contained five times as many apartments, crowding the power station in a way not seen in any previous scheme.

The power station itself – which by now only occupied one seventh of the overall site – would be a hotel, offices and retail, and for the first time it would feature residential homes, which would require significant remodelling of the exterior. It would also include a new combined cooling, heat and power plant using biofuels, waste and other renewable energy sources, with two of the chimneys reused as flues. "Key historic spaces," according to REO's press releases, would be open to the public. Surrounding the building, huge residential blocks would be built to the south and next to the railway line to the west, and there would also be a six-acre public park, a riverside walk and an urban square. Most importantly, it appeared to be viable.

"We don't embark on projects that we can't deliver," Tincknell promised with the cocksure arrogance of previous Battersea victims. "We are determined that Londoners will not be disappointed and this area will be brought back to life in the most spectacular way." Spectacular is one word for what was to follow. Inevitable is another.

As REO began the process of seeking planning permission, it was delighted with its scheme and believed Viñoly's international reputation would win over any opposition. Wandsworth Council, though, was less impressed. "Ah, the Viñoly bogbrush," says Gerald Jones. "These star architects love their prestige schemes but sightlines were a big issue. Viñoly was a disappointment, he didn't come up with anything very good, his eco-dome was a lot of nonsense and the advice we got was that it didn't really contribute to energy."

Grimshaw Architects' Neven Sidor is similarly scathing. "The Treasury guys wanted to just cram it with stuff and that piece-of-shit tower, a complete misjudgement by an architect who didn't get the British," he says.[10] It's a view hardly challenged by Viñoly's subsequent major London development, his "Walkie Talkie" skyscraper at 20 Fenchurch Street in the City, a top-heavy, bulging SpongeBob of a building that hit the headlines in September 2013 when its concave facade reflected the sun's rays on a car parked below, melting parts of it. In 2015 the building was awarded the Carbuncle Cup, bestowed by *Building Design* magazine on the worst new building in Britain, and described in *The Guardian* as "the most malignant proliferation of urban tissue that London has ever seen".

The council took a red pen to Viñoly's tower, forcing the architect to reduce its height by around 150 feet and then remove it altogether. But there were positive developments too, when in October 2008 it was announced that a new US Embassy would be built right next door to the power station, in a development led by former suitors Ballymore. At a stroke, everything changed. Whereas previously the Battersea development had been happening in isolation, now it looked like it might become part of something much bigger, what was being called the Nine Elms regeneration scheme.

"The great catalyst was when the US Embassy decided to relocate," says Richard Tracey, who worked for Parkview in community relations and then took a similar role at REO. "They'd turned Grosvenor Square into a concrete barracks and began looking all over London for a new site. Bob Tuttle, the US ambassador, sent his guys around London and they selected Nine Elms. It was nice and close to Westminster but outside the congestion zone [the US bill in unpaid congestion charges ran into the millions of pounds]. They saw it as an area with a lot of potential. Once they decided to do something all the other developers locked onto it."[11]

Edward Lister, leader of Wandsworth Council between 1992 and 2011, recalls, "The Americans went through their agents, Cushman & Wakefield, who did a land search and they came up with Nine Elms. They discovered there was some land they could buy and they came to Wandsworth and City Hall and asked what we thought. We considered it for all of about five seconds. It was just too great an opportunity to miss. We had a lot of meetings hammering through details and the various issues, which is that they wouldn't pay tax. But we weren't terribly worried about that because for us it was important just to get them there."[12]

With the US Embassy giving Nine Elms cachet, if no taxes, suddenly the post-industrial triangle of near-wasteland between river, railway and Wandsworth Road became an unlikely development hotspot. Between the power station and the embassy, Ballymore proposed to build a series of mansion blocks known as Embassy Gardens; between this and the river, another developer had drafted in architects Rogers Stirk Harbour + Partners to create Riverlight, a series of six waterside towers of descending heights. New Covent Garden fruit and vegetable market, a massive site occupied by the Royal Mail and the site occupied by gasholders to the west of the power station also received the go-ahead for redevelopment. Every month, it seemed, a new scheme was launched.

According to Boris Johnson this was now "possibly the most important regeneration story in London for the next 20 years".[13] Others claimed Nine Elms was the biggest redevelopment project since the Great Fire, spanning 480 acres along a mile-and-a-half of riverbank. Where Broome and Parkview had been sole players, attempting to solve major infrastructure and transport difficulties on their own, REO was now one of several. And while the regeneration covered a huge area it only involved a small number of landowners, making everything much simpler. To top it all off, there was a business-friendly Conservative in the mayor's office, eager to grow London's population and exploit the ferocious property market.

When REO had purchased the site, it had identified three major problems: Parkview's existing planning consent, the isolation of the power station from other residential areas and the terrible transport links. Two of these issues had now been resolved and attention turned to transport. REO looked at a few options, including a tram, monorail and shuttle from Victoria, but favoured an extension of the Underground, which it included in the 2008 masterplan more in hope than expectation. With the arrival of the US Embassy, this now became a serious option. The Irish proposed a spur of the Northern Line from Kennington with two new stations, one at the US Embassy and one at the power station. As far as Transport for London (TfL) was concerned this was a pointless bit of infrastructure as the line does not really go anywhere but for the developers it was essential, and they were prepared to pay for it.

The financial negotiations were convoluted – this would be the first tube line built with private money for 125 years – requiring every developer to pay into a fund that took into account increased business rates in the area. Each development had to be calculated separately – REO, for instance, was allowed to take into account the cost of the power station's refurbishment – but the money was needed upfront, and this £1bn was to be borrowed from City Hall in a bond due to be repaid after twenty-five years.

REO was moving at speed and in conditions that had never been more favourable, but Wandsworth remained wary. A particular concern was the chimneys, which REO wanted to replace. Wandsworth – under constant pressure from the BPSCG – wanted them to be done one at a time in case REO removed all four chimneys at once and then didn't have the cash, or intent, to replace them. "My concern was always that we kept them tied down and not to give too much away as they could always go bust like the others," says Govindia. "We'd end up with some cheap and cheerful flats and no solution to the guts of the problem."

In 2010, Viñoly submitted his revised, tower-free, £5.5bn masterplan, with residential buildings and offices swarming around a power station covered in glass and grass. Of the 3,400 apartments now in the scheme, it was promised that 500 would be affordable. The whole scheme would be built by 2020. Once again, the eternally patient officers of Wandsworth granted planning approval, which came in November 2010.

And then suddenly the ground shifted.

Ireland had not been immune to the 2008 global property market crash – far from it – and just as planning approval arrived to give the Battersea site value, Treasury found its money supply being cut off as the company's vast debts were taken over by Ireland's National Asset Management Agency (NAMA).

Viñoly's revised 2010 plan ditched the tower and glass veil but retained a heavy density of residential buildings and offices swarming around the power station, which just about keeps them at bay with a circular moat. © Rafael Viñoly Architects

NAMA had been created by the Irish government in 2009 as a "bad bank", buying up debt from Irish banks that had been busy lending €74bn to 772 Irish property developers, including Treasury and Ballymore, during the Celtic Tiger boom, only to be left exposed by the seventy percent drop in property values since 2008. Treasury believed Battersea would keep them afloat through this sticky patch, as London real estate offered billions in potential profit.

"WE'D ALL HAD A FEW DRINKS"

With Ireland's economy destroyed, a similar bubble was building in London. As a result of the international financial crisis, the Bank of England had cut interest rates to 0.5 percent making property just about the only thing with any investment value. As the euro plummeted and the rest of the world reeled from a series of political and economic shocks, wealth from Europe, China and the Middle East flooded into London, keeping the city afloat. Much of it went into property. Ronan and Barrett would stand to make a fortune from Battersea, just as long as NAMA held their nerve and didn't force them into administration.

NAMA, ironically, was headquartered in a building that had been converted and was owned by Treasury. Its distinguishing feature was a fibreglass statue of a naked woman climbing the external wall. The sculptor had originally wanted this to be a man, but after seeing the design a horrified Ronan insisted on a change of gender.

Despite sharing an office block, the relationship between Treasury and NAMA was poor. As NAMA took on more of Treasury's debts through the banks, there were regular disagreements about how this should be managed. It wasn't helped by Ronan's behaviour in March 2010, as the Irish financial crisis peaked.

It began, as these things so often do, with Sunday afternoon drinks in a Dublin hotel bar. Ronan was with friends, among them a model and former Miss World, Rosanna Davison. As Davison later recalled, "It got to about 12.30am or so and we'd all had quite a few drinks at this stage, I won't lie, and somebody suggested that we go somewhere else because the staff wanted to close the bar. Johnny suggested that we go somewhere on the jet because it was on standby, and my friend said 'Oh I've never been to Marrakech, let's go to Morocco.' It seemed like a fabulous idea at the time."[14]

Flying off in a private jet to Morocco on a whim for a whirlwind weekend with a former Miss World might not have been the wisest thing to do at a time when Ronan's role as the head of a debt-laden company was under severe scrutiny, but it got worse. Rosanna Davison also happened to be a close friend of Ronan's ex-girlfriend, an Irish TV presenter, with whom he'd had a furious row the previous night that had ended with her kicking him in the groin outside a pub in front of witnesses. Ronan was headline news and that weekend may well have cost him more than €60,000 and a pair of bruised testicles. This was just the sort of thing NAMA's head Frank Daly had in mind when he insisted that the agency would not support "the jets, the yachts, the Bentleys and whatever".[15]

NAMA began to tighten the screws while Treasury frantically looked for investors to buy its huge debt. By November 2011, this was reported to total €2.7bn, with around €1bn of that owed to NAMA. Ronan and Barrett were still sure they could rescue things and after twelve months searching for a partner had agreed terms with Malaysian property investors SP Setia, who would provide finance in return for a joint-venture stake in the power station scheme. It was at this point that NAMA called in the receivers. "The Setia deal went to Lloyds and NAMA on Friday," says Rob Tincknell. "They pulled the plug on Monday."

Treasury was furious. Tincknell remains baffled: "They didn't want to engage with the Malaysians to try and improve the offer, make it work, they just turned it down flat." But while Treasury was put through the wringer, Ballymore – with its politically sensitive US Embassy development and better personal relationships with NAMA – remained untouched. This, argued Treasury, was completely irrational. Why support one developer and destroy another? NAMA's explanation is that it ran out of patience.[16] Given Treasury's vast debt, the power station provided NAMA with its best chance to recoup some money as it was the only asset that had not dropped in value.

For Ronan and Barrett, who had come so far, this was a bitter pill, spelling the end of their business and partnership. Barrett was so angry at the way things had been handled, he moved to China and renounced his Irish citizenship; Ronan stayed in Ireland and began the long and arduous task of paying off his debt. Battersea Power Station had claimed two more scalps.

The Conservatives at Wandsworth watched all this from a distance, something they had become adept at over the decades. "We realised [Treasury] had difficulties, we were asking questions and they didn't appreciate that," says Ravi Govindia. "But if the financial papers are talking about one of the biggest developments in London going down the plughole, inevitably there'll be questions asked of the council."

As Treasury's problems mounted, Govindia had to consider the council's response. "We had neither resources nor legal authority to do anything," says Govindia. "Our interest had to be very measured. When Treasury's problems arose we would still have been perfectly happy to keep faith with them if they felt they could pull it off. They said they were in advanced discussions with potential partners and I told them I was happy to make myself available to speak to whoever their partner was."

While Ronan and Barrett departed to engage in numerous court cases and mutter darkly from the sidelines about betrayal and establishment stitch-ups, the power station was put out to tender by receivers Ernst & Young in February 2012. This was the first time Battersea Power Station had ever been offered for sale on the open market. Despite its well-documented history of chewing up would-be developers, there was considerable interest. The REO masterplan had succeeded in introducing so much residential development that the site now promised vast potential profits for anybody rich enough to see it through.

When the deadline of noon on Friday 4th May passed, there were fifteen bids on the table, but long before any announcement was made there was one clear winner when it came to generating headlines: Roman Abramovich's ambitious idea that the power station could be turned into a new home for Chelsea Football Club.

Since the club was purchased by the Russian billionaire in 2003, Chelsea had outgrown its historic Stamford Bridge stadium, located a short distance across the river in Fulham. With architects Kohn Pedersen Fox, the club cooked up a scheme to wedge a 60,000-seat stadium into the side of the power station, as well as making the usual commitments to refurbish the control room, chimneys and towers. The rest of the land would be crammed with retail, housing and offices. Given that the only way a 15,000-seat stand could fit on to the site was by knocking down pretty much the entire eastern wall of the B Station and shoving the stadium into the resulting hole, it was difficult to see how Chelsea's promise to "integrate the stadium with the power station in a sensitive, unique and powerful way" could be squared with the actual plan. It looked cool, but its general unfeasibility is readily admitted by Wandsworth, who also said it had no desire to allow a bunch of football fans to wander round Battersea every fortnight "dropping burger wrappings all over the place and having a few fist fights".[17]

Given how startling unlikely it all was, it's tempting to argue Chelsea were just flying a kite, showing reluctant supporters they were serious about moving and they had a grand vision of how to pull it off. In an era of identical new grounds, Chelsea's Battersea venture at least looked different, and it would have kept the club within its south-west London heartland. Rejection was inevitable, though. Even planning lawyer David Cooper, who had worked with John Broome and was now advising Chelsea, admits "it was a waste of time".[18]

A MANAGED RUIN

Equally unrealistic but in many ways far more compelling was a whimsical proposal by Terry Farrell, architect of the nearby MI6 building at Vauxhall, to turn the power station into a managed ruin. Inspired by the remains of Fountains Abbey in Yorkshire, Farrell's idea was to retain the north and south walls and the chimneys, but knock down the side walls, replacing them with an open colonnade. "The idea of the columns is that the gaps are invisible when you are inside," says Farrell from his office in an old Spitfire factory in Lisson Grove. "I thought you'd experience more of the space than you would if you just fill it up. The volume is the most exciting thing about it. It's going to be a shopping centre. What's the point? You'd be in a shop full of handbags and you'd have no idea where you were. This was one of the finest big volumes anywhere in Britain and the idea you wouldn't know where you were is awful."[19]

Farrell imagined that the interior would become a huge public park with key elements – control rooms A and B, and the directors' hall and staircase – refurbished and retained in their original locations, albeit now surreally suspended in mid-air as the surrounding turbine hall and switch houses had been removed. Around one hundred exclusive apartments would be fitted into the north face of the building, overlooking the Thames, while Viñoly's residential blocks would be downscaled into blocks more consistent with London's traditional streets. Instead of an expensive Underground line, new pedestrian and cycling lanes would be created, including a pedestrian bridge downriver between Nine Elms and Pimlico.

Farrell came up with his scheme on spec after a client with whom he was working on the massive Earls Court development toyed with making an offer for the power station. He intended to put the scheme forward for planning approval, so it was available as an option for any developer who wanted to take it up. Given that it would require the demolition of much of the building as well as the alteration of

Terry Farrell's scheme, which floated the idea of removing the power station's side walls to create a park within the building, otherwise leaving it as a ruin. © Farrells

the protected view of the power station from the river, it would have been tough to get planning approval.

Daft as it may sound, there's something intellectually appealing about this, deliberately constructing a man-made ruin from an industrial beast. In an extended meditation on the power station in the *London Review of Books*, Will Self speculated that the best thing do with the building might be nothing – "just make the structure safe enough for people to walk around and admire it for the Ozymandian monument that it is".[20]

While some questioned the economics of such a scheme, Farrell insists his plan was viable. "We looked at the cost and thought we could cover it easily from the flats around – or even just from the ones in the building itself," he says. "We thought all the flats would benefit from seeing a park so their values would all go up. The other thing I argued was that this could be done in just over a year. It's very simple."

As well as Fountains Abbey, Farrell was influenced by Emscher Park in the Ruhr, Germany, and Parc de la Villette in Paris, projects that created landscaped parks incorporating industrial relics. Another inspiration was the "ghost house" at the Benjamin Franklin Museum in Philadelphia, which is a steel-frame outline of Franklin's house on the site it once stood. For the power station, this would "create a memory of the building that is truer to its history than what will actually happen".

The idea was never going to fly with Wandsworth, which wouldn't have fancied the annual upkeep required to keep Farrell's scheme standing; the council had its heart set on the billions to be made from the Viñoly masterplan, regardless of who actually built it. Which is why, when an announcement was made in June 2012, the winners were SP Setia, who were prepared to pay around £400m. The Malaysian developers formerly courted by Treasury Holdings had since formed a consortium with Malaysian conglomerate Sime Darby, backed by the Malaysian state pension fund. The buyers had a bottomless pot of state cash they could call upon and they were committed to pressing ahead with the preapproved scheme inherited from REO and Viñoly.

Far from becoming a managed ruin, Battersea was now firmly part of a dynamic new high-spec London being fashioned in glass and composites for a world elite, where boutiques, offices and luxury apartments were the only games in town.

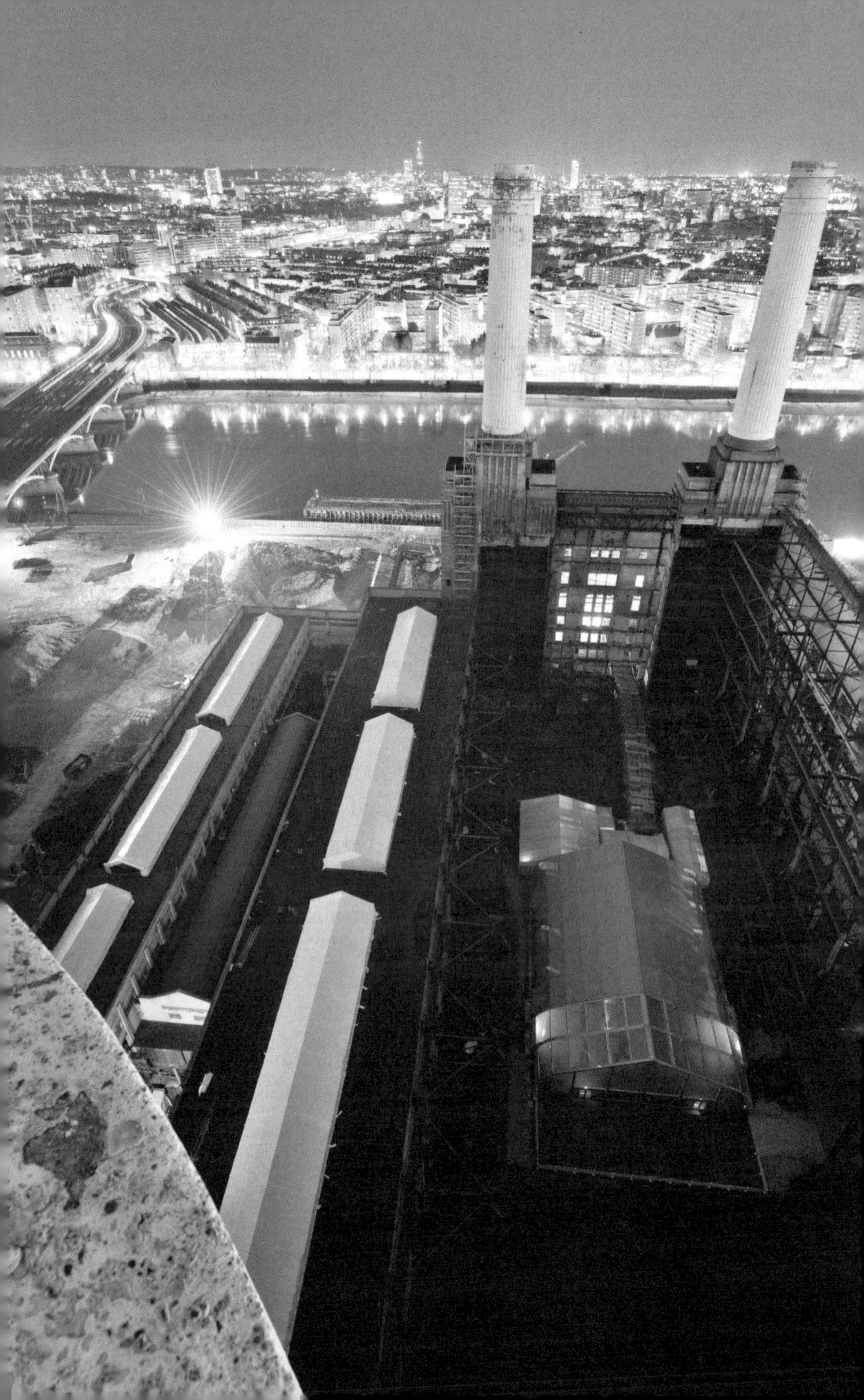

CHAPTER ELEVEN

A GOOD THING FOR LONDONERS

Developers with bottomless funds take over and it seems the building is finally saved, but at what cost?

O N 4TH JULY 2013, eighty years after Battersea Power Station had begun producing electricity and thirty years after it closed, David Cameron posed in front of the building for the official groundbreaking ceremony.

"This is a great day," said the prime minister, flanked by the Malaysian PM and London mayor Boris Johnson. "This shows Britain is open for business," he added, echoing the words spoken by his Tory predecessor Margaret Thatcher, a quarter of a century before. Johnson was more effusive: "There is no going back now. All the doubters are going to be blown away. This is going to happen."[1]

This was not Cameron's first appearance at the site. While politicians had generally tried to give the power station a swerve after Margaret Thatcher's hubristic 1988 appearance, Cameron had bravely decided to use it as the venue for the launch of the Conservative Party's election manifesto in February 2010, to predictable jokes about crumbling foundations and flying pigs.

Cameron's intention in 2010 was to draw the parallels between Treasury Holdings' massive development plan and his own objectives for Britain: "This was a building in need of regeneration in a country in need of regeneration," was the soundbite. The bitter irony that this dilapidated building had been in the care of a flagship Tory borough for three decades was missed by most commentators. Cameron's appearance was a risky strategy given Battersea's reputation for squashing grand promises and, sure enough, within eighteen months Treasury had gone bust.

The fact that Cameron could be persuaded to turn up outside the power station three years later says much about his confidence in the Malaysian consortium that had scooped up the site.

The prime minister was not the only one to have thrown his backing behind the Malaysians. In a meeting room in a converted warehouse on the power station site, Rob Tincknell fiddles with his Battersea Power Station cufflinks. He was working for Treasury when he first made contact with SP Setia, as the struggling Irish company searched for investors. He left Treasury in April 2012 – by which time the Irish involvement in Battersea was well and truly sunk – and, in an impressive feat of repositioning, joined the Malaysians as they sought local knowledge while preparing their bid for the power station. When the Malaysians won, Tincknell was able to pick up right where he had left off.

PREVIOUS SPREAD
The building as inherited by the Malaysians, devoid of roof and west wall. Also deficient in security – this photo was taken by an urban explorer who scaled the chimney. © Marc

Tincknell is ebullient and enthusiastic, a natural frontman for the new consortium. "Having Malaysian shareholders who are, to all intents and purposes, majority owned by the Malaysian government, has been so important," he says. The common factor that explains the failures of John Broome, Victor Hwang and Treasury is that none of them had enough money. Bar a political wipeout in Malaysia or demonic fluctuations in the currency market, that will not be an issue with the new owners. "The project is politically important, it's a symbol of the Malaysians' ability to play on the international stage," says Tincknell. "That's a very important thing for them."[2]

His employer is an alliance headed by SP Setia, a developer with projects in its native Malaysia, as well as Singapore, China and Australia, but for which the UK represents a big step into the international arena. It is partnered with Sime Darby, Malaysia's biggest conglomerate and the world's biggest palm-oil producer, and a company with a back story that couldn't be more colonial – it was founded in 1910 by William Middleton Sime, a 37-year-old Scottish adventurer and fortune seeker, and Henry Darby, a 50-year-old English banker, both of whom were looking to exploit the lucrative rubber market. Each party has forty percent of the Battersea Project Holding Company, with the Employees Provident Fund, Malaysia's largest pension fund, owning the remaining twenty percent.

While the chair and board of the holding company are Malaysian, Lyme Regis-born Tincknell is CEO and spokesperson for the project. He claims a personal relationship with the building that stretches back decades. When he was a child, he tells me, his father, an electrical engineer in Essex, would drive the family through central London on their way to holiday in Devon. Invariably, they would stop on the Embankment opposite Battersea Power Station. "Dad would stand looking at it for fifteen minutes, getting terribly enthusiastic about the amount of energy it produced," says Tincknell. In 1989, now at

Leicester Polytechnic where he was training as a chartered surveyor, Tincknell wrote a project about the development and regeneration of Battersea Power Station. Then, a few years after starting work on the development for Treasury Holdings, he discovered that his great-grandfather ran the Leighton Buzzard works that provided the cement for the original chimneys.

Behind the Battersea Project's reception desk stand the power station's original bronze doors, weatherworn but still impressive. Outside on the lawn sits a model of the power station that was used to represent London in the 2012 Olympics. Tincknell boasts that as soon as he saw the model in the closing ceremony, he got on the phone and bought it.

Over the past 30 years, the words in the *London A-Z* beneath Battersea Power Station have alternated between "under development" and "disused"; at the time of writing, it's very much the former. The site buzzes with traffic and workers. Foundations are in place for several surrounding blocks, some of which are already starting to rise. The much-loved view of the power station from the railway line into Victoria, the one first mentioned by the *Yorkshire Post*'s London correspondent in May 1932, is already obscured by a curtain of glass facade, not unlike the curtain drawn between economy and first class on an airliner.

Malaysian money has helped bring in the big guns. With Viñoly watching from the sidelines – his name remains on the scheme but his involvement is minimal – other stars from the architectural firmament have been drawn to the site. Ian Simpson Architects, responsible for several major developments in the ongoing regeneration of central Manchester, has taken on the railway-side site, a mix of apartments, offices and shops called Circus West. The practices headed up by Norman Foster and Frank Gehry have been invited to collaborate on a grand southern approach to the power station to be named Electric Boulevard. Their schemes were unveiled to the media in 2014: Foster + Partners has designed a large, undulating, seventeen-storey-high apartment block known as Battersea Roof Gardens (it will have London's largest roof garden); Gehry Partners' contribution is Prospect Place, five individual buildings described by Robert Booth in *The Guardian* as each having "titanium facades swinging like jiving skirts and windows staggered like towers of toppling coins".[3]

The Boulevard ends at the foot of the power station in Malaysia Square, which has been given to free-thinking Danish practice BIG, headed up by Bjarke Ingels. The studio's initial scheme, a "two-level urban canyon inspired by Malaysia's landscape and geology", was immediately compared to some of London's more unfriendly concrete roundabouts when it was revealed to the press in December 2014. It became more interesting the following July when Ingels revealed his idea to harness the energy generated by people walking across the square and transfer it up the chimneys, turning them into the world's tallest Tesla coils, complete with giant electric flashes that would zap between the stacks on the hour. "With 50,000 people walking over it every day we would actually be able to generate quite a large amount of energy," he told design journal *Dezeen*.[4] The Boulevard and its showpiece buildings constitute phase three of the £8bn project, with four more, as-yet-undesigned phases to follow that will provide a further one thousand residential properties and swathes of commercial space.

According to the current timetable, the first residents and commercial tenants move into Circus West in 2016; Battersea Power Station opens to the public in 2019, the new tube station is completed in 2020 and the whole scheme is completed by 2025.

The regeneration of Battersea has never been more real, but around London there is a curious air of disillusionment, even anger.

A GOOD THING FOR LONDONERS

On the west of the site is Foster + Partners' undulating Roof Gardens, separated by the canyon of Electric Boulevard from Gehry's Prospect Place. Between the power station and the railway is Circus West. © Battersea Power Station Development Company

Many observers see the developers as simply cashing in on a boom that has turned London home ownership into a game of investment, predominantly for rich foreigners. These will be "shiny happy flats for shiny, rich people," argues Will Self, the latest symbol of the "class-cleansing of central London".[5]

Tincknell defends his ground confidently. "Central London is an international cosmopolitan place and it will continue to be so," he says. "We can't reject that. It's driving the London economy. But we've worked hard to secure local buyers. We are running at about sixty percent local buyers – that's British passport with a London address." When this message was delivered to the assembled media at a briefing in spring 2015 the PowerPoint presentation included a photo of representative British buyers – Sting and Trudie Styler.

Since the first apartments hit the market in May 2013, Tincknell's team have sold £1.7bn of real estate in twenty months. But he is keen to emphasise that this is only one part of the story. The development – now covering forty-two acres – is fifty-seven percent residential. Of the remaining forty-three percent, 1.2 million square feet are retail and restaurants, 1.7 million square feet are offices, and the rest is hotel, leisure and community space. "This level of density has been proved all round the world as a density that works," says Tincknell. "It creates a critical mass so the shops function, the public transport works and there's a buzz, which is what people come for. We are mixed use, a proper town centre, a new London village."

Ah, the urban village. London is littered with them, a perfect example being the banal Chelsea Harbour across the Thames from the power station, a space few Londoners would claim to love. Tincknell insists that Battersea is different, that the consortium's vision goes far deeper than just real estate. The buzzword is "placemaking", a concept that originated in the 1960s but has come into its own as we increasingly require our developers to project a greater semblance of social responsibility. It advocates a community-driven process for designing public spaces, one that integrates a variety of activities for diverse audiences. In theory, the result is developments that add up to something more than the sums of their glass-and-steel parts, although the question is whether something as organic and nuanced as a community be manufactured in meeting rooms or is it all just clever PR.[6] Battersea, needless to say, has a Head of Placemaking.

One result is an ongoing programme of events, intended to give the Battersea project a buzz that might eventually take on a life of its own. To date this has included open-air cinema and street-food festivals, although a party to welcome the development's "future community" with a performance by Elton John almost had to be cancelled when a pair of peregrine falcons was discovered to be breeding in the scaffolding.

Not that Battersea Power Station requires the help of event planners when it comes to creating a buzz. Amid all the developers' guff and spiel, it continues to inspire wonder. In 2013, it was the subject of a whimsical online competition, organised by a company called ArchTriumph, which invited up-and-coming architectural firms and students to present their speculative concepts for converting the power station into, that old chestnut, a museum. The winning entry by Paris-based Atelier Zündel Cristea envisaged wrapping a rollercoaster around the building – an idea first seen in the mid-1980s on a poster satirising John Broome's theme park. AZC does it with considerable panache: the studio's visualisations show a track as high as the chimneys diving into the vast open space cleared at the centre of the building before banking around to hurtle toward the east wall and re-enter crosswise.

Others already get their thrills at Battersea, although in a more illicit fashion. As one of the last and greatest industrial ruins in London, the building has an almost mythological status among

The power of Battersea to inspire dreams is well illustrated in this scheme by French architectural office AZC. It was never intended to be built but it perfectly preserves the sense of wonder generated by the power station. © Atelier Zündel Cristea

urban explorers, that group of daredevil climbers and potholers who break into derelict or otherwise off-limits structures and photograph what they find.[7] These teams of explorers dodge security guards and clamber over fences, before they climb the scaffolding to reach the power station's roof and the base of the chimneys. Iron cleats set into the concrete allow the steely nerved to continue on upwards.[8] Author Katherine Rundell wrote about her clandestine night-time climb and of its unexpected delights in the *London Review of Books*. She discovered that the insides of the four great smoke stacks are lined with green-grey iridescent ceramic tiles – "I've seen few things as beautiful," she writes – and she was beguiled by the detailing of the brickwork around the top, too high to be appreciated from the ground. She considered the reward to be a fair return on the dangers of the climb. "As a child I wanted to fly on dragons," she writes. "The vast, brutal beauty of Battersea is the closest I am going to get."[9]

What of the power station itself in the grand new scheme of things? The much postponed chimney-replacement programme is finally underway. For much of 2015, the building had only three chimneys, the south-western one having been removed in the autumn of 2014; the developers had to pay a grant to the council as a guarantee it would be replaced. Tincknell claims it was in worse condition than engineers suspected. "It just crumbled away," he says. At the time of writing, this chimney has now been half rebuilt, and

An urban explorer descends one of Battersea's great chimneys in 2013. © Bradley Garrett

under the terms of the agreement the developers are now allowed to remove and replace the remaining three. Tincknell says he will be more nervous than anybody as he waits for them to be rebuilt.

Wilkinson Eyre, which recently refurbished Giles Gilbert Scott's Bodleian Library in Oxford, is taking care of the £1bn refurbishment. The bulk of the boiler house will, as David Roche envisaged thirty years previously, be turned into a shopping centre, with three floors of retail. Above that will come a floor of leisure; what was once seen as the raison d'être of the power station's survival is now a footnote, albeit one containing a 2,000-capacity arena. Above that will be offices. Tincknell says apartments would have been more lucrative but the developers believe it is important to put offices inside the power station to act as a magnet for the development's other office blocks. Cafes, shops and restaurants will be placed around the edges of turbine halls that will otherwise be left open. An elevator ride to the top of one of the chimneys is another holdover from past schemes. Wilkinson Eyre director Jim Eyre told *Icon* magazine, "There will be a connection between the new content and the sort of distress of the existing building which we quite like – we're not trying to clean it up particularly."[10]

There will be apartments but rather than being located within the existing building these will be banked in two-floor glass extensions that sit on the roof of the switch houses and between the chimneys above the boiler house. They will look out on rooftop gardens designed by landscaper Andy Sturgeon, a former winner of the coveted "Best in Show" at the Chelsea Flower Show. There will be 254 such apartments in all, at eye-watering prices. At the time of writing, two-bedroom apartments were being sold off-plan for close to £4m. One studio flat was sold in 2014 for £1.5m, which is what David Roche was asked to pay for the entire building and surrounding land in 1984.

One of the first tenants of the Foster + Partners designed Battersea Roof Gardens building has been announced as art'otel, the clumsily named boutique accommodation brand of the PPHE Hotel Group. © Battersea Power Station Development Company

The overall masterplan provides around 581 affordable units in three locations across the site, although much debate rages around this – including the problem that the units will only be "affordable" to those earning in the region of £40,000 a year. In August 2015, some of these affordable units were moved to a new location on the very edge of the development area, ostensibly "to speed up delivery" and ensure they will be completed by 2019 rather than 2025.

At Wandsworth there is understandable delight that the struggle over what to do with Battersea Power Station would seem to be finally over. Few probably care that the scheme in place almost entirely contradicts the council's original demands for regeneration. They would argue that London has changed massively in the interim, and a development brief that insisted the power station be used for leisure rather than retail and housing is no longer relevant. It is also somewhat ironic that the development-in-progress is only possible because it is underpinned by state cash, albeit the cash of a foreign state – something the Thatcherite council always rejected. Journalist James Meek wrote in the *London Review of Books*, "Thatcher hoped that privatisation would create globe-straddling British companies owned by small British shareholders, but instead most of the privatised firms and their small shareholders have been bought out by foreign governments and overseas pension funds." He was talking about the fishing ports of Grimsby, but it applies just as much to Battersea Power Station.[11]

So should we be celebrating? Thanks to the bounteousness of an overseas pension fund, Battersea Power Station's rebirth has never looked more likely. The wall demolished decades ago by John Broome will return, as will the roof. The great doors will be restored. The mouldering bricks, in their uncountable millions, and the rusting steel will all be renewed. Those troublesome chimneys will be reconstructed. That remarkable marble and walnut control room might even be open to the public for the first time since Halliday designed it. Battersea Power Station will be standing for many more decades than Francis Fladgate, Leonard Pearce or Giles Gilbert Scott could ever have dreamed.

Not everyone is convinced. Certainly not roof-climber Katherine Rundell: "Nobody who has seen [the power station] up close," she writes, "could believe that the solution the developers have come up with – flats, a shopping centre, a yoga studio and treatment rooms – is the right answer."[12] She is not alone.

SCANDAL OF
DERELICTION
SAVE
MICKEY
MOUSE
JOBS
&
TRAFFIC
CHAOS

CHAPTER TWELVE

POWER TO THE PEOPLE

Battersea is now privately owned by overseas interests who stand accused of turning it into an "oligarch's playground" – did it have to be like this?

CAST
Brian Barnes Artist and co-founder of the Battersea Power Station Community Group (BPSCG)
Paul Beresford MP and former leader of Wandsworth Council
Keith Garner Architect and member of the BPSCG
Ravi Govindia Wandsworth Council leader from 2011
Martin Johnson Long-time Wandsworth councillor.
Gerald Jones Former Wandsworth chief executive
Ernest Rodker Activist with a strong commitment to community politics and co-founder of the BPSCG

POWER TO THE PEOPLE

ON THE BALCONY OF THE DUCHESS PUB, over the road from the building site that is Battersea Power Station, Brian Barnes looks at the scaffolding swaddling the nearest chimney and scowls. Tall and long-haired, with an unkempt grey beard, fingers flecked with paint and a mouthful of teeth like toppled gravestones, Barnes is co-founder of the Battersea Power Station Community Group (BPSCG), which has been aggravating politicians and irritating developers since 1983 in its self-appointed role as the building's guardian.

He has not worked alone – far from it – but it is Barnes' name that keeps cropping up during interviews with MPs, architects, developers and local councillors. It is often expressed with resignation or exasperation – and, a couple of times, with the slightest flicker of anger – but sometimes it's accompanied by a note of grudging admiration. "He kept everybody on their toes," says Wandsworth councillor Martin Johnson, a regular political foe. "He was always there in the background – and sometimes in the foreground – warning us not to take any protection away from the power station."

Is Brian Barnes MBE the conscience of Battersea Power Station? Barnes laughs, bitterly. "More like the jester."[1]

According to its own records, the first meeting of what was to become the BPSCG was held on 26th October 1983, five days before the power station closed. It was called by Ernest Rodker, a long-time resident of Wandsworth. Rodker, a furniture maker by trade and a political activist by upbringing (his parents were both left-wing intellectuals), also led the Wandsworth Community Workshop, whose members included DJ Charlie Gillett. The group produced a couple of newsheets, *Pavement* and *Guttersnipe*, which focused on local issues,

PREVIOUS SPREAD
Behind their Mickey Mouse masks, members of the Battersea Power Station Community Group demonstrate outside Wandsworth Town Hall on 7th May 1986. © BPSCG

particularly housing and riverfront developments. Which is where Battersea Power Station came in.

"I had a workshop on Sleaford Street, opposite the power station," says Rodker at his house in Tooting Bec, bookshelves crammed with books about politics and housing. "I loved it. It was a great tribute to the industrial and manufacturing history of London. It had real majesty." This affection was only increased by the fact he could also visit the staff canteen if he was ever in need of a subsidised lunch.[2]

With the power station due to close, Rodker took it upon himself to organise the first public meeting about its future. It was held, he recalls, at Battersea Central Methodist Mission on Battersea Park Road. "Three people turned up," says Rodker. "Two of them were Brian Barnes and his wife. They took pity on me and that formed our group."

Barnes was an artist who studied at Ravensbourne and the Royal College of Art. A painter and silkscreen poster maker, he was also a muralist, the producer of several striking works on a massive scale, typically with a strong political message, including "Riders of the Apocalypse" in New Cross and "Nuclear Dawn" in Brixton. Barnes had previously formed the Battersea Redevelopment Action Group (BRAG), which campaigned for "jobs, housing and open space". This led to one of his first murals, "The Good, the Bad and the Ugly", which was funded partly by Wandsworth Council. It was painted on a wall beside a park that BRAG had helped create near Battersea Bridge. It was a colourful but provocative history of North Battersea that, among other things, lampooned rich property developers and their political sponsors. Unveiled by Sir Hugh Casson – later a judge in the CEGB's competition for the power station – the mural lasted barely eight months before it was demolished in 1979 by exactly the sort of developers Barnes was satirising. The site of the factory is now a luxury development called Morgan's Walk.

POWER TO THE PEOPLE

Brian Barnes' posters were an essential tool in creating awareness of developments at the power station. This one is from December 1985. © BPSCG

After the initial October meeting, Barnes and Rodker agreed to collaborate, and the Battersea Power Station Community Group was formed in November 1983. From the beginning, the BPSCG was critical of the developer-led solution demanded by the CEGB, believing the building's future would be best served if it were in the public domain. This attitude set the group at odds with Wandsworth Council, which was adamant the power station needed to be developed with private money. This essential ideological disagreement was at the heart of all that followed.

224

DIRECT ACTION

David Roche attended the BPSCG's second meeting on 28th November 1984, at Battersea County School. This came towards the end of his involvement with the consortium and he was accompanied by planning lawyer David Cooper, who would go on to work with John Broome. To advertise the meeting, Barnes had designed a poster riffing on the theme park concept that featured Mickey Mouse looming over the power station. "Everybody was very wound up," says Roche. "Afterwards, I said to Brian that I liked the poster. I offered five pounds for it. I think that confused him – he felt he was engaging in some sort of capitalist exchange. But five pounds is five pounds and he took it. I think it's real art."

Barnes has a different recollection. "Does Roche still have that?" he asks. "I made him pay for it – I said, that'll be ten quid, mate, you're not getting one for free. And he still has it? It's weird, they all love having a copy of my work. The first planning officer we had kept a derogatory cartoon I'd done of him in his office."

There is, in this exchange, the kernel of something important. Where Barnes and the BPSCG were fully committed to their battle to save the power station, those on the other side – the various councillors and developers that have come and gone – sometimes seem to view it as more of a game, albeit one with high stakes. They are also often magnanimous about the activities of the BPSCG, despite the tensions at the time. Rodker doesn't fall for this. "They may talk about having respect for us now but it's a load of baloney," he says. "If it all happened again we'd be in the same situation. It's about money and their mates. They can afford to be nice now."

The BPSCG did not limit itself to meetings and newsletters (the occasional *Battersea Bulletin*), its members also took direct action. They would disrupt meetings – "Brian and I were carried out of Wandsworth Town Hall down the long central staircase several times," says Rodker – and even took the fight to the homes of their opponents. Two of Wandsworth Council's leaders in the 1980s and 1990s – Paul Beresford and his successor Edward Lister – received visits from the group. "One of our ideas was to go to Lister's house, where he lived with his mother – which now I think was a bit irresponsible of us – and we built a wall in front of his door late at night," says Rodker. "It wasn't a particularly good wall, but it was about four-foot high and it gave him a shock when he opened the door." The group also visited Beresford's house "with pick axes and hammers at 8am", having put in a planning application to turn his house into a theme park, remembers Barnes.

For Beresford, a droll New Zealander who went on to become an MP, this was part of the game. "It was just something we dealt with," he says. "I quickly learnt that if you're at a public meeting you stand up, because then you can see anything that's being thrown at you. At Wandsworth, at that point it wasn't unusual for me to have a council meeting and find 3,000 people outside screaming and yelling at me. The Battersea lot came to my home with picks, shovels and wheelbarrows, and said they were going to knock it down because we were going to knock down Battersea Power Station. They also barricaded themselves outside my surgery. My patients thought it was terrifically entertaining having to cross a picket line on their way to the dentist."

More productively, the BPSCG also kept a watchful eye on the various development schemes, pointing out when the sums didn't add up – as in the case of John Broome's inflated promises of jobs, traffic and attendance. It kept preservation groups, such as English Heritage, updated and successfully lobbied for the power station's listed building status to be upgraded from II to II*. It got the power station included on the World Monuments Fund danger list. The BPSCG claim it was they who first alerted Wandsworth to the dangers of knocking down the chimneys without any assurance or

The first two issues of the BPSCG newsletter, intended to keep Battersea residents up to date with developments at the power station. The tone is sceptical but not totally dismissive, and the main thrust is for more public consultation. © BPSCG

guarantee they would be reconstructed. They also commissioned a survey to examine their exact condition. And they turned up to council meetings every time another development went down the pan to crow, "We told you so."

No wonder they weren't too popular at the town hall.

"What have we done?" says Barnes. "We've seen off three developers and everything we've said has come true. [The power station] is only still there because we've been campaigning for it. If we hadn't, somebody would have got rid of it by now."

When the BPSCG came into being, Conservative-held Wandsworth was leading the charge in London to privatise council assets and put contracts out to tender, overturning a consensus built over the previous century that councils should spend on services that benefit everybody, rather than cut back in a determination to keep taxes as low as possible. Wandsworth was the standard bearer for this new approach, and under Beresford would charge the lowest rates in the country thanks to a dedication to cost cutting.

"Wandsworth was the flagship, the best in the world," says Gerald Jones, who was the council's chief executive for twenty-four years. "Why do you think he became Sir Paul Beresford? He was Thatcher's blue-eyed boy and he got that knighthood on the back of Wandsworth being at the cutting edge of privatisation. But we weren't the hard guys we were represented as, we didn't privatise refuse or street sweeping, we did easy things like horticulture. We sacked contractors if they weren't up to the mark because Paul wanted everything to be best quality. People came from all round the world to see how we did things."

At Battersea Power Station, power, property and politics were inextricably intertwined. The power station became the frontline when Margaret Thatcher herself was invited by John Broome to the launch of his theme park. Campaigners believed the Conservatives disliked the power station simply because of what it stood for: a state-owned monolith with links to the moribund coal industry, with a suspiciously Soviet-style socialist look about it. (It is interesting how film-makers have tended to see Battersea as the sort of building only a totalitarian could love, hence its roles in *Richard III*, *Nineteen Eighty-Four*, *Children of Men* and *The Dark Knight*.)

On this, Barnes is typically blunt. "I don't have any personal animosity towards any of them, Beresford or Lister, and when I meet them I'm mister nice guy," he says. "But they are Tories and I'm not a Tory and we're never going to agree."

Rodker accepts this atmosphere of ideological enmity was not particularly helpful for the power station. "This was a serious issue for a very important building but you get into these confrontational situations and nobody wants to back down to lose face. The antagonism creates a condition that makes it impossible for change."

The group may also have erred in its belief that all developers were equally bad. As Paul Beresford notes, "It didn't matter what we came up with, they wouldn't like it." There was perhaps a missed opportunity when the power station was owned by the relatively benign Victor Hwang. But, typically, the relationship got off to a bad start when a small group of BPSCG protestors occupied the boardroom of Parkview's Mayfair office. From there, things never really recovered.

There was no common ground. The campaigners had an explicit distrust of Conservatives and private enterprise; the council was committed to a radical restructuring that embraced the market and rejected state ownership. This meant Wandsworth would never step in when the market failed, because by its ideology the market did not fail. Once Battersea passed into private hands, it was never going to be renationalised.

"The suggestion made was that we as a council should have compulsory purchased the power station," says Ravi Govindia, Conservative council leader from 2011. "But in terms of the size of the land it wasn't something we could contemplate. We were non-interventionist and had a clear view that while the post-industrial land of Wandsworth needed redeveloping, we were not going to be stepping in to do it ourselves. I don't believe we would have had the resources. Nor did we have the political appetite. If it had been a flat site, it would have been a different matter but then Broome would have developed it. It was the power station that was his problem and it would have been our problem too. There was no plan B."

Instead, Wandsworth washed their hands of the problem by passing it on to various entrepreneurs, constantly affirming their dedication to a developer-led solution even after decades of disappointment. "There was never a hint of state money being used, we were there solely for planning," insists Beresford.

An August 1989 poster by Brian Barnes makes life uncomfortable for John Broome. © BPSCG

The closest anyone involved with Wandsworth Council came to suggesting things might have been done otherwise is Gerald Jones, the shrewd former chief executive: "If a developer had made a case with experts stating why it could never be developed viably without a grant from the government, if somebody had made that presentation, the council may have stood behind them. It wouldn't have been popular but at least something would have happened."

Govindia's view is more typical of the three Conservatives who have led the council since 1983. "I've known Brian three decades or more, we get on well and I understand his arguments, which are quite unreconstructed – he says it is a public asset that should have public benefit and it should hark back to the Battersea of yesterday rather than the Battersea of tomorrow. I respect the position but I think it's wrong. The time has passed for them."

Ernest Rodker believes Wandsworth was naive: "They said they were pro-entrepreneur and open to ideas, but they weren't. They were totally locked in to what they wanted, which was to get in a property developer. They should have stepped in when Broome went under, or when Parkview sold up. But I don't think they had the imagination. They couldn't see the possibilities of developing something magnificent, something memorable. They were locked into Tory ideas of using the building for commercial use, then later for luxury housing."

Rodker's view finds a degree of support from Gerald Jones. Unlike the elected councillors, Jones was a non-political appointment and while he expresses admiration for Beresford and Lister, he is also one of the few at Wandsworth prepared to admit the council's arms-length approach had its flaws. "I was very lucky to be at Wandsworth with them and they were great people to work with but we never had a clear picture [of the condition of the power station]. We didn't do our own feasibility study. Maybe if we had, we'd have uncovered the problems. But that wasn't our job. We believed in the private sector. The developers were the experts. But it turned out three of them let us down."

Jones acknowledges that the end result of Wandsworth's laissez-faire philosophy could be a development that embodies many of the worst features of modern London: luxury real estate for wealthy investors to dump their money into, high-spec apartments that serve the needs of investment portfolios rather than home seekers, vanity projects that in their architectural inadequacy, damage the fabric and integrity of the power station itself.

"My employees were Conservative but the BPSCG were good guys," says Jones. "I have a lot of time for them. You need people like that in a community to stand up for things. They want affordable housing and they oppose a total gentrification project, and I have sympathy with that. None of my kids will be able to afford to live there. Should London's future be an oligarch's playground? Is that what London wants? I'm not happy with that."

So, what then would the BPSCG have had Wandsworth do with Battersea? In 1986, the group launched *The People's Plan for Battersea Power Station*, written in collaboration with architect Francis Graves. This had two purposes: to demonstrate there were possibilities for the site other than the unpopular theme park idea, which they were already convinced would fail, and to safeguard the building against potential demolition by gaining alternative planning permission. "We consulted local people and held meetings every month for more than a year before we submitted a formal planning application," says Barnes. "Basically it was going to be a million square feet of anything we thought was good for Battersea. There was going to be an art gallery, sculpture corner, cinema, conference centre and loads of small industrial units with the address No.1 Battersea, which could be used for anything."

The plan promised to create jobs, as well as offering a range of sports, leisure and cultural activities, including squash courts, a pool, a Museum of Power, health clinic, crèche, vocational training centre, Women's Business Advisory Centre, shops and a nightclub. Offices and studios were to occupy the switch houses, and there would be flats installed in the south end of the boiler house overlooking an internal courtyard. As with the luxury development rejected by the CEGB panel in 1984, the coal store would be turned into a boating lake. The borough planner reported that it was "imaginative" but noted there would be a "credibility" problem that a community group could actually fund and construct the scheme. (The BPSCG claimed it would be through a mix of private, public and charitable finance.)

Beresford, council leader at the time, is more scathing: "They told us they wanted to set up an arts and crafts workshop. It would take up one tiny corner [of the power station] and nobody would ever visit it."

It does sound airily utopian, but in his 1993 dissertation on Battersea Power Station, conservation architect Keith Garner described the BPSCG mixed-use plan "as the best scheme proposed for the power station up to this date". He was so impressed he joined the group. "I was doing my master's at York on Battersea Power Station because that was the big conservation issue at that time," he says. "The only people who came out of it all with any credit were Brian and his group, so I became a member."[3]

Suited, smartly spoken and with a flat across Battersea Park offering a perfect view of the power station, Garner makes for an intriguing double act with Barnes. At one point on the balcony of the Duchess, Garner points to the immense southern wall of the power station and tells me, "If you look closely, you can see the join where Battersea A meets Battersea B".

"You can't see the fucking join, Keith," laughs Barnes, who has clearly heard it all before.

But Garner was able to point the BPSCG in the direction of successful conservation projects such as the Dean Clough mixed-use complex created from a derelict mill in Halifax. The group visited, met the developer Sir Ernest Hall and fed back its findings to Wandsworth. Garner insists that despite the complaints of developers, who have sunk wads of cash into the black pit of Battersea, "there is no technical impediment to doing something nice here. This is a simple, straightforward matter. If it was treated like a public works exercise or National Lottery-funded project it would be dealt with, but it's fallen into the hands of rogues. That's the problem."

While you could take issue with the blanket characterisation of all developers as "rogues", the idea of turning Battersea into a public institution deserved more scrutiny. As early as July 1985, the BPSCG suggested that the National Gallery should use the gift of £50m it had just received from the philanthropist Paul Getty to buy the power station as a south-of-the-river annex. Then in 1993, it wrote to the directors of the Tate suggesting they consider the building as the location for the proposed new Tate Modern gallery. In fact, the Tate very much liked the idea of moving part of its collection into the voluminous spaces of a former power station, however, the power station it favoured was Giles Gilbert Scott's later work, Bankside.

The fate of Bankside offers a vision of what might have been had circumstances been different at Battersea. Bankside was also in private hands after 1989, when it had been given to Nuclear Electric "as an asset to exploit".[4] Nuclear Electric's architectural advisor was Andrew Derbyshire, the man who five years earlier had advised the CEGB to organise a competition to decide the future of Battersea because this would demonstrate that nothing could be done with the building and they would therefore be able to knock it down.

With Derbyshire's approval, Bankside was also heading for demolition – indeed, the bulldozers had already set to work – only to be halted by a public outcry. Even so, the building was only secured when the Tate sized it up at the end of 1993 and completed the purchase in early 1994. Bankside was saved by several factors that saw it differ in crucial ways from Battersea. For one, it was not listed, which meant that once the immediate threat of demolition had passed it was far easier to convert, with few restraints on what the architects could and could not do. It was also half the size of

Battersea and, as a younger building, in far better shape. Crucially, it was in a much better location with plenty of walkable transport links, meaning there was no need to create car parking or invest in major infrastructure.

Ironically, Bankside has since proved too small for the Tate's needs and has required the commissioning and building of a significant £215m extension.

That aside, from the day it opened, on 12th May 2000, Tate Modern has been one of London's most popular attractions, proof, if it were needed, that private enterprise is not the answer to every problem and that public enterprise has much to offer. But let's not be too quick to deliver a hearty back slap to New Labour, under whose patronage Tate Modern came into being: it was, after all, also responsible for the woefully ill-conceived financial sink-pit that was the Millennium Experience at the Millennium Dome. Perhaps the public just prefers art to theme parks?

There were ample chances to learn from the success of Tate Modern, according to Keith Garner. There were at least two occasions, he points out, when the power station fell into the hands of the banks and the opportunity arose to unpick the building from the site at large. The power station, he says, could have been restored to the public realm and fixed with National Lottery money, while the land around could have been sold to recoup the money owed. By far the best chance came in 2011, when then-owners Treasury Holdings went bankrupt and the whole site was in the hands of the state-owned Lloyds bank and the Irish government. Garner, on behalf of the BPSCG, wrote to administrators Ernst & Young offering them one pound for the freehold of Battersea Power Station.

Around the same time, and in a similar spirit, Marcus Binney of SAVE and Graham Morrison of Allies and Morrison Architects, offered a plan that developed the ideas they had back in 1981. They

In 2012 SAVE and architects Allies and Morrison offered a practical scheme in which the boiler house would become an arena, while the turbine halls would be used for exhibitions and receptions. The rest of the site would be sold. © Allies and Morrison

too thought that the power station could be separated from the rest of the site and filled with an ampitheatre in the central boiler house space. Initially this would be open-air but as part of a second phase it would be roofed and more facilities added. The arena would hold about 11,000 and could be used for the sort of events that regularly take place at The O2 arena (finally, a suitable use was found for the Millennium Dome). Neither the BPSCG's bid or the SAVE scheme was given serious consideration.

While Barnes and Rodker reserve most of their anger for the Tory councillors, Garner is particularly critical of English Heritage, the national cultural preservation body, which he argues in the case of Battersea "turned a blind eye to neglect". In his view English Heritage granted concessions where none should have been given. "They gave permission to knock down the chimneys and they've said nothing about the massive new buildings that will destroy the sightlines," says Garner. "They've let them put in windows and they've let them put pavilions on the roof. They've stood by and let this happen to one of the most famous and loved buildings in the world."

For the members of the BPSCG, there are conflicted emotions about the power station today. If the current development continues to completion – and with Battersea Power Station there are no certainties – the building will survive, albeit as little more than a useful brandmark for an otherwise unremarkable swathe of riverside shopping, some swanky office space and lots of luxury homes for the international super-rich. It is an issue Garner was addressing even as he wrote his dissertation in 1993, asking presciently, "Would the power station as an enclave of privilege be worth keeping?"

It certainly is in the view of Wandsworth Council, for which it represents a triumph for its limpet-like faith in the market, albeit one that has taken three decades to come to fruition and has resulted in a scheme entirely at odds with its original vision for the power station in 1983. And if this latest scheme should fail – as three others did before it? "I would like nothing done for twenty-five years," says Garner. "It's perfectly viable to consolidate the ruin and then come back when somebody has a better idea. One of the great fallacies is the use fallacy – that the power station needs a use. It doesn't. Its function is that it exists and that it is beautiful. That's enough."

AFTERWORD

WHEN I BEGAN VISITING HOMES, pubs and restaurants around the power station to conduct interviews for this book, the builders were just arriving at Battersea. At first, in accordance with thirty years of stasis, nothing seemed to change. The power station still squatted monumentally on its vast territory of wasteland, with small groups of workers and their vehicles scurrying around its base. Slowly, though, things began to happen. Huge holes appeared in the ground surrounded by immense pipes and great rods of steel, tall cranes arrived, and the termites multiplied and intensified their activities: digging, lifting, mixing, filling.

Progress became visible. Then the power station was wrapped in scaffolding and the entire site surrounded by billboards that boasted in the characterless language of corporate marketing about the wonders being conjured within. The view that had delighted me since childhood began to disappear behind an undulating stockade of flats. I could still see its reassuring silhouette from my local park until one Sunday I noticed that one of the chimneys was shrinking, getting shorter every day, like a smoked cigarette. Before long there were just three of the famous cream-coloured stacks standing. It was disorienting, like listening to a favourite song with the drumbeat removed. Close up, more of the power station became obscured, until soon my cherished childhood view from the railway tracks had vanished. Looking at the developer's renderings, when the project is completed, the only place from where you will be able to see the power station properly is over the river in Chelsea, once home to the very people who tried so hard to get its construction blocked.

I was not alone in finding this dispiriting. Battersea Power Station exerts a pull on Londoners greater possibly than that of any other London building. It is rare to find a resident who does not have something to say about it. While writing this book everybody I talked to without exception had an opinion – and I am not talking only about those people who were professionally involved. I do mean everybody.

I often pondered why that was. There is no question Battersea is a striking piece of architecture, a hulking mass of brickwork that inspires genuine awe. Alone on the riverside, it dominated the horizon. It looked lonely but dignified, like some sort of sentinel or lighthouse. Its appearance was honest and square, with those magnificent chimneys to admire from afar and the subtle but ornate brickwork to observe from up close. The chimneys gave it an instantly recognisable profile, as ingeniously simple and immediate as a McDonald's arch or Nike swoosh.

But I suspect the answer lies more in its decades of ruin. Abandoned buildings are charged with intrigue and potential in a way that ordinary, occupied buildings rarely are. Why are they empty? What happened? Where did everybody go? The absence of occupation leaves space for the imagination, hence the profusion of books and articles about Chernobyl and Detroit or, closer to home, London Underground's disused "ghost" stations. There is also the frisson that comes from contemplating somewhere that is off-limits, possibly even unsafe – combine that with the city centre location and the vertiginous challenge of those chimneys and it's no wonder infiltrating Battersea tops the urban explorers' hit list. Even for those

AFTERWORD

content to gaze from a distance, Battersea is the ultimate empty shell, the greatest of blank canvases, the biggest invitation there could be to dream the most fantastic possibilities. There is not another building in London that has come close to inspiring fantasies in the way Battersea has, from giant serpentine rollercoasters to thirty-foot cleavages. It's no wonder John Broome and Victor Hwang did not want to let go, and that Cecil Balmond was so distraught when his masterplan was dropped.

At the heart of all this was the hope that something magnificent might happen here. Something appropriate to the architectural, industrial and cultural weight carried by those masses of bricks. Something inspirational. After all, this is the place where pigs *do* fly. In their own ways John Broome and Victor Hwang recognised this. Their schemes may have been gauche or simply unbuildable, but at least there was passion and a vision. It is hard to view what came after as being about anything other than money. As the overall footprint of the development grew, the significance of the power station diminished to the point where it now seems like little more than a brandmark. The current marketing people love to refer to the power station as "iconic" and you cannot help but think they mean icon as in a pictogram, a visual shorthand for the brand that can be stamped on something that can be sold.

As it stands, when the development is finished, the power station will be one element in an oversized sculpture park celebrating the egocentric excesses of 21st-century architecture while remaining wholly generic in content. It will offer nothing to London that the city doesn't already have to excess, namely expensive and exclusive accommodation, office space and shops. A gated community with a Harrods sub-branch.

"When we contemplate ruins," writes historian Christopher Woodward, "we contemplate our own future."[1] In all those years

A BETTER FUTURE

spent looking at Battersea, I think many of us had in mind a better future than this.

The best that can be said is that the building itself survives. If the work carried out by the developers is done well, reinstating the missing west wall and roof, as well as every bit of chipped brick, smashed window, rusted girder and crumbling ring of ferroconcrete, then it could be that Battersea Power Station outlives the shortcomings of second-decade-of-the-21st-century developers. It survived the attempts of kings and archbishops to have it aborted before building could begin, German bombs, fire, flying pigs and obsolescence, followed by over three decades of neglect, left roofless and exposed to the elements, and still it stands.

Its tempting to imagine the site a century from now, when the glass towers currently under construction have collapsed or fallen to the wrecking ball of redevelopment. One can see Battersea Power Station still intact amid the rubble, as indominitable as the Thames and London clay, issuing a challenge to Londoners to dream again, embrace its magnificence and make London proud.

BATTERSEA POWER STATION TIMELINE

1840s A waterworks plant is built in Battersea beside the Thames on the future site of the power station

1858 Chelsea Bridge opens next to the future site of Battersea Power Station to provide access to the new Battersea Park, which is created over the marsh of Battersea Fields

1882 On 11th April, the world's first power station enters operation at 57 Holborn Viaduct, London

1891 London's first large-scale, purpose-built power station goes into operation at Deptford

1903 Battersea waterworks becomes obsolete

1907 JWF Bennett announces Dream City, a fun park to be constructed on the site of Battersea waterworks

1927 The London Power Company acquires the site of the former waterworks and applies for consent to build a power station there

1928 On 15th February, the Central Electricity Board agrees to Battersea as the site for a new large power station and chief engineer Leonard Pearce presents his initial plans for a building with sixteen chimneys, subsequently revised to eight chimneys, then six and finally four

1929 The digging of the foundations for the power station begins

1930 An announcement is made of the appointment of Sir Giles Gilbert Scott, of red telephone box fame, as the architect of Battersea Power Station

1931 On 2nd April *The Times* publishes Sir Giles Gilbert Scott's first designs for the exterior of the power station. Later that month the foundation stone for the power station is laid

1933 Topped by two chimneys, Battersea's A Station enters into service in June

1937 Construction begins on the B Station

1941 The third chimney goes up

1952 The first phase of Bankside Power Station is completed and it starts generating electricity

1955 The fourth chimney goes up and the power station finally takes on its famous four-square appearance

1964 On 20th April a power outage delays the launch of BBC2

1965 Battersea makes a brief appearance as "A Well-Known Power Station" in the Beatles film *Help!*

1975 On 17th March Battersea's A Station is taken out of service

1976 Over three days in December, design studio Hipgnosis floats a giant pink pig over the power station for the cover shoot accompanying Pink Floyd's album *Animals*

1978 In October a fire takes out turbine No 4 rendering Battersea Power Station close to redundant

1980 On 14th October, Battersea Power Station is given Grade II listed-building status by the Secretary of State for the Environment, Michael Heseltine, which means that owners the CEGB cannot demolish it

1981 SAVE publish *The Colossus of Battersea*, the first and highly influential blueprint for a future for the power station once the electricity was turned off

1983 On 31st October, after fifty years of service, Battersea Power Station is fully decommissioned. The same month, the Battersea Power Station Community Group is formed

1984 On 3rd July, the CEGB holds a press conference at Battersea to announce that a competition to redevelop the power station has been won by the Roche & Co consortium, which will pay £1.5m for the building and fifteen acres of surrounding land. The bid is promptly hijacked by one of the consortium, John Broome, developer of Alton Towers theme park

1985 Broome's Battersea Leisure company issues a promotional broadsheet describing its plans to turn the power station into Alton Towers-on-Thames with a mix of theme rides and shopping

1988 On 8th June, Margaret Thatcher fires a laser gun at the power station to launch The Battersea, Broome's vision for the building and its site, which he promises will open on 21st May 1990

1990 The May deadline passes and John Broome is forced to sell Alton Towers to finance a last-ditch scheme to save The Battersea

1993 Victor Hwang's Parkview purchases John Broome's debt for £9.5m and becomes the owner of Battersea Power Station

1994 The Tate Gallery announces that Bankside will be the home for the new Tate Modern

1997 An outline masterplan by Arup Associates produced for Parkview receives planning permission from Wandsworth Council

2000 Parkview gain planning consent for a scheme by Grimshaw Architects that includes a permanent base for the Cirque du Soleil troupe. Meanwhile, on 12th May, Tate Modern opens in the former Bankside Power Station

TIMELINE

2006 Parkview sells Battersea Power Station to Irish development company Real Estate Opportunities (a subsidiary of Treasury Holdings) for £400m

2007 REO announces the appointment of Uruguayan architect Rafael Viñoly to produce a new £4bn masterplan for the site

2008 The Viñoly masterplan is unveiled featuring a soaring, transparent "eco-tower". Later this year plans for the US Embassy to relocate to Nine Elms, a next-door neighbour to the power station, are made public, triggering massive investment in the area

2010 On 15th February, leader of the Conservatives David Cameron uses Battersea Power Station as the venue to launch his party's election manifesto

2011 In November it is officially announced that the REO scheme has collapsed with the debt called in by its lenders and creditors, putting Battersea in administration

2012 In February, the power station is put out on the open market by receivers Ernst & Young; one of the bids comes from Russian oligarch Roman Abramovich, who wants to convert the building into a new home for Chelsea Football Club

2012 In June it is announced that a consortium of two Malaysian developers backed by the Malaysian state pension fund is the winning bidder for the power station and site, paying around £400m

2013 On 4th July Prime Minister David Cameron is back at Battersea for the official groundbreaking ceremony for the Malaysian's scheme, which is based on the Rafael Viñoly masterplan with additional contributions from starry international architects, including Frank Gehry and Norman Foster

BIBLIOGRAPHY

When writing about the power station's design and construction, I relied heavily upon Andrew Saint and Colin Thom's magnificent *Survey of London* on Battersea, as well as *Landmark of London*, the useful short book on the power station produced by the state electricity board as it prepared to close down Battersea. A fuller and more detailed bibliography is given below. For everything that came after the decommissioning, I was able to speak to the developers, architects, designers, solicitors, councillors, politicians and campaigners who had roles in the story – well, most of them anyway; they are all thanked in the acknowledgements and their names appear in the source notes that follow.

I am also grateful to have been able to draw on Keith Garner's thesis for the University of York Institute of Advanced Architectural Studies, *A Well-Known Power Station* (August 1993).

Barker, Felix and Jackson, Peter, *Pleasures of London* (London Topographical Society, 2008)

Binney, Marcus, *The Colossus of Battersea: A Report by SAVE Britain's Heritage* (SAVE Britain's Heritage, 1981)

Boyd Harte, Glynn, and Stamp, Gavin, *Temples of Power* (Cygnet Press, 1979)

Cochrane, Rob, *Landmark of London: The Story of Battersea Power Station* (CEGB, 1983)

Gaffney, Mike, *That'll Never Work: Success Stories From Private Irish Business* (The Mercier Press, 2008)

Garrett, Bradley L, *Explore Everything: Place-Hacking the City* (Verso, 2013)

Glinert, Ed, *The London Compendium* (Penguin, 2004)

Green, Jonathon, *All Dressed Up: The Sixties and the Counterculture* (Jonathan Cape, 1998)

Haward, Sir Harry, *The London County Council from Within* (Chapman & Hall Ltd, 1932)

Hibbert, Christopher, (editor), *The London Encyclopaedia, 3rd Edition* (Macmillan, 2008)

Inglis, Simon, *Played in London: Charting the Heritage of a City at Play* (English Heritage, 2014)

Jackson, Lee, *Dirty Old London: The Victorian Fight Against Filth* (Yale University Press, 2014)

Kynaston, David, *Austerity Britain* (Bloomsbury, 2007)

Macqueen, Adam, *The Prime Minister's Ironing Board and Other State Secrets* (Little, Brown, 2013)

Matthews, Peter, *London's Bridges* (Shire, 2008)

Moore, Rowan, *Building Tate Modern* (Tate Gallery Publishing, 2000)

Pedroche, Ben, *London's Lost Power Stations and Gasworks* (The History Press, 2013)

Roberts, Chris, *Cross River Traffic* (Granta Books, 2005)

Rosenberg, David, *Rebel Footprints* (Pluto Press, 2015)

Saint, Andrew, and Thom, Colin, *Survey of London: Battersea* (Yale University Press, 2013)

Sandbrook, Dominic, *Never Had it So Good* (Little, Brown, 2005)

Sandbrook, Dominic, *State of Emergency: The Way We Were, Britain 1970–74* (Allen Lane, 2010)

Sexby, John, *The Municipal Parks, Gardens and Open Spaces of London* (Elliot Stock, 1898)

Weightman, Gavin, *Children of Light: How Electricity Changed Britain Forever* (Atlantic Books, 2011)

Woodward, Christopher, *In Ruins* (Chatto & Windus, 2001)

FILMOGRAPHY

In addition to the films below, Battersea Power Station has also appeared in episodes of the TV series *Ashes to Ashes*, *Doctor Who* (1964's "The Dalek Invasion of Earth" and 2006's "Rise of the Cybermen" and "The Age of Steel") and *Sherlock* ("A Scandal in Belgravia").

1936 *Sabotage* (dir. Alfred Hitchcock)
1951 *High Treason* (dir. Roy Boulting)
1965 *Help!* (dir. Richard Lester)
1967 *Poor Cow* (dir. Ken Loach)
1967 *Smashing Time* (dir. Desmond Davis)
1983 *The Meaning of Life* (dir. Terry Jones, Terry Gilliam)
1984 *Nineteen Eighty-Four* (dir. Michael Radford)
1995 *Richard III* (dir. Richard Loncraine)
2001 *Lara Croft: Tomb Raider* (dir. Simon West)
2006 *Children of Men* (dir. Alfonso Cuarón)
2008 *The Dark Knight* (dir. Christopher Nolan)
2008 *RocknRolla* (dir. Guy Ritchie)
2009 *The Imaginarium of Doctor Parnassus* (dir. Terry Gilliam)
2010 *Another Year* (dir. Mike Leigh)
2010 *The King's Speech* (dir. Tom Hooper)
2010 *Shanghai* (dir. Mikael Håfström)

NOTES

INTRODUCTION (pp14–21)
1   Margaret Thatcher's words were quoted in Hansard, March 1995.
2   Brian Barnes of the Battersea Power Station Community Group related this quote to me and the BPSCG used it several times in its published material, although Barnes forgets who first told it to him.
3   "And if you think this is good…" From an interview with John Gidman, John Broome's project manager from 1986-1988, conducted by telephone, March 2014.
4   When I interviewed Paul Beresford, the leader of Wandsworth Council at the time of Margaret Thatcher's visit to Battersea, he told me, "Maggie got a lot of publicity out of it, standing there in her hard-hat and wellies. We all smiled, but it was never going to happen."
5   "It was once a testament…" Quoted in Hansard, October 1991.
6   "There is always the danger…" From a speech given by Robert Bernays MP, quoted in Hansard, November 1936.
7   *King Rat* by China Miéville, p83.
8   Prince Philip's typically irascible comment was recalled by Victor Hwang when I interviewed him in April 2014.

CHAPTER ONE: TOGETHER IN ELECTRIC DREAMS (pp22–35)
1   Arthur Hill Hassall's condemnation of the Southwark and Vauxhall's water comes from a piece entitled "A Microscopic Examination of the Water Supplied to the Inhabitants of London and the Suburban Districts" published in *The Lancet* in 1850.
2   The description of Dream City as "an up-to-date, healthy and popular-priced place of amusement" comes from the *Maitland Daily Mercury*, 21st December 1907, a newspaper published in New South Wales, Australia. That a newspaper on the far side of the world should be reporting on the scheme perhaps indicates the degree of excitement with which it was met.
3   Fladgate's negotiations with the Duke of Northumberland were reported in *The Times*, 15th May 1929.
4   Reported in a cabinet memorandum of April 1929, held at the National Archive in Kew.
5   Thomas Kirk's fulminations against the goings-on at the Red House

in Battersea are quoted in Sexby's 1898 *The Municipal Parks, Gardens and Open Spaces of London.*

CHAPTER TWO: AN EVIL SCHEME (pp36–47)
For general background for this chapter I made use of *Battersea Power Station and Environmental Issues 1929-1989*, an academic paper by Catherine Bowler and Peter Brimblecombe of the School of Environmental Sciences, University of East Anglia.

1   The content of the Most Reverend Cosmo Lang's telegram was reported in *The Times*, April 1929.
2   The background to how Pearce and Allott arrived at their design is told in Cochrane's *Landmark of London: The Story of Battersea Power Station.*
3   Hilton Young's letter and the possibly not-quite-serious reply from Geoffrey Fry are quoted in a wry account of the "Blight on Battersea" in Adam Macqueen's *The Prime Minister's Ironing Board.*
4   Ibid, p104.
5   The invitation to Sir Herbert Baker to submit plans for the power station and their subsequent rejection, comes from a letter to *Building Design*, 23rd January 1981, provided to me Paddy Browne, an architect who worked on John Broome's development scheme. The letter was written by LB Ollier of Allott and Lomax outlining the role of Henry Newmarch Allott in the construction of Battersea Power Station. He writes, "In view of the prestigious position the power station was going to occupy on the London river front, the London Power Company deemed it necessary to appoint as consultant architect a person of some eminence in the architectural field in order to help overcome the objections which were bound to arise in connection with such a proposed development. This position was first filled by Sir Herbert Baker but I believe he was unable to gain acceptance of his ideas by the London Power Company and when his association with the project terminated he was followed by Giles Gilbert Scott."

CHAPTER THREE: A FLAMING ALTAR (pp48–61)
1   The quote from Gilbert Scott comes from *The Builder*, May 1947.
2   The quote from Gilbert Scott is recounted in the notes by Gavin

NOTES

Stamp to Glynn Boyd Harte's *Temples of Power*, a portfolio of the artist's drawings of power stations, printed in a limited edition of 250 copies. Boyd Harte was a brilliant, flamboyant artist who once lived in a house lit only by candles, where he held extravagant costume parties, one of which saw his house redecorated as revolutionary Mexico, complete with cacti and bullet holes, and ended with Boyd Harte, dressed as the Emperor Maximilian, being mock executed by firing squad on the stroke of midnight. Stamp and Boyd Harte would later fall out when Stamp's wife shoved her dessert into Boyd Harte's face after a row at a party. "I have to record, the assault was well deserved," insisted Stamp in his obituary for Boyd Harte, who died of leukaemia in 2003. The pair are credited with playing a key part in spurring the serious interest in power stations that led eventually to the remodelling of Bankside as Tate Modern.

3   As well as writing on Battersea in *Temples of Power*, Stamp has written extensively on the Gilbert Scott dynasty, including most recently *Gothic for the Steam Age: An Illustrated Biography of George Gilbert Scott* (Aurum Press Ltd, 2015).

4   The figure of 352 feet as the height of the chimneys comes from a paper, *The Constructional Works of the Battersea Power Station of the London Power Company*, prepared by engineers Charles Seager Berry and Arthur Creswell Dean and published in *Proceedings of the Institute of Civil Engineers*, vol 240, 1934–35, pp37–120. Other sources differ: the *Architects' Journal* of 2nd November 1933, for example, gives the height of the chimneys themselves as 181 feet from base to top, with the top 337 feet above ground level.

5   *Wonders of World Engineering*, March and April 1937.

CHAPTER FOUR: NEW POWER GENERATION (pp62–79)

1   The quote is from Spender's 1933 poem "The Pylons".

2   One of the men who crewed these boats is quoted in the CEGB's official Battersea book, *Landmark of London*: "It seemed your feet were always wet. You were a little above or just below the waterline for most of the time – in anything like a sea it would come up green over the bows and sweep the length of the ship."

3   *Wonders of World Engineering* appeared in fifty-three weekly instalments from 2nd March 1937 to 1st March 1938. It was intended

to be a comprehensive encyclopaedia of engineering. The magazines are archived online at wondersofworldengineering.com.
4   A briefing document prepared in the 1980s by Paddy Browne, the architect for developer John Broome, suggests that Battersea "provides a unique example in architectural terms whereby the quality of the similar spaces within the two stations are significantly different, although the client, the architect and the building's function and location were the same... In A, the quality of the architecture reflects the high standards of design and detailing prevalent in the 1920s and 1930s, whereas the quality of the interiors within the B Station is somewhat utilitarian and minimal, which is in direct response to the conditions imposed by the austerity of the war period."
5   Quoted from Weightman's *Children of Light*, p181.
6   Quoted from Kynaston's *Austerity Britain*, p191.
7   Quoted from Cochrane's *Landmark of London: The Story of Battersea Power Station*.
8   The cats are mentioned in "Battersea: Loser in the Generation Game" by Fred Pearce, a story that ran in *New Scientist*, 4th November 1982, reporting on life at the power station in the week after the official announcement was made that it was to close.
9   Quoted from Cochrane's *Landmark of London: The Story of Battersea Power Station*.
10 Quoted from Weightman's *Children of Light*, p222.
11 An item in the *New Scientist* column "It Seems to Me" by Geminus in the 30th April 1964 issue (p299) begins, "My belief that Battersea Power Station should now be evacuated will, I am sure, be shared by the moguls of television..." In the wake of the power outage that delayed the BBC's launch of BBC2, the author's conclusion is that the CEGB should be compelled by law to justify its continued use of the site every decade or so.

CHAPTER FIVE: PIGS MIGHT FLY (pp80–93)
1   Interview with Michael Sharp by telephone, May 2015.
2   Interview with Aubrey Powell, April 2014, conducted at Powell's apartment in Pimlico. Powell still designs album covers for Pink Floyd and had to fit our interview between jobs, including creating a Pink Floyd museum exhibition for an Italian gallery and directing the

NOTES

film of Monty Python's Flying Circus reunion at the 02 (the Python script sat on the coffee table, temptingly, throughout our interview). In a later conversation, Powell revealed he had been approached by the current owners of the power station who wished to celebrate the *Animals* shoot but, he told me, he declined to help because of his dislike of their development.

3   Interview with Theo Botschuijver by Skype, March 2014. Botschuijver also sent me several photographs he took of the pig and other inflatables for Pink Floyd.

4   Interview with Rob Brimson in Finsbury Park, March 2014. Brimson was one of the few photographers who retained any personal prints from the episode, getting them made before he handed over the negatives to Hipgnosis, as he knew from previous experience he wouldn't otherwise ever see them again.

5   Interview with Dennis Waugh by telephone, February 2014.

6   Email interview with Robert Ellis, March 2014.

7   Interview with Howard Bartrop by telephone, March 2014.

8   Waters' comments come from Austin Scaggs' "A Pig's Tale: Roger Waters Traces the History of Rock's Most Famous Prop", published in *Rolling Stone*, 29th May 2008. Waters was approached for an interview for this book and although the message came back that he was willing, sadly he never actually found the time to talk to me.

9   A first listen-through of Pink Floyd's *Animals* album was staged for a small invited gathering of the UK press at the power station's social club on 19th January 1977. It's not known whether the band were present at the event.

CHAPTER SIX: POWERING DOWN (pp94–109)

1   From an interview with former Battersea Power Station workers, June 2014, arranged via Peter Hill.

2   The information on the filming of the "Brave New World" video comes from a transcript of a 2006 ITV interview with Toyah, archived online as part of the Toyah Willcox Interview Archive.

3   Interview with Delcia Keate by email, January 2014.

4   Interview with Martin Johnson in his office at Wandsworth Town Hall, January 2014.

5   Interview with Ravi Govindia in his office at Wandsworth Town

Hall, March 2014. He has been leader of the council since 2011, and a local councillor for many years before that. He graciously spent an hour and a half discussing the history of the power station with me. Pleasingly, he has a reproduction of the cover of Pink Floyd's *Animals* hanging prominently on one of his walls.

CHAPTER SEVEN: A CUNNING PLAN (pp110–29)

1. In a conversation that took place in June 1993, Andrew Derbyshire told Battersea Power Station Community Group member Keith Garner that he had advised the CEGB against appealing the power station's listing and instead proposed the notion of a competition because he was convinced it would demonstrate that there was no suitable use for the building and permission would inevitably follow for its demolition. This is related in Garner's 1993 thesis.
2. Interview with Mark Leslie via Skype, January 2014.
3. Battersea Fun Fair features prominently in the excellent 1961 film *The Day the Earth Caught Fire*. The power station appears in the background during one scene.
4. Interview with David Roche, February 2014 at Roche's central London mews house. Roche has kept several souvenirs of his time as brief owner of Battersea Power Station, including a poster designed by Brian Barnes of the BPSCG.
5. The story about Broome buying a house aged sixteen, which has a more than whiff of myth-making about it, comes from an interview the developer gave to journalist Chris Blackhurst, published in *The Independent*, 30th May 1993.
6. Interview with Martin Johnson, January 2014.
7. Interview with Lord Dubs at the House of Lords, November 2013. An energetic and inspirational figure, Lord Dubs has followed the developments at Battersea from the start and has maintained a close relationship with campaigning groups.

CHAPTER EIGHT: THE BROOME YEARS (pp130–53)

1. Interview with John Gidman, March 2014.
2. Interview with Paddy Browne in Vauxhall, July 2014. Browne talked at length about the project and his disappointment at the way it ended. He kindly supplied me with several helpful articles and documents.

NOTES

3 The figures are quoted in Keith Garner's thesis *A Well-Known Power Station*; Garner says they originate with Peter Kreamer, the man behind the failed waste-burning scheme.
4 Interview with David Cooper by telephone, February 2014.
5 Interview with Gerald Jones at the Charing Cross Hotel, April 2014. Jones talked for some time and offered an interesting perspective, being the man who had to put Wandworth's plans into action.
6 Interview with Michael Jenkins via email, October 2014. Jenkins also kindly sent me some of the publications he created for Broome during their time working together on the project.
7 Interview with Paul Beresford, March 2014. Beresford, a mischievous New Zealander, also helped put me in contact with several other interviewees.
8 The various alternative names for the scheme are mentioned in the story "Thatcher's Laser Launch" by Robin Young, which ran in *The Times* on 9th June 1988.
9 Interview with Alex McCuaig by telephone, January 2014.
10 Interview with Michael Jenkins, October 2014.
11 Quoted by Phil Clark in "The Pig is Taxiing for Take-Off", published in *Building*, issue 17, in 2003.
12 John Williams' company Mason Williams is doing the PR for John Broome's new scheme, Camel Creek, which is a 300-acre site near Newquay in north Cornwall, on which it is planned to develop 200 luxury holiday villas. Perhaps Broome does not want the new project tainted by discussion of past failure.
13 The full text of Will Broome's article on his father and Battersea can be found at www.londonlaunch.com in the Be Inspired/Wills Week section. It is a strange read in which he seems to hint at a romantic liaison between John Broome and Margaret Thatcher. He also suggests his father deserves a Disney-style statue as the saviour of the power station and reveals that plans included a family penthouse, a "gigantic glass palace on the roof with Batman-style searchlights mounted on each of the fluted chimneys".
14 Interview with Edward Lister at City Hall, February 2014. Lister was extremely helpful at explaining the implications of the Nine Elms development on Battersea and the complex network of funding that will pay for the new Northern Line extension.

CHAPTER NINE: THE PARKVIEW YEARS (pp154–81)

1. Interview with Michael Roberts at his central London apartment, January 2014. The interview went on so long it was extended into a second day.
2. Interview with Victor Hwang via Skype, April 2014. Hwang's office also supplied me with a copy of the huge red book I refer to in the opening paragraphs of the chapter, for which I am most grateful.
3. The two financial scandals were reported, among many other places, in a story headed "Power Station Runs Out of Puff" by David Hencke and Rob Evans in *The Guardian*, 8th November 2002.
4. John Outram Associates involvement with Parkview is documented on the company's website at www.johnoutram.com/batter.html.
5. Interview with Edward Lister, February 2014.
6. Interview with Steve Kennard in a Fitzrovia hotel, December 2013. We had a follow-up conversation on the telephone a few weeks later.
7. Interview with Neven Sidor, January 2014. The interview took place at the architectural firm's offices in Farringdon and I was shown numerous images of the various schemes Sidor and his predecessor had planned for the power station. Simon Beames was approached for interview and initially accepted but then went quiet.
8. Interview with Cecil Balmond via telephone, September 2014.
9. In its April 2014 issue, international design magazine *Icon* published a story "Pipe Dreams" by Christopher Turner, revisiting some of the fantastical unrealised schemes dreamt up by various architectural practices for Battersea over the years.

CHAPTER TEN: THE TREASURY YEARS (pp182–205)

1. Interview with Gerald Jones, April 2014.
2. Interview with Rob Tincknell at Battersea Power Station, December 2014. Tincknell sent me home with numerous items including several books and a power station-branded foam brick.
3. The book to which Barrett contributed was Mike Gaffney's *That'll Never Work: Success Stories From Private Irish Business*.
4. Interview with Victor Hwang, April 2014.
5. In February 2012, the property consultancy EC Harris calculated that the Battersea site would be worth an extra £470m if the power station were knocked down.

NOTES

6   Interview with Martin Johnson, January 2014.
7   Interview with Paul Beresford, March 2014.
8   Interview with Ravi Govindia, March 2014.
9   These claims are made in an REO press release of June 2008.
10   Interview with Neven Sidor, January 2014.
11   Interview with Richard Tracey in Clapham, December 2014. Tracey also helped me locate some former workers at the power station for interview.
12   Interview with Edward Lister, February 2014.
13   The Boris Johnson quote comes from "Redeveloping London: What's the Plan?" a story that ran in *The Economist*, 16th February 2013. "Unusually," comments the writer, "Mr Johnson is not guilty of hyperbole," noting that the last time so large and so central an area of London was redeveloped was after the Great Fire in 1666. At 195 hectares, the site is bigger than Hyde Park, and spans a mile and a half of riverbank. By comparison, the World Trade Center site in New York is barely seven hectares.
14   The Rosanna Davison quotes come from an article in the *Irish Independent* of 12th May 2010, which ran under the headline "Rosanna says 'I Don't Regret Morocco Jaunt With Ronan'". The story records that "Johnny Ronan has since temporarily stepped away from his company Treasury Holdings, a subject of NAMA, due to media attention following the trip".
15   "The jets, the yachts, the Bentleys and whatever." Quoted from "Developers will have to sell off their jets, yachts and Bentleys" by Michael Brennan in the *Irish Independent*, 19th November 2010.
16   Caroline Madden writing for the Business Diary of the *Irish Independent*, 20th February 2012, records that, "In January, the National Asset Management Agency finally ran out of patience with Treasury, one of its ten biggest debtors, and decided it was time to call in the cavalry".
17   Interview with Gerald Jones, April 2014.
18   Interview with David Cooper, February 2014.
19   Interview with Terry Farrell at his Lisson Grove office, January 2014. Farrell also showed me a model of his power station proposal as well as providing me with his original concept sketches for the scheme.
20   Self is not a huge admirer of the power station: the quote, from the

London Review of Books, 18th July 2013, continues "Or, failing that, raze it to the ground and build the social housing so desperately needed by less affluent Londoners".

CHAPTER ELEVEN: A GOOD THING FOR LONDONERS (pp206–19)

1. Cameron & Co's visit was widely reported and video clips are online. The chapter title comes from an on-site interview with Boris Johnson, as he sought to convince (himself?) that the scheme those present were there to endorse really was all for the best: "There are going to be hotels, there are going to be restaurants, there are going to be 3,800 homes, many of them affordable. It shows that around the world there is massive confidence and interest in London and that international investment is not a bad thing. It is a good thing for Londoners."
2. Interview with Rob Tincknell, December 2014.
3. Robert Booth, "Frank Gehry Unveils Plans for His First Buildings in England" in *The Guardian*, 8th April 2014.
4. "Bjarke Ingels Could Turn Battersea Power Station's Chimneys Into Sparkling Tesla Coils" published by online magazine *Dezeen*, 14th July 2015.
5. Will Self in the *London Review of Books*, 18th July 2013.
6. One of leading proponents of placemaking is the US-based PPS (Project for Public Spaces); the company states, "The goal is to create a place that has both a strong sense of community and a comfortable image, as well as a setting and activities and uses that collectively add up to something more than the sum of its often simple parts."
7. The statement that Battersea Power Station has "an almost mythological status among urban explorers" comes from *Explore Everything* by Bradley L Garrett, a leading spokesman for urban exploration. His excellent website contains more stunning Battersea images, as well as an essay he wrote on the power station for the collection *Mount London: Ascents in the Vertical City* (Penned in the Margins, 2014).
8. Urban explorer Marc, who shot the incredible image on p206, took the time to explain how it is possible to ascend the chimneys: "There are no rungs but a series of spits bolted into the chimney about two feet apart from each other. They are too small to climb directly but you can clip a carabiner into the metal loop: this makes it possible to climb the chimney with just two short rope ladders. The climber

attaches one of the ladders to the first spit, climbs it to reach the next spit, and attaches the other ladder there. A buddy belays the climber for safety, just like in rock climbing. It took about two hours to climb the chimney." The chimney at the top, he says, is just a single brick thick.

9   Katherine Rundell is a children's book author whose most acclaimed book to date is called, appropriately enough, *Rooftoppers*. Her essay describing a nocturnal ascent of Battersea, "Night Climbing", appeared in the *London Review of Books*, 23rd April 2015.

10 *Icon*, April 2014, p77.

11 Meek's essay "Why Are You Still Here?" appeared in the *London Review of Books*, 23rd April 2015. A collection of his essays on the privatisation of Britain, drawn largely from the *LRB*, was published as *Private Island* (Verso Books, 2014).

12 *London Review of Books*, 23rd April 2015.

CHAPTER TWELVE: POWER TO THE PEOPLE (pp220–37)

1   Interview with Brian Barnes at the Duchess pub in Battersea, March 2014. I spoke at length with Barnes and Keith Garner on the pub's balcony, and also on several other occasions. Barnes also supplied me back issues of the *Battersea Bulletin*, which were extremely useful.

2   Interview with Ernest Rodker at his house in South London, July 2014. On hearing of this book, Rodker contacted me as he was keen to explain his role in the formation of the pressure group, and discuss a political life that included involvement with the CND, the Committee of 100 and numerous anti-apartheid and squatters' rights groups. We also talked about his extraordinary family history: his maternal grandfather was a conscientious objector as well as a poet and publisher who worked with the likes of TS Eliot and Ezra Pound. His father was Gerard Heinz, a German Communist actor who was incarcerated by the Nazis before fleeing to the East and then eventually arriving in the UK during the Second World War, where he resumed a successful acting career. His mother was a peace activist whose home was described in one obituary as "the nearest Britain ever possessed to a Communist salon". Doris Lessing was a regular visitor. It's little surprise that Ernest developed such an active interest in politics.

3   Interview with Keith Garner, March 2014, plus numerous follow-up interviews and emails. Garner also lent me a copy of his dissertation about the power station, which was of great use. He was always available as a sounding board for ideas and theories about the power station's non-development.
4   The background to the redevelopment of Bankside into the Tate Modern comes from Moore's *Building Tate Modern*.

AFTERWORD (pp238–41)
1   *In Ruins* by Christopher Woodward.

ACKNOWLEDGEMENTS

Thank you to all the people who gave up their time to speak to me while I was researching this book, including Cecil Balmond, Brian Barnes, Howard Bartrop, Cora Bennett, Sir Paul Beresford, Theo Botschuijver, Rob Brimson, Paddy Browne, David Cooper, Lord Dubs, Robert Ellis, Sir Terry Farrell, Keith Garner, John Gidman, Ravi Govindia, Peter Hill, Jon Herbert, Dave Hislop, Victor Hwang, Michael Jenkins, Martin Johnson, Gerald Jones, Delcia Keate, Steve Kennard, Peter Legge, Mark Leslie, Nigel Lesmoir-Gordon, Sir Edward Lister, Alex McCuaig, Aubrey Powell, Michael Roberts, Sir David Roche, Ernest Rodker, Michael Sharp, Neven Sidor, Terry Smith, Rob Tincknell, Richard Tracey, Nic Tucker, Dennis Waugh, Carinthia West and Terry Whatley.

Thanks also to all those others who lent their time and energy to helping unpick the story of Battersea Power Station, including Matt Brown, Wilfred Camenzuli, John Clark, Mark Greaves, Jon Herbert, Niall Hobhouse, Lee Jackson, SF Said, Jeffrey Shaw, Paula Stainton, Wendy Tse and Carl Williams.

A thank you also to my inspirational editor and publisher, Andrew Humphreys, and to my proofreader Omer Ali. Lastly, thank you to Cathy Irving, Meg Irving, and Daisy and Graham Watts for all their continued support.

From the publisher
A heartfelt thanks to the following people for assistance in sourcing and providing images for this book: Brian Barnes, Theo Botschuijver, Clementine Cecil of SAVE, Terry Farrell, Charlotte Fox of the Battersea Power Station Development Company, Bradley Garrett, Raymond Lee of Rafael Viñoly Architects, Mark Leslie, Marcia Mihotich, Neil Miller, Carol Morgan of the Institution of Civil Engineers, John Outram, Juliette Rey of AZC, Neven Sidor of Grimshaw Architects and Chris Richardson.

INDEX

PROPOSED SCHEMES AND IDEAS FOR BATTERSEA

aeronautical museum, 103
amphitheatre/arena (SAVE scheme of 2012), 236, *236*
Arup mixed-use scheme (hotels, theatres, housing, business, retail), 162
AZC's giant rollercoaster, 214, *215*
BatHat, The, 126, *126*
boating lake on the roof, 171
British Empire-themed attraction, 124–25
Cecil Balmond's fractal masterplan, 174–75, *176*
Chelsea FC's new ground, 202
church, 104
Cirque du Soleil home, 169–70
conference centre, 122
European Parliament, new home, 104
exposition hall, 108
flats for the elderly, 104
Grimshaw Architects mixed-use masterplan, 169, *170*, *172–73*
Houses of Parliament, replacement for, 104
John Outram Associates mixed-use masterplan, 164–65
leisure complex (SAVE scheme of 1981), 105–106
luxury flats and a hotel, 123
Michael Jackson sponsored "fantasy centre", 162
mosque, 108
museum, 104
National Gallery extension, 234
NoddyLand theme park, 161–62
nuclear power station, 104
People's Plan for Battersea Power Station, 232
Rafael Viñoly mixed-use masterplan, *182*, 191–94, *193*, 197, *198*
refuse-burning centre, 108, 123–24, 127
religious theme park, 161
restaurant in a chimney, 170–71
Ron Arad's Upper World, 176–77
shopping centre, 122
sports centre, 104
Tate extension, 234
technology theme park (Mark Leslie scheme of 1983–84), 114–15, *115*, *116*, *121*
Terry Farrell's managed ruin, 203–205, *204*
theatre, 123
theme park with shopping (John Broome scheme), 134–36, *137*, 144–45
Warner Bros super cinema, 162
Warner Bros theme park, 147

GENERAL INDEX

Abramovich, Roman, 183, 202
Adavanced Geometry Unit, 175
Alexander Kennedy (flattie), 66, 72
Alfie (1963 novel), 76
Algie, the Pink Floyd pig, *80*, 81–93
Allies and Morrison Architects, 235, *236*
Allot, Henry Newmarch (civil engineer), 39, 250
Alton Group, 148
Alton Towers, 117–18, 132, 135–36, 143, 149
Ambrose, John (station manager), 56, 96

American Embassy, *see* US Embassy
Amos, Tori (singer), 161
Animal Farm (1945 novel), 84
Animals (1977 album), 18, 83–93, 253
Applegate, George (dowser), 169
Arad, Ron (designer), 155, 176–77
Archbishop of Canterbury, 17, 37–38
ArchTriumph, 214
Arup, 161, 162, 165, *170*, 174–75
Arup masterplan, 162
art'otel London, *218*
Atelier Zündel Cristea (AZC), 214, *215*
atomic energy, 18, 75, 104

BAA, 162
Baker, Sir Herbert (architect), 47, 250
Ballonfabrik, 86
Ballymore, 185, 195, 198, 200
Balmond, Cecil (architect), 155, 174–75, 177, 180–81
Bank of England, 17, 72
Banks, Tony (MP), 16
Bankside Power Station, 51, 100, 109, 234–35
Barnes, Brian (BPSCG co-founder), 221–23, 225–28, 232–33
Barrett, Richard (developer), 183–86, 190, 199, 201
Barton Power Station, Manchester, 39, 45–46
Bartrop, Howard (photographer), 86, 88–89, 91
Bathat, The, *126*, 126
Batman & Robin (1997 film), 163
Battersea:
  industry, 33; market gardens, 33; radical politics, 35; taint of disrepute, 34
Battersea, The, 15–16, 144
Battersea, The (newsletter), *150*
Battersea Bullet, 144, *145*
Battersea Bulletin, 225, *227*
Battersea Fields, 34, 113
Battersea Fun Fair, *110*, 113, 254
Battersea Leisure, 132, 140, 148
Battersea Park, 25, 34, 43, *77*, *110*, 187, 233
Battersea Park Road, 25, 223
Battersea Park station, 26, 167
Battersea Power House, 133–35, *134*
Battersea Power Station:
  descriptions of, 18; uses of likeness, 20; popular uses for, 103–104; choice of Battersea as a site, 33; campaign against, 37–39, 41–44; layout of, 39–41; arrangement of chimneys, 40–41, *42*, *43*; gas-washing 46–47; Giles Gilbert Scott's contribution, 48–54; design of chimneys, 53–54; construction of A Station, 54–56; blackouts 63–64, 78–79; how it worked, 66; construction of B Station, 69–74; third chimney, 70; bombing during WWII, 71–72; burning of banknotes, 72; fourth chimney, 74; closure of A Station, 96; Grade II listing, 100–102; the SAVE proposal, 105–107; closure of B Station, 109; CEGB competition, 112–29; removal of absestos and west wall, 140–41; exploitation of, 161; falcons in the chimneys, 168; consideration of demolition, 186; Grade II* listing, 188; replacement of chimneys, 216; the allure of its ruin, 239
Battersea Power Station (1969 album), 85
Battersea Power Station Community Group (BPSCG), 149, 163, 167–68, 180, 188, 192, 197, *220*, 222–37
Battersea Power Station Development Brief, 108

Battersea Power Station and Environmental Issues 1929–1989 (paper), 250
Battersea Project Holding Company, 209–10
Battersea Redevelopment Action Group (BRAG), 223
Battersea Roof Gardens, 211, *212*
BBC2, delayed station launch, 78–79
Beames, Simon (architect), 169, 171
Bennett, John Walter Frink (engineer), 23–24, 26, 27
Benson & Forsyth, 175
Beresford, Paul (Wandsworth Council leader), 120, 131, 142–44, 183, 187, 221, 226, 228–29
Bernays, Robert (MP), 249
Berry, Charles Seager (engineer), 58, 251
Betjeman, John (poet and critic), 51
BIG (architectural practice), 211
Big Freeze, 72–73
Binney, Marcus (chairman of SAVE), 105, 235
blackouts, 63–64, 78–79
Bloomfield, Paul (developer), 148–49
Blunt, Reginald (founder of Chelsea Society), 41
Booth, Handel, Mrs, of Chelsea, 38
Booth, Robert (critic), 211
Botschuijver, Theo (inflatable structure designer), 85–88, 89–90
Boyd Harte, Glynn (artist), 251
Branson, Richard, 144
British Electricity Authority (BEA), 73
Brimson, Rob (photographer), 86, 88–89, 91–92
Broadcasting House, 17
Broome, John (developer), 15, 24, 111, 112, 117, *130*, 130–53, 158: joins Roche consortium, 118; takes over consortium, 128; purchase of Battersea, 132; gains planning permission, 137; sale of Alton Towers, 149; sale of Battersea, 150; refusal to speak, 151; career post Battersea, 153
Broome, Will (son of John), 151–52, 255
Browne, Paddy (architect), 131, 133, 138–39, 146, 148, 252
Business Design Centre, 149
Butler, Rab (Lord Privy Seal), 75

Cameron, David, 192, 207–208
Casson, Sir Hugh (president of the Royal Academy), 119, 223
Central Electricity Authority, 73
Central Electricity Board (CEB), 33
Central Electricity Generating Board (CEGB), 18, 73, 95, 100–101, 112–29
Chambellan, Rene Paul (sculptor), 60
Chamberlain, Neville (Minister of Health), 43
Chanin Building, New York, 61
Charing Cross Electricity Supply Company, 27, 32
Chelsea Bridge, 34, 166
Chelsea Football Club, 202
Chelsea Harbour, 213
Chelsea Hospital, 34
Chelsea Monster, 38
Chelsea Physic Garden, 43
Chelsea Society, 41
Children of Men (2006 film), 81–82, *83*, 84
Chrysler Building, 54
Churchill Gardens estate, 74–75, 103, 109
Circus West, 210–11, *212*
Cirque du Soleil, 169–70, 173
Clapcott, Charles, Mayor of Chelsea, 37, 42
Clark, Kenneth (National Gallery director), 61

INDEX

Cleese, John, 95
Clooney, George, 163
Colossus of Battersea, The (book), 105
Cooper, David (solicitor), 131, 137–38, 140, 202, 225
County Bank, 122
CS Allott & Son, 39
Cuarón, Alfonso (director), 81–82, 84

Dark Knight, The (2008 film), 228
Davison, Rosanna (former Miss World), 199–200
Day the Earth Caught Fire, The (1961 film), 254
Dean, Arthur Cresswell (engineer), 39, 58, 251
Dembo, Bernard (*Times* reader), 104
Deptford Power Station, 30, *31*, 64
Deptford West, *see Deptford Power Station*
Derbyshire, Andrew (CEGB architect, 112, 119, 127, 234, 254
Doctor Who, 78
Dolphin Square, 74, 103
Dowson, Sir Philip (Arup), 161, 165
Dream City, *22*, 23–26, 113
Dubs, Lord Alf (MP), 111, 120, 254
Duchess, The (pub), 222, 233
Dunn, Nell (writer), 76

Eco-Tower, Viñoly's, *182*, 192, *193*
Edison, Thomas (inventor), 27–30
Edwards, Eddie "the Eagle", 132
Electric Boulevard, 211, *212*
electricity:
    invention of 27; arrival in London 27–28; first public power station 29; Electric Lighting Act of 1882, 29; Grosvenor Gallery, 29; first execution by, 30; confusion of suppliers, 31; consolidation of suppliers, 32

Ellis, Robert (photographer), 86, 88
Embankment, The, *28*
Embassy Gardens, 195
Empire State Building, 54
Employees Provident Fund, 205, 209
English Heritage, 18, 100, 167, 176, 226, 236
Ernest & Young, 201, 235
Exposition Universelle of 1900, Paris, 25
Ezra, Lord (chairman of the NCB), 119

Farrell, Terry (architect), 183, 203–205
Ferranti, Sebastian Pietro Innocenzo Adhemar Ziani de (engineer), 29–30
Firestone factory, 101–102
Fitzroy Robinson Partnership, 133, 140–41, 148
Fladgate, Francis (LPC director), 27, 32–33, 44, 47, 64, 219
Flanagan's (pub), 96
flatties (flat-iron barges), 66, 72
Foster + Partners, 169, 190, 210–12
Fox, Samantha, 156, 161
Franco-British Exhibition of 1908, 27
Frederick Snow & Partners, 133
Fry, Geoffrey (private secretary to PM), 41
Fulham Power Station, 66, 140
Furst, Herbert (art historian), 53

Garner, Keith (BPSCG activist), 221, 233–37
Garrett, Bradley L (urban explorer and academic), 258
gas-washing, 46–47
Gehry Partners, 210–11, 212
George V, King, 39, 43
Getty, Paul (philanthropist), 234
Gidman, John (project manager), 16, 131–32, 139, 141–44, 146–48

265

Gilbert Scott, George (architect), 50, 76, 171
Gilbert Scott, George Jr (architect), 50
Gilbert Scott, Giles (architect), 17, 47, 50–54, 57, 76, 104, 219
global property market crash, 197
Gordon Group, The, 162–63
Govindia, Ravi (Wandsworth councillor), 108, 171, 183, 191, 197, 201, 221, 229–30, 253–54
Graves, Francis (architect), 232
Great Train Robbers, 78
Griffiths McGee, 140–41
Grimshaw Architects, 169, *170*, 171, *172–73*, 180
Grimshaw, Nicholas (architect), 166
Grosvenor Gallery, 29
Grove Road Power Station, 44, 46
Gustafson Porter, 175

Hall, Sir Ernest (developer), 233
Halliday & Agate, 17, 52, 57
Halliday, James Theodore (architect), 17, 52, 60
Hanson (band), 93, 161
Haward, Sir Harry (comptroller of the LLC), 31
Hawkwind (band), 93
Help! (1965 film), 78, 85
Hercock, Stuart (Wandsworth councillor), 119–20
Herzigova, Eva (model), *160*, 161
Heseltine, Michael (Secretary of State for Environment), 100–101, 112
High Treason (1951 film), 77
Hill Hassall, Arthur (chemist), 24
Hill, Peter (Battersea worker), 96–97, 99
Hilton Young, Edward (MP), 41
Hipgnosis, 84–86, 90, 93
Hislop, Dave (Battersea worker), 96–99
Hitchcock, Alfred, 77

Holborn Viaduct, 29
Holy Trinity Church, 161
Hong Kong Parkview, 157
Hutchinson, Maxwell (president of RIBA), 149
Hwang, Chou-Shiuan (developer), 155, 157–58, 174, 178
Hwang, George, 157–58, 174
Hwang, Richard, 157–58
Hwang, Sally, 157
Hwang, Tony, 157–58
Hwang, Vicky, 177
Hwang, Victor (developer), 20, 155–81, 185–86: childhood and schooling, 157–58; purchase of Battersea, 159; financial scandal, 163; consumption of architects, 165; sale of Battersea, 186

Ian Simpson Architects, 210
Ingels, Bjarke (architect), 211
International Exposition of Electricity of 1881, Paris, 28
Isherwood, Christopher (writer), 73
Ito, Toyo (architect), 174

Jackson, Michael, 156, 162
Jam, The (band), 93
Januszczak, Waldemar (critic), 18
Jenkins, Michael (LARC owner), 124, 131, 142, 147
Jenkins, Simon (columnist), 102
Jet Set Willy (computer game), 20, 84
John, Elton, 214
John Outram Associates (JOA), 163–64, *164–65*
John Portman & Associates, 163, 175
Johnson, Boris, 192, 196, 207, 257–58
Johnson, Martin (Wandsworth councillor), 101–102, 111, 119–21, 125, 131, 142–43, 153, 183, 187, 221–22

INDEX

Jones, Gerald (chief executive of Wandsworth Council), 131, 140, 155, 159–60, 167, 169, 183–84, 188–89, 194, 221, 228, 230–32
Jordan, Robert Furneaux (architect), 76
Junior's Eyes (band), 85

K2 telephone kiosk, 51
Keate, Delcia (senior advisor at English Heritage), 100, 254
Kemmler, William, execution of, 30
Kennard, Steve (architect), 155, 169, 174
King Crimson (band), 82
Kirby, Louis (editor of the *Evening Standard*), 119
Kirk, Thomas (letter writer), 34
Kohn Pedersen Fox, 202

Laliberté, Guy (founder of Cirque du Soleil), 169
Lampl, Sir Frank (chairman of Bovis), 165
Lancaster, Osbert (artist), 113
Landmark of London (book), 58, 73, 99, 250, 251
Lang, Cosmo, Archbishop of Canterbury, 37–38
LARC, *see Leisure and Recreation Concepts*
Laughton, Charles (actor), 61
Lawrence, Sir Robert (British Rail board member), 119
Lee, Joseph (cartoonist), 76
Legge, Peter (architect), 111–14, 128–29
Lehrer McGovern, 147
Leisure and Recreation Concepts (LARC), 113, 118, 124, 133, 142, 147–48
Leslie, Mark (architect), 111–16, 118, 128–29

Lesmoir-Gordon, Nigel (cameraman), 90
Lesser Group, The, 108
LG Mouchel and Partners, 56
Lincoln's Inn Fields, 30, *36*
Lister, Edward (leader of Wandsworth Council), 152, 166, 183, 195, 226, 228
Lloyd Webber, Andrew, 162, 173
London 2012 Olympics, 210
London County Council (LCC), 26, 32, 39, 56
London Electric Supply Corporation, 30
London Power Company (LPC), 27, 32–33, 39, 44, 51, 57
Lots Road Power Station, 31, 38, 66
Lutyens, Edwin, 47

MacCormac Jamieson Prichard, 163
Magic World, 113
Malaysia Square, 211
Malaysian consortium, 208–209
Malaysian state pension fund, *see Employees Provident Fund*
Marshall, Walter (chairman of the CEGB), 109
Masters, David (journalist), 68–69
Maxim, Hiram (inventor), 28
McAlpine, 146, 160
McCuaig, Alex (director of MET Studio), 131, 142, 146–47
Meek, James (journalist), 219, 259
Mellor, David (MP and developer), 188–89
MET Studio, 142, 147
Miéville, China (writer), 249
Millennium Dome, 118, 171, 185, 235–36
Montague, Michael (chairman of the English Tourist Board), 103
Monty Python's *The Meaning of Life*, 95, 109

267

Moore, Rowan (architecture critic), 187
Morgan Grenfell, 117
Morrissey (singer), 93
Morrison, Graham (architect), 105, 235
Morrison, Herbert (Minister for Transport), 55
Mosley, Oswald (politician), 17
Mowlem, 56, 117
Municipal Parks, Gardens and Open Spaces of London, The (book), 250
Muse (band), 93
music videos shot at Battersea Power Station, 85, 93, 96, 161

National Asset Management Agency (NAMA), 197–200
National Gallery, 27, 75, 234
National Grid, 65, 97, 161
National Lottery, 235
Naughton, Bill (writer), 76
Network Rail, 167
New Covent Garden market, 196
Nine Elms regeneration scheme, 195–96
Nineteen Eighty-Four (1984 film), 228
Noddyland theme park, 161–62
Northern Line extension, 196–97
Nuclear Electric, 234
nuclear power, *see atomic energy*

Old Bailey, 29
Old Red House (pub), 96
Open House, 20
Ormsby-Gore, William (First Commisioner of Works), 57
Orwell, George, 84
Ove Arup & Partners, *see Arup*
Owen, Clive (actor), 81

Palmer, Arthur (station worker), 71
Parkview International, 150–81, 185

Pearce, Leonard (engineer), 39–41, 46–47, 52–53, 57, 73, 219
People's Plan for Battersea Power Station, The, 232
peregrine falcons, 168, 214
Peter Jones department store, 61
Peter Legge Associates, 112
Peyton-Jones, Julia (director of the Serpentine Gallery), 177
Pink Floyd, 18, 83–93
Piper, John (artist), 113
placemaking, 213–14, 258
Portman International, 163
Powell, Aubrey (of design agency Hipgnosis), 84–85, 87, 89, 91–93, 252–53
power cuts, *see blackouts*
Power Plex, 162
Power Station Journal, The, 156
power stations:
  Bankside, 51, 100, 109, 234–35; Barton, 39, 45–46; Deptford, 30, *31*, 64; Fulham, 66, 140; Greenwich, 31; Grove Road, 44, 46; Lombard Road, 35; Lots Road, 31, 38, 66; Neasden, 31; Notting Hill, 31
Price, Cedric (architect), 125–26
Prime Minister's Ironing Board, The (book), 250
Prince Philip, 20
Prospect Place, 211, *212*
pylons, 65

Quadrophenia (1973 album), 85
Quatermass Experiment, The (1955 film), 78
Queenstown Road station, 167
Quidam, 170

Railtrack, 166
Real Estate Opportunities (REO), 190–97

INDEX

Really Useful Company, The, 162, 173
Rebel Footprints (book), 35
Red House, inn at Battersea, 34, 113
refuse-burning plant scheme, 108, 123–24, 127
Rendel, Palmer & Tritton, 122
Renton Howard Wood Levine, 148
RHWL Architects, 163
Richard III (1995 film), 228
Roberts, Michael (CEO of Parkview), 155, 157–60, 162, 166, 168, 174, 178–79, 187
Roche, David (developer), 111, 116–19, 122, 125, 127–29, 225
Roche Leisure, 116
Rodker, Ernest (BPSCG co-founder), 221–23, 225–26, 228, 231, 259
Rogers Sirk Harbour + Partners, 196
Rogers, Vivian B, Mayor of Westminster, 42
Ronan, Johnny (developer), 183–85, 190, 199–201
Rosenberg, David (historian), 35
Rundell, Katherine (writer), 215–16, 219, 259

Sabotage (1936 film), 77
SAVE Britain's Heritage, 102, 105–107, 117, 235–36
Savoy Court, 38
Savoy Theatre, 28
Sceno Plus, 165
Schwarzenegger, Arnold, 163
Self, Will (writer), 204, 213, 257
Sellafield, *see Windscale atomic power station*
Serpentine Gallery, 174, 177
Sharp, Michael (location manager), 82
Sidor, Neven (architect), 155, 171, 172, 174–77, 180, 183, 194
Sime Darby, 205, 209
Simon, Mel (developer), 147–48
Simon Properties, 147–48

Simpsons Movie, The, 84
Skidmore, Owings & Merrill (SOM), 190
Slade (band), 85
Smashing Time (1967 film), 78
Smith, Terry (Battersea worker), 96, 109
Snow, John (physician), 24
Southwark and Vauxhall Waterworks Company, 24, 25
Spender, Stephen (poet), 65
Sprigge, Squire, editor of *The Lancet*, 42
SP Setia, 200, 205, 208–209
Stamp, Gavin (historian), 53, 103–105, 108, 251
Sting (musician), 213
Sturgeon, Andy (landscaper), 217
Super Furry Animals (band), 93
Super Grid, 97
Superman III (1983 film), 96
Swales, Francis (architect), 23–24, 26
Swan, Joseph (inventor), 27–28

Tahara, Keiichi, 175
Tapper, Walter, President of RIBA, 42
Tate Modern, 171, 234–35
Taylor Woodrow, 73, 112
Teddington Lock, 24
Temples of Power (book), 105, 251
Texas (band), 161
Thatcher, Margaret, *15*, 15, 24, 132, 142
Thirties Society, The, 102
Thorgerson, Storm (of design agency Hipgnosis), 84
Thurman, Uma (actor), 163
Tincknell, Rob (developer), 183, 185–86, 190–91, 194, 200, 208–10, 213, 216–17
Touche Ross, 117
Tracey, Richard (community liaison), 183, 195

Transport for London (TfL), 196
Treasury Holdings, 184–205, 208
Trentham Gardens, 118
Twentieth Century Society, The, 102

UFO (band), 93
UNStudio, 175
Up the Junction (1963 novel), 76
urban explorers, 215–16, *216*
US Embassy, 99, 166, 194–96

Victoria Bridge, 34
Victorian Society, 102
Viñoly masterplan, *182*, 191–94, *193*, 197, *198*
Viñoly, Rafael (architect), 183, 190, 194, 210

Wakeman Trower & Partners, 122
Walkie Talkie, 194
War, Reginald (chief executive of the London Docklands Development Corporation), 119
Waring-White Building Company, 25
Warner Bros, 147, 162–63, 173
Warren, Michael (artist), 146

Waters, Roger (musician), 84–85, 92, 253
Waugh, Dennis (photographer), 86, 88
Weightman, Gavin (historian), 29
West 8, 175
WG Curtin & Partners, 122
Whatley, Terry (Battersea worker), 96, 100
Who, The, 85
Wimberly Allison Tong & Goo, 165
Wilkinson Eyre, 217
Willcox, Toyah (singer), 96, 253
Williams, John (PR), 151–52
Wilson, Sir Hugh (architect), 122
Windscale atomic power station, 18, 75
Wonderbra, *160*, 161
Wonders of World Engineering (magazine), 68, *68*, 251
Woodward, Christopher (writer), 240
Woolf, David (architect), 139, 147
World Monuments Fund, 226
Wyman, Bill (musician), 93

Zunz, Sir Jack (Arup), 165

Paradise Road is devoted to publishing non-fiction books about London. *Up in Smoke: The Failed Dreams of Battersea Power Station* is our first title. More titles will follow in 2016.

To discover more, please visit
www.paradiseroad.co.uk

Thank you for reading.